THOUGHT

ACTION

AND

PASSION

THOUGHT

ACTION

AND

PASSION

Richard McKeon

THE UNIVERSITY OF CHICAGO PRESS

CHICAGO & LONDON

THE UNIVERSITY OF CHICAGO PRESS, CHICAGO 60637
The University of Chicago Press, Ltd., London W.C. 1

Midway Reprint 1974

Preface

Three of the four essays published in this volume are revisions of essays that have appeared elsewhere in somewhat different forms. The fourth essay—"Imitation and Poetry"—which is almost twice the length of the other three combined, is published here for the first time. The discourse on Thomas Mann, which is published in the Appendix, has not appeared in print before. The other three essays have been revised, and material has been added to them to bring out the similarities of the problems treated and of the data used in them. The new Introduction traces the schema of transformations and varying influences of the "themes" and "techniques" that take specific form in doctrines and analytical disciplines and that supply the connections among historical processes and among applications of the liberal, and interpretations of the fine, arts. "Love and Philosophical Analysis" is based on "Symposia," which was delivered as the presidential address of the Western Division of the American Philosophical Association and was published in the *Proceedings of the American Philosophical Association for 1951–1952,* pages 18–41. "Truth and the History of Ideas" appeared as "Plato and Aristotle as Historians: A Study of Method in the History of Ideas" in *Ethics,* LI (October, 1940), 66–101. "Freedom and Disputation" appeared as "The Funeral Oration of Pericles" in *Great Expressions of Human Rights,* edited by R. M. MacIver (New York: Harper and Brothers, 1950), pages 29–41. I am grateful to the publishers for permission to reprint these articles.

RICHARD McKEON

CHICAGO, ILLINOIS

Table of Contents

Introduction

The influence of ideas and ideals is not found in patterns of actions rigidly determined, and the sensed continuity of cultures is never formulated unambiguously. What is effective on men's minds and feelings and what persists in their thought and imagination are only partially and temporarily expressed in bodies of doctrines found in one age and transmitted from age to age. The story of ideal influence and cultural continuity cannot be told definitely or finally. Doctrines and beliefs are modified as they are repeated and reinforced in traditions, and the history of the common past must be re-examined and reformulated by each age and by each community to account for the emergence of new circumstances that give ages and communities their peculiar character and spirit. Old and new, tradition and change, permanence and relativity are not simple opposites, nor are they simply discovered in the facts of human action and expression. They are encountered in the theories and histories by which the facts are explained and in which new succeeds old, old supplants new, and theory and history become themselves parts of a process in which continuity and change are mingled in the prosecution of a common inquiry and unending dialogue.

In the inquiry that has associated men in progressively larger and more interdependent groups, men have turned from investigating immediate practical problems to making and enjoying things of beauty or to speculating on eternal mysteries and enigmas—sometimes combining practical, aesthetic, and theoretic; sometimes separating the accumulations of knowledge, not only from the errors discarded and the ignorance superseded, but also from other human accomplishments classified for that purpose as emotional, imaginative, or mystic; sometimes using past acquisitions of knowledge or information as instruments for further inquiry; sometimes returning to hypotheses prematurely discarded, or refurbishing accepted doctrines to adjust them to newer data, or abandoning the old and constructing radically new theories and amassing data which were inaccessible until the concepts that marked them off were discovered or formed. In the dialogue which began before the beginning of history, interlocutors have participated for a time and then have disappeared, while others, more recently arrived, have continued the themes their predecessors had discussed and the words they had used—sometimes forgetful of the original problem or ingenious in discovering unsuspected aspects, and often insensitive to the meanings in which the words were used when they picked up the thread of discussion or inattentive to the nuances of distinctions the words once carried; sometimes introducing new problems which bent the altered words to still newer meanings and associations and which altered the old arts and techniques of statement and proof; sometimes adapting newly devised instruments to transform old problems.

The common inquiry and adventure, the continuing dialogue and co-operation are, like everything else, subject matter for theory and science. Human nature and human community have been set forth and ordered according to theological, anthropological, biological, philosophical, metaphysical, psychological, semantic, sociological, geographic, cosmological, or economic principles. Histories recount the successions or patterns of action and thought with the aid of one or another of these doctrines and in substantiation of its assumptions. But the relations of the sciences and the successions of the histories are, in turn, steps in the inquiry and phases in the dialogue. Participants in the inquiry and speakers in the dialogue proceed as if they were engaged uniquely in promoting acceptance of true doctrines and sound proofs in a context of accepted facts and established sciences; and our analyses of states of affairs, actual and past, are frequently framed as if doctrine, belief, and action fall into place by conforming to unique patterns or sequences historically determined and disputable only by the ignorant, the biased, or the malicious. Yet the ambiguity of concepts in theoretic disputations and the multiplicity of interpretations of historical facts may also suggest, not that we ought to eliminate ambiguity from our statements or that we shall ever be able to do so, if that were desirable, nor that we ought to agree on the facts of our situation, but rather that our efforts to use knowledge and history to guide actions are involved in problems similar to those of scientists faced by opposed hypotheses and to those historians faced by mutually inconsistent interpretations.

It is difficult to apply knowledge to action, not only because the motives that lead men to act are not basically, or even largely, rational, but also because what is advanced as relevant knowledge in any problematic situation is not a single consistent body of doctrine and does not indicate a unique course of action. We have almost ceased to notice, to cite one striking example, the differences and oppositions between the diagnosis of the problems of our times which traces the persistent crises of a scientific and technological age to the fact that our moral and spiritual development has not kept pace with our scientific and technological advance and the diagnosis of our troubles as due to the fact that the social sciences have lagged behind the natural sciences and that our power to control nature exceeds our power to control man. It is difficult to learn from history, not only because the past is never wholly repeated and what is relevant in analogies from the past is not easily determined, but also because what is advanced as history reflects the circumstances and convictions among which the history was conceived as well as the conditions and actions it sets forth. Historians in the West have in recent decades constructed accounts of the characteristics of civilizations, their development, decay, and death, to balance Marxist inquiries into history as part of the science of the history of society according to which society moves inevitably through fixed stages determined by relations and means of production to an ideal classless society; not only are the histories contradictory in the data selected, in the interpretations put on common data, and in the relations found to connect data, but also it is not immediately apparent how men may learn from either account to advance or prevent processes which are inevitable or, at least, to which no exceptions have been recorded. The problems which arise in applying science or history to action are not scientific or historical: in their theoretic form they are metaphysical problems of first principles; in their practical form they are rhetorical problems of persuasion.

The problems of a culture and of the relations among cultures, which are stated in theory and narrated in history, are encountered and resolved in the clash of theories and the oppositions of traditions. A community or a civilization is a product of antecedent circumstances; it is also an expression of a set of beliefs concerning the nature of things and an evaluation of what is worth while. Within the community or the culture, the antecedent conditions are interpreted in a variety of histories, and the common beliefs concerning reality and values are interpreted in a variety of theories. Commitments and convictions concerning what is true and what is important are mingled in the operation of historical processes, and those processes, in turn, are expounded in histories committed to principles which result in variant historical interpretations of the consequences of convictions. They have their grounds in reality and processes, but those grounds are formulated in philosophies and sciences which are constructed to take account, in the sphere of human and social actions, of the differences among philosophies and among the organizations of sciences. Tradition has been the channel as well as the obstacle of change. Revolutions have sought the new by a return to the old, and, when they have sought to avoid the old, they have rediscovered old ways and values, old predicaments and problems at the peak of their revolutionary success. Philosophers and scientists have organized symbols in demonstrative systems, have sought the verification of systems in facts and experience, and have promoted doctrines and methods in an effort to secure acceptance for them by a consensus of all men, or of the experts or the educated or the elite, or, at least, of a school or a sect or a party, but they have also recognized that their systems of symbols, their empirical verifications, and their proofs depend on the formation of concepts which face out on the unexplored and determine the alterations or revolutions of their systems.

In the processes of objective history (which include among historical phenomena the construction of histories by historians) and in the processes of objective nature (which include among empirical social facts the formation of theories by scientists and philosophers) continuity and change are found in themes and concepts, arts and techniques, data and purposes. A civilization which has a common past and a common set of values is bound together by symbols which are the source of common action and mutual confidence and understanding. So long as the symbols are viable, the civilization is vital, and the symbols are a source only of concepts for inquiry and themes for discussion. The symbols of a civilization by which men live and act are elaborated in myth and history, in belief and knowledge. A crisis of civilization is a failure of symbols as a bond binding men in the community they previously recognized and as an inspiration leading them to common action for common purposes. New histories are then composed and new efforts are made to convert all men or an elite or a sect to one of the doctrines which interpret reality and values. Such efforts succeed sometimes, but they never secure more than partial and temporary consensus, and their success in the past has usually been due less to the values or the truths they celebrate than to some species of force—the influence of material and economic circumstance, social pressure, political control, or military power. Even when they are successful, moreover, the form and content of doctrine and belief are modified by the same processes that lead to the resolution of differences of belief and doctrine by conviction and force, by influence and resistance— the success of peaceful and violent social change is due to the efficacy of the themes and the concepts, the arts and the techniques, which are the sources of the interpretations we give to the nature of things and to their operation and development.

The four themes which are treated in the essays brought together in this volume—love, truth, freedom, and imitation—are themes which were first given a prominent place in the inquiry and the dialogue of Western civilization by Greek poets, statesmen, and philosophers. They have continued since antiquity to be concepts about which men have organized inquiry into, and discussion of, our common lives and purposes. The history of the influence of the Greeks has been retold in every age from Alexandria and Rome to present-day formulations of an emerging world community, but the different judgments of the adequacy of their ideals and conceptions have themselves been parts of the discussion of common themes. The influence of the Greeks has been exalted and disputed for qualities attributed to them and for reasons alleged to account for or to diminish their accomplishments. The miracle of Greece was that one small community of men—not indeed of all Greeks but of Greeks resident in Athens during a few generations—developed so many themes and perfected so many techniques that have continued to occupy men in their individual lives, their arts, their association, and their pursuit of knowledge, wisdom, and spiritual values.

Love, truth, freedom, and imitation have been defined, developed, and applied in theories which depart from Greek conceptions; and the histories which recount the development of those themes find Greek practices and doctrines deficient in many respects. The Greek doctrine of love, despite the lofty reaches and subtle elaborations of the Platonic theory, was supplemented by the Christian conception of divine love and charity. Yet St. Augustine found the themes and the dialectic for the systematic formulation of Christian charity in the doctrines of Plotinus.

Greek mathematicians, astronomers, physicians, and philosophers, despite the progress they made in formalizing, systematizing, and advancing knowledge in astronomy, mathematics, physics, meteorology, and biology, and despite their monumental construction of logical devices and techniques and their profound explorations of the nature and requirements of truth, did not succeed in elaborating the instruments, in defining the concepts, or in making the measurements required for the establishment of empirical and experimental sciences. Yet at each stage of the development of modern science the themes and the problems on which the Greeks exercised their ingenuity reappear, sometimes in explicit reference, sometimes in distant echo, sometimes in distorted refutation: Copernicus quotes Greek astronomical theories which he learned about from Cicero; Galileo developed his mechanics in the context of the disputes of Aristotelians and Averroists in Padua; Descartes invented his geometry to solve problems posed by Greek mathematicians and Fermat laid the foundations of number theory to translate their insights into new symbolic forms; Cuvier and Darwin expressed admiration for the observations and theories of Aristotle; Whitehead borrowed inspiration and terminology from Plato to express the organic interrelations of his philosophy of science; and modern scientists frequently clarify the basic assumptions of their theories by quarreling with concepts they attribute to Aristotle.

Greek society and polity had their economic foundation in slavery; the love of freedom which Pericles celebrated in his Funeral Oration did not extend to all residents of Athens, and the Athenian democracy was an oligarchy; Plato, Aristotle, and other political theorists in Athens did not number "democracy" among the "perfect" forms of government. Yet Western man learned to talk about freedom and justice, order and the rule of law from Greek poets, thinkers, and men of action; and eighteenth-century philosophers and revolutionists justified democracy by means of distinctions, arguments, and principles that had their origins in Greek theory and practice.

The concept of imitation occupied a fundamental place in Greek theories of science, morals, art, and rhetoric; it was displaced from that central position and found inadequate in later critical, phenomenological, and pragmatic theories of truth and in creative and expressive theories of art and beauty. Yet the influence of the various doctrines of imitation is apparent, not only negatively in the doctrines set up to supplant them, but positively in the exemplary uses to which history was put by precepts applied in practical action, in the dialectical and operational criteria by which the truth of hypotheses was tested by application in natural processes, and in the techniques which were adapted to different objects of imitation in academic, impressionistic, imagistic, expressionistic, surrealistic, and futuristic art.

A theme or a concept is an instrument in the development, defense, and refutation of doctrines and theories. The history of themes is longer in extent and broader in scope than the history of the doctrines that specify the theme in any field or in any form of action, since the development of themes includes the significances and implications which relate disparate doctrines, connect the histories of separated theories and sciences, and explain heterogeneous applications of developed doctrines in other fields than those in which they originally appeared. Some themes which were first elaborated by the Greeks have influenced later developments of doctrine by the *pattern of interrelations* they suggested or laid bare. It would be absurd to argue that Greek philosophers, poets, or rhetoricians anticipated the Christian doctrine of charity, or the psychiatric doctrine of sexual urges, or the doctrines of courtly love or of romantic love. They did explore ingeniously and imaginatively the loves that relate man to man, to woman, to ideas, ideals, and God and that bind men in families, friendships, and communities; and the names of Oedipus, Helen, Aphrodite, Antigone, Hippolytus, Damon and Pythias, Orpheus, Alcestis, Achilles, Orestes, and Socrates have continued to evoke in the minds of later men the vast complexity of human loves. Later discussions of the themes of love as subconscious drive, individual desire, community bond, or transcendent attraction, not only extended early concepts to new meanings and applications using Greek examples or borrowing Greek names to form technical terms, but played on the interdependences of forms of love, making one form or another fundamental to the rest.

Other themes that bear the marks of Greek origin have influenced later developments of doctrines by *basic distinctions and data*, and further development has consisted in sharpening of the distinctions in doctrines, correcting and adjusting theories, and supplementing hypothesis by hypothesis as new data have been accumulated in the successive applications of more refined theories. Aristotle discussed motion in terms of time, space, matter, infinity, and cause, but his distinction between upward and downward motion prevented him from giving importance to the idea of inertia, and his distinction between violent and natural motion, between alteration, increase, and local motion stood in the way of his forming a concept of force. He examined the kinds, structures, functions, and parts of animals, basing his distinctions in many cases on extraordinarily acute empirical observations, and he concentrated attention on problems of nutrition, growth, modes of locomotion, reproduction, heredity, struggle for existence, survival, disease, and death; but at best he prepared for the later concepts of classification, function, and evolution on which biological inquiry has proceeded since the eighteenth and nineteenth centuries. The character of the themes which have guided the progress of science is obscured by the importance of the data on which concepts are employed and to which they are adjusted; and the suggestive power of the interrelations which they conceal in their ambiguities, which are as frequently liberating as obstructive, appears only occasionally in the insights explored in new discoveries.

Still other themes explored by the Greeks have influenced later developments of doctrines by the enlarging *scope of application* which they acquired with changing circumstances, beliefs, and institutions. Cynics and Stoics conceived the equality and brotherhood of man; Christians related the brotherhood of man and the heavenly city to the Judeo-Christian conception of God; but only in recent times have economic and political changes permitted the extension by which the concept of freedom is applied to all men and the enlargement by which it includes economic, social, and cultural as well as political and civil rights. Modern man has rediscovered in his efforts to comprehend and encompass the four freedoms some of the perplexities of Antigone's appeal to an unwritten law which underlies, and comes into conflict with, the laws of states.

Finally, some themes of the Greeks have influenced later developments of doctrines by moving from field to field, losing significant application in one to acquire new applications in another, often without attracting attention to the *relations between the fields.* Plato and Aristotle discussed art as an imitation of nature; aesthetics and criticism made little sympathetic use of imitation during some periods, including the nineteenth century, yet the theme has had a long continuing career: Hellenistic and Roman rhetoricians and poets advised poets, historians, and philosophers to imitate the great models in their art; Christian writers moved the concept into morals and theology and advocated the imitation of Christ; imitation returned to a central importance in the doctrines of the Renaissance, and among other applications political philosophers based their doctrines on the imitation of the past or the imitation of nature; and the models which scientists constructed and the operations they employed and described had a relation to nature and its processes which the Greeks could have named imitation.

The discussion and application of themes which can be traced back to the Greeks have been carried on for centuries by arts and techniques which the Greeks invented to develop and variegate the themes in which they were employed. They still retain the names given to them by Greek thinkers—logic and dialectic, mathematics, rhetoric, grammar, poetic, history, logistic, sophistic, eristic, criticism, philosophy. Just as the themes of inquiry and discussion tend to assume a fixity and rigidity in doctrines, conclusions, and beliefs, so too the techniques of inquiry and discussion tend to lose their character as arts and to become methods, instruments, and organa of verification and proof by which postulates, hypotheses, and beliefs are attached to bodies of data and by which inquiry and inference are transformed into formalized sciences. The processes employed in these methods are in turn combined and transformed by similar methods— those which in the past led to the construction of metaphysics, theologies, critical philosophies, philosophical anthropologies, and epistemologies, or to the elaboration of the ideals of the communion of saints, the republic of letters, and the consensus of experts, or, more recently, to the promulgation of the unity of sciences, the homogeneity of cultures or ages or the patterns and successions of cultures, societies, and epochs, and the integration of the whole man. On the other hand, just as themes are fertile sources of diverse and even contradictory doctrines, so too techniques are moved from field to field in heterogeneous application to subjects for which they were not designed in their previous uses: the devices of rhetoric are applied to things as well as to words, to the construction of methods of discovery in science as well as to the formation of arguments for persuasion in practical problems or to the invention of forms and figures in poetry; treatises on the grammar of science or the grammar of politics follow more than a figure of speech in their search for least parts and simple connections; dialectic, whether it finds its foundation in spirit or in matter, supplies a method for all problems; theologians and poets have professed sometimes to express truths beyond the scope of reason or science, sometimes to give form to insights accessible to common sense, philosophy, and science in the language of everyday life; philosophy is reduced to logic or to historiography or to art.

There is no way to participate in the inquiry or the dialogue, in which themes are developed and techniques are employed, except by taking a stand on a doctrine which is one expression of a theme and by using a method which is one development of a technique or an art. The history of the processes which lead to that doctrine—that belief or philosophy or science—and to the method by which it is established, extended, and defended, relates what went before to the assumptions and convictions that form the last stage of the evolution. Yet actual processes transcend the fixities of doctrines and the oppositions of historical accounts of their evolution. The themes that connect the successive doctrines are ambiguous from the point of view of the precisions attained in systematic formulation; and the techniques which move, usually undetected, from one application to another are haphazard from the point of view of rigorous method. Yet the very ambiguity of the themes and the freedom of the techniques from commitment to principle or subject matter give them a double value—a *heuristic* value as instruments of discovery of doctrines and principles, which may then be verified and applied in determinate and definite form, and an *expressive* value as grounds of common purposes providing a means of communication and mutual understanding to proponents of different forms of expression, different contents of value, and different systems of proof. The invention and discovery of new hypotheses and principles, when they are not purely fortuitous, arise out of new variants of themes and new applications of techniques; and communication, when it is more than the elaboration of the shared beliefs and postulates that unite communities, sects, and schools, depends on the discovery of the common themes to which particular doctrines give different concretion, the common values to which different communities give different expression, and the common techniques to which different methods give different principles, employments, and systems.

Four themes—love, truth, freedom, and imitation—and four arts or techniques—philosophy, history, rhetoric, and poetry—are presented in this volume in four aspects of their operation in the processes of discovery and communication, of concealment and deception, which elude single definition and simple reduction to the rules of methods. By the criteria of clear, distinct, and adequate ideas, the themes are equivocal, yet they are the thesaurus out of which univocal and analogical definitions evolve and achieve precision of significance and application. Philosophers criticize the presuppositions and refute the conclusions of other philosophers according to the requirements of their own definitions and theories, yet the relations which give relevance and significance to their exchange of compliments arise from the themes by which they are joined rather than from the definitions by which they are separated. By the criteria of methods whose presumptions are stated in advance and whose operations are reduced to rules conforming to requirements and criteria, the techniques are indeterminate, inasmuch as their starting points are undefined, enigmatic, and mysterious, and their operations inventive, creative, and unpredictable. Yet the techniques provide not only the connections between the stages by which grammar, rhetoric, logic, dialectic, and poetic have evolved in practice and in the application of normative rules to practice, but also the connections between the arts which make heterogeneous applications possible—poetic has afforded the devices to make philosophy an art, dialectic has determined successions of history and patterns of cultures, logic has supplied categories for metaphysics, rhetoric has constructed the "proper places" of inductive method on the analogies of the "common places" of discourse, and grammar has suggested the "syntax" of modern logic.

The theme treated in the first essay is *love;* the technique by which it is developed is *philosophy*, but in the course of the treatment and in its manner it is apparent that this is properly a theme for *poetry*. The interrelations of the treatment of one theme by two techniques, however, run counter to the interrelations of things discovered in the development of themes and the use of techniques. We have tended in recent decades, in spite of our devotion to philosophies of events, relations, wholes, and organisms, and in spite of our avoidance of misplaced concreteness, substances, separations, and abstractions, to separate the disciplines we practice and the purposes for which they are employed. Science, and philosophy in so far as it is made scientific, treat truth and probability and are cognitive; history sets forth the interrelations and successions of concrete events; ethics has recently borrowed an orientation from rhetoric, as politics has in the past, to become ejaculatory or persuasive; while poetry arouses emotions. These four methods, nonetheless, are not distinct in the context or in the techniques from which they arise, and according to many philosophies—which we easily forget when we seek our unities and wholes in the unity of science, or of culture, or of man—to separate them is to be guilty of unwarranted dichotomies and abstractions.

The essay on "Love and Philosophical Analysis" takes its beginning, therefore, in interrelations and interdependences of loves and methods explored in Greek philosophy. The techniques of poetry and rhetoric lie, as it were, midway between—or in some other manner beyond the reaches of—both the factual determinations of history and the theoretic precisions of philosophy. To bring out the character of techniques that involve more than opinion but less than proof, the problems of knowledge and motivation, of objective fact and transcendent insight are focused in this essay, not on the large themes of *experience* or *intuition*, which might be used to provide the matrix in which contemplation and action are joined, but on the theme of *love*, which is the stimulus to the pursuit of knowledge, the prosecution of action, and the creation or appreciation of art.

Plato argued that there is a single method by which truth is achieved in philosophy, science, practical action, and common discussion; that that method, dialectic, is a method of discovery, of proof, of communication, of teaching, and of expression; that the use of dialectic simultaneously defines terms, clarifies ideas, prepares and persuades minds, and analyzes the objective situation. It follows, therefore, that practical problems are solved best by dialectic employed by philosopher-kings or, failing that ideal solution, by right opinion applied by statesmen and enforced by the persuasion and penalties of laws; that poets should properly be banished from the state and that dialecticians and lawgivers should be recognized to be sounder and better poets or, if the dialogues be taken seriously as examples of dialectic, that Homer, Hesiod, and Pindar should be rectified, interpreted, and applied by dialecticians; that history is a myth which either applies the truths of dialectic in likely stories or uses the truths of what actually happened to interpret dialectical proof as a likely story. These are complexities of interrelations and mysteries of transformation which few "Platonists" have preserved in their use of the dialectical method or in their translation of Platonic themes into Neoplatonic doctrines. They have frozen the dialectic of Plato to make it an instrument by which to ascend the ladder of loves, the chain of inspirations, or the parts of the divided line, which in turn have been ontologized into sharply divided stages of being and becoming, knowledge and opinion, reality and process; or they have made the equivalence of the processes of reality and the processes of thought into an identity of historical evolution and intellectual demonstration. Only the constant and recurrent influence of Plato himself has saved Platonists from the consequences of scientific or religious dogmatisms and practical skepticisms by reproducing in the varieties of doctrines inspired by the dialogues the richness of the themes they explore.

The fact that Plato applied the term "Ideas" to the realities, which are imitated by things and by thoughts, has led many of his interpreters and admirers to conceive his philosophy in purely, or in fundamentally, intellectual terms. This is the more surprising, since few philosophers, not even Augustine and Ambrose, or Rousseau and Kierkegaard, whose arguments reflect Plato's dialectic and whose inquiries echo Socrates' ironic questions, have devoted more thought than Plato to nonrational springs of human action and to nonintellectual insights into transcendent values—to love, poetry, intoxication, and the mystical perceptions of intuition and religion. The theme of love, rather than the Idea of the Good, or the One, or the Beautiful, is suited to focus in human action on motivation and inspiration instead of on the rational analysis of means and ends; and the techniques of poetry, religion, rhetoric, and drinking, which find their perfection in dialectic and philosophy, are appropriate to focus attention on the persuasion of men to action instead of on the analysis of truths by which love operates and in which it finds its ultimate justification. The theme of love carries the analysis, not simply through varying doctrines of love, but through varying methods, circumstances, and subject matters made relevant to those doctrines in ancient, medieval, and modern discussions. That exploration of the theme permits the statement of modern problems which arise from lacunae in modern doctrines of love and which indicate desiderata in methods of developing and understanding it: the rich varieties of conceptions of love developed in past discussions of the theme have tended to be reduced in modern times to a basic sexual concept, and it has become difficult to treat effectively the loves which bind men in communities, attach man to ideals, or draw him into mysteries which exceed self-interest or subconscious

self-assertion; the techniques by which men engage in inquiry about
love and attempt to effect communication have tended to be reduced
to methods of objective verification of erotic aberrations or social
frustrations, insecurities, and tensions, or, when they have resisted
such reduction in the techniques of poetry and politics, to be treated
as void of cognitive content. It has become difficult to state the
problems that are involved in establishing purposes, plans, measures, policies, or cultural values as genuine and grounded propositions in relevant sciences, for problems of action and mutual understanding depend not only on persuading people who are frequently
separated by doctrines and beliefs but also on the adequacy of purposes and statements, on the one hand, to common values that
underlie differences and on their fidelity, on the other hand, to an
objective situation whatever the differences of the views by which
it is approached.

The theme treated in the second essay is *truth;* the technique by
which it is developed is *history,* for although truth is properly a
theme for *philosophy* it is treated historically more frequently than
philosophically, and even the accounts philosophers give of the doctrines of other men as stages or as elements in the development of
their own positions are histories of doctrines that have been presented as true rather than demonstrations designed to exhibit their
truth. History is not concerned only with facts and with the interpretation of what men have done and said, after the manner of
Thucydides and of most writers classified in libraries as "historians"; it is also concerned with the doctrines, communities, and
fantasies men have constructed and with the methods they have
employed in those constructions. The ideas men have used to interpret and to alter facts become themselves facts in history. The
ideas of historians, poets, prophets, scientists, and philosophers, no
less than the ideas of statesmen and the ideas attributed to peoples,
are data for history. History and rhetoric, viewed as techniques,
have a double relation in the treatment of facts and the planning of
action: the past facts of history are a guide to future action, and the
present attitudes of times and of peoples determine the interpreta-

tion of history and the past. History and philosophy have likewise a double relation when they are viewed as techniques: every formulation of history is guided by basic ideas which may be expressed in a philosophy of history; every philosophy is developed and set forth in a context of other philosophies which may be related in a history of philosophy.

Ideas are transformed when they are stated as historical events in a historical context. The significance and the truth of a doctrine depend on its proof and verification; when ideas are viewed in the circumstances of their occurrence and the influences that contributed to their formation, they are facts and events to which truth or falsity are relevant only indirectly and accidentally. Yet we usually treat ideas "historically" rather than intellectually, and we seldom note the transformation we work on them. Only rarely do we restate the presuppositions on which a doctrine other than our own is based or examine the evidence that is advanced to support it and the data to which it is applied. Our usual procedure is to state other men's theories and doctrines in the context and on the presuppositions of our own, to show the irrelevance of their arguments to our principles, the inadequacy of their conclusions to our data, and then to account for the peculiarities of the doctrine by the circumstances, interests, or prejudices of its author, or his times, his nation, people, or class. The influence of philosophies on history, conversely, determines the relevant data and the taxonomy or causal relations which are sought among data. When histories depend on dialectical presuppositions, they tend to be epochal and to trace the spirit, climate, or character of times and peoples in the manner of Herodotus, Augustine, Hegel, Marx, Spengler, or Toynbee. When histories depend on the causes treated in some particular science or branch of knowledge—such as politics, economics, sociology, or the military art—they tend to trace a causal line of progress or decline that cuts across distinctions of periods and ages in the manner of Polybius, Gibbon, Buckle, or Henry Adams. When histories concentrate on the actions of outstanding men or peoples, they tend to be exemplary narratives presented for imitation or avoidance in the manner of Plutarch, Machiavelli, or Carlyle. Finally, when histories are concerned with problems and with the doctrines which men evolved in the solution of problems, they tend to be disciplinary in the manner of Diogenes Laertius, Prantl, and Ueberweg, in the history of philosophy and logic, or of like historians of the sciences, the arts, and literature.

The techniques of philosophy and history are focused, in the essay on "Truth and the History of Ideas," not on the large themes of *fact* or *event* or *reality*, which might be used to explore the data or irreducible materials on which history, science, action, and art are employed, but rather on the theme of *truth*, in which men justify in varying ways what they say in varying situations by reference to what they conceive to be the relevant and compelling facts. Plato treated the history of his predecessors dialectically and concentrated therefore on what has been taken to be the spirit and the significance of their philosophies; Aristotle treated the history of his predecessors problematically and concentrated on the details of the doctrines they developed to resolve particular problems. Plato and Aristotle both treated history in the interest of philosophy, and there is good reason to doubt the accuracy of their presentation of either the spirit or the doctrines as they were developed and without reference to Plato's or Aristotle's philosophy. Yet later historians, working as historians rather than as philosophers, have been dependent largely on their testimony and have composed the history of Greek philosophy prior to them by mingling the two in proportions and according to criteria supplied by the philosophies of successive historians. Plato and Aristotle choose, in accordance with their respective philosophies, the facts they report concerning earlier philosophy: they concentrate attention on different philosophers, on different ideas of the same philosophers, and on different interpretations of the same ideas; the relations they reveal among the ideas of any one philosopher or any group of philosophers are different; and they differ even on the question of the beginning of philosophy, Plato finding it in Greek thought, Aristotle extending his inquiries to the barbarians. But if their philosophical assumptions determine the facts available to later historians, their philosophies likewise become facts in a context of other facts and with scant remnants of proof or verification, when the history of philosophy is extended to include them and to pass beyond them to their successors.

The theme treated in the third essay is *freedom;* the technique by which it is developed is *rhetoric,* but the rhetoric is that of speeches used in a *history* to reconstruct the conditions and intentions that moved men to action. As the subject of the first essay is the theme of love presented philosophically for poetic purposes, and as the subject of the second essay is the theme of truth presented historically for philosophic purposes, so the theme of freedom is presented in the third essay in the rhetorical development of Pericles' Funeral Oration, and of the opposed speeches by which it is framed, for the historical purpose of setting what men thought against the background of the causes that led them into conflict. The problems involved in the resulting juxtapositions are not problems of the theoretic interrelations of themes and techniques in an organic philosophy in which all things may be thought to be interdependent, all sciences unified, and all methods one, if being is distinguished from becoming, and knowledge from opinion; they are problems of the practical interrelations of knowledge applied to particulars and knowledge used in action, if knowledge is applied to the conditions of men and used to influence their motives. Thucydides had a theory by which he combined history and rhetoric in order to relate, in the treatment of practical problems, knowledge applied to particulars historically and knowledge used in action rhetorically. His history is an effort to present both the immediate causes and the real issues of the war. The immediate causes are what men thought and said, and they are expressed rhetorically in the speeches which Thucydides reproduces and reconstructs, while the real issues emerge in the circumstances and relations of the opposed powers which become inseparably mingled with what men think the issues to be. But if rhetoric is employed to construct the particular knowledge which constitutes history, the purpose of the history is to contribute to the practical knowledge employed in plans for action which is set forth by rhetoric. Thucydides hoped that, if he succeeded in exposing the real cause of the war, exact knowledge of the past might facilitate the interpretation of the future and the discussion of possible courses of action.

These two interrelated problems—the historical determination of what happened and why and the practical determination of what should be done and how—have led to the use of many other methods, some similar, others in radical opposition, to those developed by Thucydides. To bring out the character of the techniques of rhetoric and history that underlie those opposed methods, the problems of historical knowledge and practical action are focused in the essay on "Freedom and Disputation," not on the large themes of *human behavior* or *society*, which might be used to bring fact and belief, motivation and persuasion to bear on one another, but on the theme of *freedom*, which men of different persuasions have long conceived to be the condition and the end of human action. The historical development of doctrines expressing the theme of *freedom* runs a course almost directly contrary to the historical development of doctrines of *love*. All the varieties of love and all their applications are intelligible today, but apart from the conception of love developed and applied in psychology and psychiatry they have little effective application in the analysis and planning of our individual or social actions, and the term is not used without hesitation in most of its meanings. The doctrines of freedom—the definitions and applications which the theme has received in historical evolution after the Greek phase—have undergone almost total transformation in their actual and possible applications; but, whereas a modern speaker or writer would feel embarrassment in repeating the theme of any except the satiric speeches of Plato's *Symposium*, he can and does repeat the theme of Pericles' Funeral Oration in almost unaltered form and details of expression. In their historical development as themes, *freedom* and *truth* have come frequently into contact with each other; and, in the optimistic philosophies of dialecticians, truth leads inevitably to freedom (since freedom is action in

accordance with wisdom), while, in the philosophies of progress of
logistic philosophers, freedom is a necessary condition for the discovery of truth (since freedom is action in accordance with the laws
of one's own nature). Yet the two histories exhibit the basic differences that separate knowledge and action: the development of
knowledge has consisted in the multiplication of truths that men
can verify and the extension of the methods of inquiry and verification to the problems of all aspects of human life, and the discovery
of later truths has led both to the abandonment of earlier doctrines
and to the discovery of interrelations and interdependences among
the branches of knowledge; the development of human relations has
consisted in the multiplication of freedoms that men can justify and
to the extension of freedoms, in principle and promulgation, to all
men without distinction or restriction of any kind, and the recognition of later rights—economic, social, and cultural—has not neces-
sitated the abrogation of rights earlier recognized—political, civil,
and religious—yet the question of the priority of the earlier or the
later freedoms is one that separates Soviet philosophers and statesmen from those of the West, and the extension of freedoms to all
mankind has proceeded by dividing and opposing men in parties,
sects, races, nations, and peoples for the vindication of some freedoms for some men.

Greek conceptions of freedom divided men into freemen and
slaves. Even those Greeks who formed an idea of the brotherhood
and equality of all men found no plausible or effective means in
their civilization of attacking the institution of slavery or the conviction of Greeks that Hellenes were fundamentally different from
barbarians. The Greek development of the theme did include the
doctrine that freedom is a "right" based on the nature of man and
on the law of nature. Men had to wait until the eighteenth century
for the development of the concept of a Bill of Rights which enumerates the forms of freedom and charges responsible governments
with providing guaranties against their violation. The developments of the next two centuries vastly increased the number of
rights or freedoms and the spread of their application without dis-

crimination based on race, previous status, religion, sex, or nationality. Yet these differences of circumstance, doctrine, definition, and application do not affect the applications that can be given to Pericles' exposition of the ideal of freedom and its problems. Today, rhetoric is being re-employed and history is being repeated in the development of the theme of freedom. Part of the world has attached itself to the Athenian ideal of freedom; part of the world views that development of the theme with the suspicions expressed by the Corinthians, who thought it a deceptive cloak for the interests and aggressions of the rich and the powerful. Yet in both interchanges of fear and suspicion, ancient and modern, both versions of the theme had been united, only a short time before, in the defense of freedom against a common tyrannical danger. The opposed notions led ultimately, in the ancient development, to a war from which Greek political forms and cultural life and civilization never fully recovered. In the retrospect of over two thousand years the war, which found its "immediate causes" in what men said and did, was clearly a tragedy in which the "real" issues did not justify the extremes to which men were carried, and they were not resolved by the actions men took.

The theme treated in the final essay is *imitation;* it is a theme used to explain the techniques of *poetry*, but if art is viewed as itself an object of imitation rather than as an imitation of nature, all human arts and all human activities are guided by criteria of imitation employed by techniques developed in *rhetoric*. Like love, imitation is a theme that can be applied to all human actions. Love is attachment in action to something valued; imitation is action designed to embody or produce a value. Differences in loves and in theories of love are due to differences in the objects of love; differences in imitations and in theories of imitation are due to differences in the objects of imitation. The different loves and imitations are assimilated to philosophy and distinguished from each other in the dialectic of Plato. Love is a madness which may turn man to the vision of the Good and the Beautiful or to the pursuit of pleasure—and poetry and rhetoric, which may be dangerous and immoral instruments, assume their perfect forms as dialectic and philosophy. Imitation is the process by which all things are made, from the creation of the cosmos by the demiurge imitating eternal forms to the imitation of an imitation in which a poet imitates a lie in the soul—and the errors of poetry are corrected by knowledge in philosophy and by persuasion and force in laws. The analogies and ambiguities of love and imitation are reduced in the "scientific" analyses of Aristotle's philosophy. Love becomes a passion treated in psychology and exploited in rhetoric, with only analogical extensions and indirect uses in morals, politics, and poetry. Imitation becomes the process by which the arts are distinguished from the theoretic and practical sciences. After Aristotle, love, even in its analogical extensions in theory, practice, and art, tends to be only one of the passions defined by its object; and imitation, even in its literal restriction to art, tends to be, not the processes of art copying and extending nature, but the devices of artists copying artists, in which poetry, history, science, and philosophy are all alike arts, and poetry with its more supple and delicate means of imitation attains to higher truths than science or philosophy or at least to a higher expression of the same truths. The modern doctrines in which both themes are expressed tend to conceal them by recourse to their contraries. Love has fallen out of the central place which Socrates gave it in philosophy except as it is reflected or implied by the contraries found for it in particular doctrines—hate, anxiety, fear. Imitation is a theme which has fallen from the central place in the aesthetics of poetry except in its negation by one of its doctrinal contraries—creation, expression, communication. As the consideration of the theme of love serves to recall, among other things, that there are philosophies which deny the distinctions, which other philosophies labor to construct, between knowing, doing, and making, between science, practice, and art, between cognitive, persuasive, and emotive, so too the theme of imitation serves to bring to attention forms of literature and poetry that are composed on the assumption that the true, the good, and the beautiful are not, and cannot be, separated.

Thought, Action, and Passion

There are philosophies whose exposition could not easily be confused with the development of a poem or the plot of a novel. There are novels which could be differentiated from histories (and indeed their authors often call them "histories" in the course of their fictions) only by determining whether or not their characters ever existed or performed the actions narrated. There are philosophers like Plato, Lucretius, Dante, Rousseau, Kierkegaard, Nietzsche, and Santayana whose mode of expression is poetic, aphoristic, or literary and philosophers like Hume and Sartre who use comparable techniques to develop comparable themes successively in philosophy and history or in philosophy, fiction, and drama. The novels of Fielding, Balzac, or Hemingway present actions; the development of characters is appropriate to the action and makes it plausible; what the characters think and say is appropriate to the characters in their situations; whatever philosophy is expressed in the course of the narrative is easily identified as the thought of one of the characters or of the author. The novels of Rabelais, Melville, Dickens, James, Dostoevski, Kafka, Joyce, on the contrary, present actions that emerge into literal focus from the complexities of character, thought, and language; and the connections which they develop, far from being determined by events in time and space, supplant literal facts and give them meaning when they emerge. It would be idle to ask whether Everyman, or Christian, who represent the characteristics of all men or all men of faith, is more or less abstract than Tamberlane, or Tom Jones, or Cousin Pons, whose characters are based on the development of one human quality. The characters that Christian encounters in his pilgrim's progress are likewise motivated by simple traits, and rounded characters are sometimes formed on the model of the complexities of actual characters by placing a dominant characteristic in a variety of circumstances or by a necessity and probability suggested by poetic or ideal models. The world of Captain Ahab is no less real than the world of Clarissa Harlowe, but it is a world in which events are merged with ideas and in which puzzled critics try to find their bearings by identifying the compulsion or ideal symbolized by the white whale. Literal narratives separate the real from the illusory, but it is no less legitimate or effective, as truth and as art, to recognize the relativities of the processes reported and to leave the resolution of the issue of fact and fancy, as Dostoevski does, in the balance of characters who interpret, oppose their interpretation to that of other characters whom they interpret, then doubt and change their interpretations, and in which illusion may easily be truth or truth illusion. The symbolism of the world may be reflected in the symbols the artist uses, as Bunyan and Kafka built their worlds in dreams, or as the nervous sentence structure of James conveys and justifies states of mind and attitude, or as the learned puns and buried levels of symbolic structure of Joyce suggest the inexhaustibly rich content of daily and apparently trivial action. There are forms of artistic expression which have no univocal literal interpretation and which cannot be translated into emotional responses independent of thought or unrelated to action; and, what is even more important, the methods of interpretation and criticism that are adapted to such works apply no less effectively to works that have a literal meaning and an emotive purpose and make them bearers of truth and causes of action.

The techniques of poetry and rhetoric are focused in the essay on "Imitation and Poetry," not on the large themes of *necessity* or *beauty*, which might be used to mark the basic principles in which knowledge, action, and art are joined, but rather on the theme of *imitation*, which provides one of the lines of continuity in efforts to explain the nature of art, action, and knowledge, including the arts of science, philosophy, and life, and the sciences of history, art, and practical action. For Plato, imitation is a broad concept—things, ideas, and virtues as well as poetry are imitations. For Aristotle it is a narrow concept, limited to art and used to distinguish the natural bases of a poem or any other artificial object from the natural bases of a virtue or a science. Plato used the concept of imitation to relate theory, practice, and art. Aristotle used the same concept to distinguish art from knowledge and action. Yet for both, what was imitated was nature or reality. In the concepts developed later in the evolution of the theme, imitation changed its meanings with the change in the object of imitation: writers were enjoined to imitate the genius of other writers or the art evident in their works or to adapt great or common themes to appropriate language newly devised or borrowed from common language. The applications of imitation move from art to practice (as when Machiavelli expounds his new method of basing political action on the emulation of great men or great peoples, or Hobbes bases his new science of the state on the assumption that the commonwealth imitates the art of God) and to theory (as when scientists resort to the construction of models, or dialectical materialists and operationalists seek the test of theory in the reproduction or control of natural processes, in what Aristotle would have called the use of art to imitate and extend natural processes).

The inquiries of men concerning the things that surround them and the dialogue in which they communicate with each other are guided and influenced by themes. The terms and concepts in which those themes are expressed are ambiguous, and the relations of terms and concepts to one another in the development or expression of the theme alter and change. The theme may for a time bring together in one concept many related ideas and data, and then the unity may break and the connections be lost. The theme may for a time set up basic distinctions which, with changes of definitions, are abandoned as unwarranted dichotomies and abstractions, separating facts into parts without basis in reality. The theme may for a time take the form of a concept or theory that is applied to facts to which it later seems irrelevant. Changes in concepts following the development of a single theme may affect the relations among ideas, the meanings of individual ideas, and the facts accepted as relevant or warranted as real. Inquiry and discussion are affected and determined, not only by these changes, but also by the relations among the themes and the techniques. The four techniques and the four themes by which these interrelations are explored in the following essays are sometimes used to distinguish and separate fields and activities. Philosophy or science then employs a scientific method or a logic in the determination and statement of truth; poetry employs figurative language to depict and to arouse emotions, including the emotion of love; history is constructed of singular propositions which designate or imitate individual things, events, and their interconnections; practical propositions use a rhetorical or persuasive mode of discourse to stir men to action or to turn them from actions they had contemplated. Or, on the other hand, truth, instead of being distinguished from the facts of history, the constructions of poetry, or the operations of practical action, may be identified with any one of them, or all four may be conceived to be the same; and, in that reduction, any one of the four—truth, love, freedom, or imitation—may take precedence.

Similarly methods may be distinguished according to their principles, purposes, and data: history may be conceived as a method by which to reproduce individual happenings in their individuality; rhetoric may be conceived as a method by which a speaker influences an audience by starting from its preconceptions and attitudes; logic, dialectic, or the scientific method may be conceived as a method by which theories are formed to account for regularities or recurrences in a group of phenomena, to relate them to other regularities in systems of laws, and to derive consequences in application and prediction; poetry may be conceived to be a method of creating an object of art whose unity is not the same as the facts to which it is related but is created by the artist and appropriate to his medium and whose effects are not practical actions induced by playing on prejudice and preconception but aesthetic contemplation and purgation of passions and their impulsions to action. Or, in turn, each of the methods may borrow from the others: philosophic and scientific methods are often treated as arts, reduced to history, or adapted to rhetorical devices of discovery; poetry is often treated as a vehicle of truths, an instrument of social control or change, or a method of recounting history; practical devices of agreement or persuasion are often sought in a campaign of truth, in adherence and conformity to facts, or in poetic adornments; history has become a dialectic and a science, an art and an instrument for practical action.

The influence of Athens on the culture of the West has been set

forth in poetry that celebrates the glory of Greece while imitating
its themes, meters, and forms; it has been traced in histories that
follow the development of influences, distinguish stages, periods,
epochs, and cultures, set forth the example of Greek heroes,
geniuses, and institutions, or expound the formulations of problems
and the inventions of hypotheses to solve them, while employing the
historical methods originated by the Greeks and the historical data
assembled in their histories; it has been explained in philosophies
that acknowledge the influence or refute the errors of Plato, Aristotle, Democritus, or the Sophists; it has been illustrated or advocated in practical action and statement that pursue ideals dreamed
of by Greek sages, poets, and politicians in circumstances, with instruments, and by institutions which the Greeks did not imagine.
But all these statements and actions are part of the dialogue and the
inquiry in which the themes of the Greeks assume many definitions
and their techniques take on many forms. In a significant sense the
real influence is in themes and techniques which elude and exceed
literal restatement. The influence of Greek philosophy is not found
in literal fidelity to doctrines or methods even by those who have
professed to follow the positions or to use the methods of Greek
philosophers; it is found rather in the living influence of Greek
themes and techniques that is encountered even in the modification
of concepts and the transformation of methods by men who know
Greek philosophy only indirectly in doctrines and proofs influenced
by ancient philosophy and who often rediscover ancient doctrines
when they refute what they conceived to be the doctrine of Plato,
Aristotle, or Democritus. The influence of Greek poetry is not
found in literal imitation of Greek epic, tragedy, comedy, pastoral,
or ode; it is found rather in the inspiration by which poetic themes
and poetic devices have led to the creation of other forms or the use
of other materials to attain like poetic ends. The influence of Greek
practical ideals and human relations is found, not in the survival of
Greek political, social, or economic institutions, but in the adaptabil-
ity to changing circumstances of ideals which the Greeks expressed
and modes of communication which they used and in forms of

homogeneity that have emerged in the Western world as a result of the experiences and the expressions of the ancient Greeks. History, finally, has continued to discover characteristic periods, causal lines, exemplary models, and developments in the arts and disciplines; yet the influence of Greek history is found in no one statement of subsequent events as continuations of those which the Greeks recorded but rather in the aid which their insights and hypotheses have afforded to each succeeding age in rewriting history to the requirements and aspirations of later times, different places, and strange people.

I

Love and Philosophical Analysis

The guests of Agathon, after they had dined and had poured a libation to Dionysus, discussed whether or not they should drink and listen to the music of a flute-girl and decided instead to speak, one after the other, in praise of love. The course of action which Plato describes in the *Symposium* would have little plausibility as a modern narrative. It would have scant ground in modern habits, expectations, or institutions—apart from changes in the conventions of dining, drinking, and conversing and in the relations of classes in society, the communication and concourse of friends, and the status of poetry and poetic competitions in the state, the subject matter discussed by Socrates and his companions has undergone profound alterations. The argument by which Eryximachus supported the topic, that no poet had yet written a song in praise of Eros, has long ceased to be true; and few philosophers would welcome the topic enthusiastically today for the reason given by Socrates, that he professed to understand nothing except love matters—ἐρωτικά. Those modern philosophers who do profess to understand love prefer to talk about it by treating one of its contraries. Dr. Menninger, thus, hesitated before naming his recent book *Love against Hate*, because there is a general tendency to shrink from the use of the word "love" as being sentimental, romantic, or weak. Titles using the words "hate," "war," "conflict," and the like (Dr. Menninger for some reason does not include "fear" and "tension" explicitly in his list) are considered more acceptable because they sound strong, scientific, and dignified and at the same time somewhat deterrent. This attitude toward "love" epitomizes for Dr. Menninger the chief message of his book and its commentary on our

civilization.[1] Love has continued to be a theme for poets and psy-
chiatrists, and recollection of the Platonic *Symposium* suggests today, not a philosophy of love, as it has at various times in the past,
but reflections on the ways in which men have talked about love—
the different arts and techniques by which it has been developed in
application to the relations of men to women, friends, and societies,
to mankind, the universe, and God—and the different circumstances in which the discussions have occurred—the methods, manners, and persistent yet altering subject matters of discussion of
symposia.

In antiquity the symposium was recognized both as a literary
form and as a social institution. Hermogenes of Tarsus, the rhetori-
cian, writing in the second century A.D., treats the symposium as
one of five literary forms—Socratic symposium, oration, dialogue,
comedy, and tragedy—defining each according to the double method which it employs. Popular oratory combines reprehension with
consolation; comedy conjoins the bitter and the ridiculous; tragedy
links pity and wonder; the Socratic symposium joins the serious
and the ridiculous in persons and in things; the dialogue employs
arguments which exhibit character and arguments designed for investigation and dispute.[2] Athenaeus of Naucratis, writing in the
third century A.D., examines the banquet exhaustively as a social
institution, seeking evidence and data from all sources: the messes
at Sparta and Crete and the dinners of heroes celebrated by Homer
and the poets as well as the conversations of philosophers. Hermogenes finds the models of his literary form in the symposia of
Plato and Xenophon; Athenaeus, on the contrary, finds the customs,
actions, characters, sentiments, and manners portrayed by Homer
preferable to those set forth by the philosophers—by Plato,
Xenophon, and Epicurus.[3] Much that is irrelevant to the treatment
of the style of the symposium, considered as a literary form, becomes important in accounts of symposia, treated as a social institution. Athenaeus' *Deipnosophistae* touches on almost every conceivable subject, including recipes and table etiquette. Other
writers, like Plutarch, collect the topics discussed at symposia and

argue that the philosophic queries and discourses recorded by Plato and Xenophon have a lasting quality that renders inappropriate accounts of the costly dishes, sauces, and wines served at the houses of Agathon and Callias.[4] The form of the symposium may be examined as a literary genre; the institution of the symposium may be studied for insight into a culture and for inspiration to pursue like values; the subject matters discussed may be preserved for utility and erudition; but if the symposium is to be examined for a structure of philosophical argument, the *Symposium* of Plato stands apart, not only from the symposia of poets, satirists, and scholars, but also from those of other philosophers, for the Platonic argument binds together and transforms the method, the circumstances, and the subject matter of discussion and lights up the literary criticism of the symposium as art form, the sociological traits of dining and drinking together, and the erudite collections of table talk.

The method of dialectic, as Plato conceived it, does more than construct a formal statement or adapt an argument to data and principles: it is adjusted to the character of the disputants no less than to the peculiarities of their subjects; and the solution of the problem, the clarification of the understanding, and the development of the argument are inseparable parts of one process. The speeches in the *Symposium* are composed in distinctive styles, each appropriate to the speaker who uses it precisely because it is adapted to the position he wishes to express concerning the common subject, love. The truth about love, in so far as it is attained, is found in no one speech, but rather in the development and context in which the variety of meanings of love is explored. In a significant sense it is Alcibiades, not Socrates, who has the last word, while the violent piety and traditionalism to which Aristophanes gives comic expression contain a threat which is not lessened by the argument of Socrates.

All the chief participants in the *Symposium*, except Aristophanes, were present in the *Protagoras* as silent observers during the discussion of whether or not virtue can be taught. Phaedrus, whose enthusiasm for Lysias' discourse on the advantages of the nonlover as lover is described in the dialogue that bears Phaedrus' name, echoes

Lysias' style. He quotes the poets to support a conception of love as the cause of the greatest good to man in life and in death; by it lovers are led to deaths celebrated and interpreted by poets—the death of Alcestis, the lover who died for love; the death of Orpheus, the lover who did not dare to die; the death of Achilles, beloved but not a lover, who sacrificed his life for Patroclus the lover. Pausanias, the friend and lover of Agathon and his companion in exile at the court of Archelaus, employs the rhetoric of Prodicus in his speech. He touches on the paradox of the love which Phaedrus described by criticizing him for failing to state what kind of love he praised. Pausanias differentiates two kinds: a heavenly and an earthly love whose differences are apparent in their objects and in the associations and societies of men. The political institutions of Elis, Boeotia, and Ionia and of tyrannies in general reflect the earthly love as contrasted with the path of the heavenly love practiced in Athens. The speech of Eryximachus, a physician, recalls the rhetoric of Hippias. He approves the distinction of Pausanias but criticizes the narrow restriction of love to men, and his speech extends it, on the evidence of the sciences—of medicine, music, astronomy, and the mantic art—to the attraction of all things to a variety of things, which works in the bodies of all animals and all growths upon the earth. His is a cosmic love, but he does not neglect the motions of love in its sexual or political applications. Aristophanes had satirized the philosophy of Socrates in his *Clouds*, and his speech in the *Symposium* imitates the method of his comic art, setting forth a myth of separation, search, and return, which accords with the love encountered in poetry, politics, and nature.

The discourses after Aristophanes' natural history of love place a new emphasis on the need to define its essence before examining its processes and operations. Agathon, the tragic poet whose victory was the occasion of the symposium, uses a figurative style in his speech in which Socrates humorously finds borrowings from the rhetoric of Gorgias. Agathon's criticism of all the speeches is that they have not praised the god or stated his nature. He therefore presents the nature of love, with generous quotations from the poets, as most beautiful and most virtuous and for that reason the source of all good things. Socrates confesses that the preceding speeches convinced him that he was ignorant of the method of praising love, although he had thought himself expert on love matters and had been prepared to give a fine speech because he knew the truth, and he therefore secures permission to use his customary method, the cross-questioning elenchus. His dialogue with Agathon demonstrates that love is not beautiful, and his speech recounts a dialogue with Diotima, who was expert in matters of love and who had helped the Athenians delay the coming of the plague. In that dialogue love is shown to be neither beautiful nor ugly, neither good nor bad, neither god nor man. Many kinds of love and many kinds of poetry are distinguished, since the whole cause of whatever passes from not being into being is poetry, so that the productions of all arts are kinds of poetry and their craftsmen are all poets. A ladder of such loves is constructed from beautiful bodies, to beautiful habits, to beautiful learning, and at last to the study of beauty itself, which makes possible the reinterpretation of the insights of the poets, the practices of the politicians, and the knowledge of the scientists. Alcibiades was known for beauty, talents, and dissipation and, to the reader of the dialogue, for the disaster his ambitions brought on Athens. His speech is a myth which sets forth the uniqueness of Socrates as a lover to balance the myth constructed by Aristophanes to show the common urge implanted by love in all men. All five of the literary forms distinguished by Hermogenes are here: there are rhetorical speeches, not deliberative orations, to be sure, but encomia, combining praise and blame; there are dialogues in which the arguments are moral and investigatory, since they both show forth the characters of the speakers and advance inquiry and dispute; the work itself is a symposium combining the serious and the ridiculous in men and in things; and it closes with the argument of Socrates to demonstrate to Agathon and Aristophanes that the knowledge required to write comedy and tragedy is the same, recalling briefly in that episode the identity for dialectic of oration, dialogue, symposium, comedy, and tragedy.

Love and Philosophical Analysis

When one turns from the form to the circumstances of the discussion of love, the prominent part played by drinking and drunkenness is obtrusive. The speakers complain, at the beginning of the dialogue, of the effects of excessive drinking the night before, and some of them slip away to escape the drinking that is resumed after the entrance of Alcibiades. Drink is of particular importance in characterizing three of the speakers. Aristophanes acknowledges that he was among those who went to extremes on the previous day; he is prevented from taking his proper turn as speaker by an attack of hiccoughs; and he is one of those still drinking at the end of the dialogue until he drops off to sleep. Alcibiades bursts into the party drunk and in love, protests that the company looks sober, persuades them to drink, and chooses his subject, the praise of Socrates rather than the praise of love, after remarking the injustice of pitting a drunken man against sober tongues. In the preliminary discussion of whether the company should drink or talk Socrates is left out of consideration, since drinking or not drinking is a matter of indifference to him, and at the end he leaves to go about his business after the hardiest drinkers have fallen asleep.

One is tempted, so prominent is the place of drinking in the discussion, to find a difference of literary genre in the difference between drinking together and eating together, between symposia and banquets, but that temptation encounters the philological impediment that the word "συμπόσιον" does not occur in Plato's *Symposium* except as its title; Agathon's party is called a dinner (δεῖπνον), a dining-together (σύνδειπνον), and a being-together (συνουσία), but never a symposium. Indeed, the temptation probably reflects a memory of the orderliness of Hellenistic pedantries or the simplicities of Roman common sense which we usually fall back on in our contact with Hellenic wisdom. Cicero invented the word "compotatio" to distinguish the symposium from the "concenatio" or banquet and to make clear the superiority of the Roman over the Greek tradition:

For our fathers did well in calling the reclining of friends at feasts a *convivium*, because it implies a communion of life, which is a better designation than that of the Greeks, who call it sometimes a "drinking together" (*compotatio*) and sometimes an "eating together" (*concenatio*), thereby apparently exalting what is of least value in these associations above that which gives them their greatest charm.[5]

For Plato the relations among drink, love, virtue, poetry, and philosophy are more subtle and more deeply laid. In the *Phaedrus* Socrates differentiates two kinds of madness, one arising from human diseases, the other from a divine release from customary habits; and of the divine madness he finds four kinds: prophecy inspired by Apollo, the mystic madness by Dionysus, the poetic by the Muses, and the madness of love, inspired by Aphrodite and Eros.[6] One of the great problems which Socrates pursued throughout his life was whether virtue can be taught. It can be taught, under the perfect conditions of the ideal state, by dialectic and philosophy. But Socrates also learned from Diotima that love is engendering and begetting in beauty;[7] that true love or even true pederasty is the ascent from beautiful things, to beautiful souls, to beauty; and that love teaches virtue;[8] and he argued that to hate what ought to be hated and to love what ought to be loved is the mark of true education.[9] Wine, too, assists in teaching virtue, for it serves a function for the old in inculcating virtue or its use, similar to that of music for the young;[10] and in the actual or second best state described in the *Laws* the good legislator will lay down the laws of drinking and of music,[11] and the state itself is ruled not by dialecticians but by a Nocturnal Council of older men.

Love, the subject, displays all the complexities discovered in the method and circumstances of the discussion. Plato's starting point is the partial truths of poets and sophists: the dark, mysterious love celebrated by poets which is the source of good and of destruction, the self-centered love which finds its end in the satisfaction of desires and impedes true goods in the pursuit of its pleasures, the bonds of association which practical politicians and sophists would reduce to the operation of power, and the impulsions and motions of things which scientists would reduce to congeries of bodies. Love is a madness comparable to the madness or inspiration of poetry, of

wine, or of prophecy. Those madnesses have a bearing on the analyses of practical and of theoretic knowledge. Callicles undertakes, in
the *Gorgias*, to defend his doctrine that luxury and licentiousness
and liberty, if they have the support of force, are virtue and happiness, by the fact that the stronger are able to benefit their friends
out of their accumulations,[12] while Socrates argues, in the course of
his refutation of that doctrine, that such a man cannot be the friend
of man or God, "since he cannot commune with any, and where
there is no communion, there can be no friendship (φιλία). And
wise men tell us, Callicles, that heaven and earth and gods and men
are held together by communion and friendship, by orderliness, and
temperance, and justice; and that is the reason, my friend, why they
call the whole of this world by the name of order (κόσμος), not of
disorder or dissoluteness."[13] In the *Republic* Plato seeks to unify the
state by binding the ruling class together by the love that characterizes members of a family[14] and by assimilating all their loves to
philosophy, the love of wisdom.[15] Even in the second best state of
the *Laws* one of the necessary ingredients of a state is found to be
friendship.[16] The knowledge which is the basis for practical action
is identical with science and wisdom. Sexual love, pleasure in the
satisfaction of desires, affection or friendship are all given their
grounds, their rectification, and their completion in the love of
eternal forms and beauty.

There is an order of loves that runs from the divine love inspired
by the highest values, dimly discerned and rarely approximated, to
the lowest degradation and perversion that man can suffer in lust
and madness. In that order there are contradictions and antagonisms, not only among desires on the same plane, but also among the
levels by which man mounts to wisdom or falls to folly. Each of the
four madnesses runs this range from wisdom to folly, confusion,
and degradation. Poets may teach virtue, but unguided by dialectic
they may teach vice and so merit banishment from states that benefit by the rule of philosopher-kings or prudent legislators; wine may
assist in teaching virtue, but drunkenness brutalizes man; mystic
possession may be religious inspiration or lunacy; and love, finally,

may be directed to beauty and the good, or it may be directed to the objects of the various passions. After Plato has set forth the characteristics of the perfect state and of the corresponding "philosophic man" in the *Republic*, he traces the line of progressive degradation that may come to states and to men as they fall in the scale of loves or desires or pleasures. The principle governing the process in individual men is that each of the three parts of the soul—the rational, the spirited, and the appetitive—has its own form of pleasure and its peculiar desire, and any one of the three may govern the whole of man. There are, therefore, three classes of men: the knowledge-loving or philosophic, the honor-loving or ambitious, and the men who satisfy appetites so multifarious that the class can be designated best as money-loving, since money is the principal means of satisfying desires of this kind.[17] The perfect state corresponds to philosophic natures, the timocratic state to ambitious natures, and three kinds of appetites serve to distinguish three kinds of men and states: the necessary appetites corresponding to the oligarchical state, the unnecessary appetites corresponding to the democratic state, and the lawless appetites corresponding to the despotic state.[18] It is at that lowest level—the man ruled by lawless desires and the despotic state—that the four madnesses make their reappearance in completely perverted forms: the tragedians are banished because they praise despotism,[19] and the master-passion that rules the lawless soul combines the traits of drunkenness (μεθυστικός), lust (ἐρωτικός), and lunacy (μελαγχολικός).[20]

The history of symposia, considered as philosophic arguments, may be traced by following the development of methods of discourse adjusted, under the constant circumstances of the dinner table, to a variety of objects of love. The *Symposium* of Xenophon centers about Socrates, but the loves that inspire it are not those revealed by Diotima. Xenophon gives as his purpose in writing the dialogue the intention to relate not only the serious acts of great and good men but also what they do in their lighter moods. The dinner is held, not in the house of a tragic poet to celebrate the victory of one of his tragedies, but in the house of Callias, the patron of

sophists, and was assembled on the spur of the moment to celebrate
the victory in the pancratium of the boy Autolycus of whom Callias
was enamored. The dancing girl is not sent away, but on the contrary her dexterity is one of the subjects of conversation, and wine
is praised, in "Gorgian" rhetorical figures, for bringing us by
gentle persuasion to a more sportive mood. Love is discussed on a
level which does not stray far from application to the love of Callias,
even when the earthly is distinguished from the divine love, or
when the influence of love on political and military virtues is remarked. There is evidence that the love which inspired other philosophical dinners was the love of technical erudition or of philosophical discussion: Aristotle's *Symposium* seems, on the testimony of
the ancients, to have been a treatise on drunkenness, while the
philosophers talk shop in many of the surviving fragments of
Epicurus' *Symposium*.

A different direction is taken in pursuit of different loves in the
symposia of Menippos, the Cynic satirist, and of his imitators—
Meleager, Lucilius, Varro, Horace, Petronius, Lucian, and Julian.
Many of these exist in more than disjointed fragments: they are
dinners in which the objects of love are luxury, wine, woman, and
song, and in which excesses are tempered only by comedy and
satire. Horace recounts, in the eighth satire of Book ii of his *Satires*,
the fiasco of a symposium in which the love of food (described in
detail) vies with the love of ostentation and of affected erudition in
the discourse and behavior of wealthy epicures. In Petronius' *Feast
of Trimalchio* the ostentation is even greater and the gluttony and
lechery without curb. Lucian's *Symposium or the Lapiths* varies the
pattern by assembling philosophers of all schools at dinner and ex-
hibiting the quarrels that arise from the antagonisms of their baser
loves.

Still another direction is taken in the erudite collections of table
talk of Plutarch, Athenaeus, and Macrobius, which reflect, not a
love of wisdom or of knowledge, but a love of information, of the
records of the past, and of odd facts observed or alleged. Plutarch
justifies his zeal in assembling the varieties of topics discussed at

symposia in the vast compilation of the nine books of his *Symposiac Problems* on the grounds that, although it is wise to forget absurdities, as Euripides says, nevertheless to deliver to oblivion all that is said under the influence of wine is not only repugnant to the conciliating influence attributed to entertainment but also contrary to the known practice of the greatest philosophers—Plato, Xenophon, Aristotle, Speusippus, Epicurus, Prytanis, Hieronymus, Dion the Academic—who thought it worth while to record the discourses they had at table.[21] In his *Symposium of the Seven Wise Men* Plutarch takes advantage of the tradition that the seven sages met and dined at Delphi to assemble them at table where they discourse in the extant fragments of their wisdom. In *Men Learned about Dinner*, the *Deipnosophistae*, Athenaeus organizes a sprawling encyclopedic body of information in a dinner conversation about themes appropriate to cookbooks and to the etiquette of the table and of table talk. The *Saturnalia* of Macrobius records a vast amount of antiquarian knowledge: analyses of Virgil, the arts of rhetoric, literature, and linguistics, religious observances and practices of the augural art, items from the philosophic and the astronomic sciences; and, when the question is raised at the beginning of the seventh book concerning whether or not it is appropriate to philosophize at table, one of the interlocutors, the philosopher Eustathius, advances the principle that it is inappropriate to disturb the gaiety of convivia with discord, and therefore, although no word was pronounced at the symposia of Plato, Xenophon, and Plutarch which did not savor of philosophy, philosophic considerations would have spoiled the charm of the symposia of the Phaeacians and the Carthaginians recorded by Homer and Virgil. The history of symposia, and of the kinds of love they celebrate, comes to an appropriate end with the *Banquet of the Ten Virgins* of St. Methodius. There are echoes of Plato in both the doctrine and the manner of this chaste feast: the account of the dinner is given by a wise woman who resembles Diotima, in some respects, and the gathering occurs in the garden of Arete, the daughter of Philosophy; but the ten discourses of the virgins and the eleventh discourse of Arete are in praise of chastity, which the first speaker characterizes as the best and noblest manner of life, the only root of immortality, and the specifically Christian virtue, since Christ was the first to teach virginity.[22] At the beginning of the discourse, Arete, the hostess, remarks that they have had all kinds of food and a variety of festivities. But there is no mention of wine.

In antiquity the symposium was a literary form based on a social institution. During the Middle Ages the supper became a sacrament based on the celebration of a religious holiday. The Synoptic Gospels recount the consecration of bread and wine by Christ on the Passover, while the Fourth Gospel sets forth the discourse in which Christ instituted a new commandment: "That ye love one another; as I have loved you, that ye also love one another,"[23] and set forth a new ladder of love: "As the Father hath loved me, so have I loved you: continue ye in my love. If ye keep my commandments, ye shall abide in my love; even as I have kept my Father's commandments, and abide in his love."[24] The word used to express this love is not ἔρως, or στέρξις, which carry the association of sexual passion, nor στοργή, which connotes parental affection, nor φιλία, which is the affection which binds friends or social groups together, but ἀγάπη, which is the attachment which members of a family feel for each other, although in tragedy it seems to have been used only of affection for the dead. It was translated by *caritas* and *charity*, and the gatherings in which the early Christians celebrated the memory of Christ's injunctions were called ἀγάπαι. In the latter use, the term went through a development and reversal familiar in the dialectic of love: early apologists, like Tertullian and Minucius Felix, complained that the critics of the Christians think of their gatherings as orgies, such as were common among the pagans, heightened by illicit and perverted practices: incest, the adoration of the genital organs of the priest, and the sacrifice of children; a century or two later St. Gregory Nazianzen admonishes the innocent, in his *Precepts to Virgins*, to avoid ἀγάπαι, and Augustine condemns drunken *convivia* in honor of the martyrs and in memory of the dead.[25]

The two traditions of love whose beginnings were sensed in the *Symposium* of Plato—the tradition of the dark and mysterious love of the mystic and the poet by which the lover is carried to his perfection and to his destruction and the practical self-centered love of the man of affairs and the scientist directed to the attainment of what is desired—influenced the development of the Christian conception of love. They were held in check, moreover, both in the construction of the community of the church and in the formation of the doctrine of the faith, by devices that show the influence of the Platonic dialectic and doctrine. But although there was place in Christianity for the insights of the Eastern mystery religions and for the clarities of Greek philosophy, there was no place for symposia. The new conception of charity gave new force to the conception of the brotherhood of man by relating the fatherhood of God to a free gift of divine love. The unity of the organization of the church was, like that which Plato advocated in the *Republic*, the unity of one family, but it was a mystic marriage, in which the virtues of the human bridegroom or bride included chastity and virginity, temperance and abstinence, and in which faith excluded the trifles of vain philosophy. The tradition of dining did not encourage random conversation among the clergy, and, when the religious orders were formed, silence was frequently enjoined at meals. The doctrine of love, as it was elaborated by St. Augustine, fresh from his reading of Plotinus, found philosophic grounds for the distinction between two loves: concupiscence and charity.[26] St. Augustine analogized the motions of bodies and souls and defined love as the weight by which the soul is borne wherever it is borne.[27] Many objects of love attract men, and they are united in polities—in terrestrial cities and in the City of God—which differ according to the objects of love by which they are ordered. Charity, however, is the love by which one loves that which should be loved.[28] The prescription of the Christian life is, "Love and do what you will," for all loves are mediated by the love of God, and God is charity.

The great antagonists in the development of this doctrine during the early centuries of Christianity were the Gnostics and the Manichaeans, who built their doctrines on dualisms rather than on the single principle of love. Christian opponents record that the first principle of the Gnostic, Simon Magus, was fire, which has a double aspect, one evident, the other secret, one visible, the other invisible. It was this distinction, according to Simon, that Plato had in mind when he distinguished the sensible from the intelligible, and Aristotle formulated it in the distinction between potentiality and actuality. Divine fire manifests itself in six eons, which proceed in pairs, one male, the other female. The first pair are νοῦς and ἐπίνοια, Mind and Thought. Epinoia had been taken prisoner by the angels and had been incarnated by them, after many sufferings, in a human body destined to pass through the centuries from woman to woman. It was Epinoia who was Helen of Troy, and in the time of Simon she was a prostitute, whom Simon delivered in the person of Helen and made his companion. Salvation depends wholly on belief in Simon and Helen, and human works, good or bad, are indifferent; indeed, promiscuity constitutes the perfect ἀγάπη, the reciprocal sanctification.[29] The dualism of the Manichaeans consisted in two eternal, opposed principles, Good and Evil, Light and Darkness. Man, like the world, is moved by two principles, for he possesses two souls, one incapable of evil, the other subject to all the impulsions of concupiscence. Jesus alone can impart the knowledge by which man can separate the luminous from the dark elements in himself and so escape the consequences of the deeds of the seductress Eve. Marriage and all propagation are prohibited to Manichaeans, since birth encases the luminous in the darkness of body, and the practice of virginity is therefore a duty imposed on all.[30]

Philosophers during the Middle Ages turned their attention and their inquiries both to the sacrament of the Holy Supper and to the doctrine of charity. When John Scotus Eriugena went to Paris in the ninth century, he accepted the invitation of canon lawyers to resolve the controversy raging concerning the Eucharist. His book has not survived, and his doctrine—that we eat the body of Christ intellectually with mind, not physically with teeth—was condemned. In the eleventh century Berengar of Tours wrote a treatise *De Coena Sacra* to answer Lanfranc's charge that he had destroyed the sacrament by analyzing the changes undergone by the bread and wine in terms of matter and form, substance, subject, and accident and by applying the principle of contradiction. The interchange between Lanfranc and Berengar was a stage in the development of the dispute concerning universals in the twelfth century. The scholastic method, by which arguments are presented on either side of a question and their oppositions are balanced and resolved, was developed by canon lawyers, theologians, and philosophers to treat such controversies; and the nature of the Eucharist was treated in the twelfth, thirteenth, and fourteenth centuries in *Decreta, Commentaries on the Sentences of Peter Lombard*, and in *Summae theologicae*.

Philosophers developed philosophic analyses of the doctrines of charity to extend and apply, in varying ways, Augustine's insight that charity excludes concupiscence and cupidity but is consistent with many kinds of love and that love does not cause one to cease desiring one's own good when one loves the good of another or when one loves the source of love without thought of recompense. Mystical philosophies mount gradations of love to the love of God, often with imagery appropriate to the psychology of sexual love, and the ruses of Ovid are transmuted in allegory to mystical stratagems. Other philosophic analyses distinguish varieties of love: Thomas Aquinas places love between delectation, which is merely one form taken by love, and charity, which is its perfection; Duns Scotus differentiates three loves on the authority of Augustine: a love of the useful, a love of the delectable, and a love of the honorable; loves are also differentiated by their objects—beauty, order, and goodness—and by the relations they establish among men in their associations, friendships, and cities. During the eleventh and twelfth centuries, moreover, dualistic doctrines were revived in the Catharist and Albigensian heresies, in which many scholars see extensions of Gnosticism and Manichaeism, and poets sang in the language and the mood of those doctrines of a courtly love in which the lover is victim of a destiny, imposed by love, which leads him to humiliation and destruction. The conflict of the two traditions is brought together vividly in the legend of a dinner given by Louis IX: one of his guests, Thomas Aquinas, who had not spoken throughout the meal, disclosed the direction of his thoughts when at last he interrupted his silent preoccupation and exclaimed: "That disposes finally of the Manichaeans."

As the Middle Ages came to their close, symposia were revived in a fashion characteristic of the changing conception of love. The *Convivio* of Dante affords a transition between his *Vita nuova* and his *Divina commedia*. In the *Vita nuova* the poet's passion for a living woman, Beatrice, is given an allegorical interpretation. In the *Convivio* the thought of Beatrice has been superseded in the poet's mind by a love of philosophy, but, although the meat and the bread of the feast he prepares are symbolic, the lady who affords him consolation for his loss of Beatrice emerges as somewhat more than an allegorical figure symbolizing the truths of philosophy in their application to life and somewhat more than a symbol of the second Person of the Trinity. In the *Divina commedia* his early love is finally restored to him, transformed into the object of his spiritual devotion, and she leaves her place in heaven to be his monitress and guide. Marsilio Ficino's *Commentary on the Symposium of Plato on the Subject of Love* is itself a symposium, organized by Lorenzo de' Medici in the villa of Careggi about 1470 to celebrate Plato's birthday, at which the guests deliver speeches interpreting the speeches of the original symposium. What Agathon's guests said is placed by Lorenzo's guests in a context of Neoplatonic erudition which makes their statements consistent parts of a cosmology, stated in terms of Mind, Soul, Nature, and Matter ruled by Love.[31] Pico della Mirandola's *Platonic Discourse upon Love* is not a symposium but a commentary on a poem—the *Canzone dello amore secondo la mente e opinione de' Platonici*, in which Girolamo Benivieni tries to reproduce in poetic summary what Marsilio Ficino had set forth in his commentary on the *Symposium*.[32] During the Renaissance the erudition and philosophy of love were expounded in accounts of allusive and learned conversations and in parabolic and cryptic interpretations of poetry, myth, and history (and indeed Bacon listed the insufficient development of the parabolical interpretation of poetry among the deficiencies of learning); but, although the quest for learning and analogies which characterized one tradition of symposia continued from the Renaissance to the modern period, the symposium did not survive as a widely cultivated literary form.

Sacrificial elements were present in the ancient symposium—the libations and the chant to the god between the close of the dinner and the beginning of the drinking—which provide at least a tenuous link with the celebration of the Passover and the sacrifice of the Mass. The heritage which survived in the modern period has equally tenuous links with the ancient symposium, yet the history of that heritage throws some light on the larger problems of love in the modern world. If the heritage is sought in literary genres, the modern form of the symposium is the "Table Talk," that is, the collections of unpublished sayings of men thought wise in religion, politics, or literature, such as Luther, Selden, Coleridge, or Holmes, or the similar collections in the vast literature of "Ana," such as *Baconiana, Scaligeriana, Valesiana,* which culminates significantly in the *Omniana,* published usually together with Coleridge's *Table Talk.* These miscellanies merge easily with the diaries, like Pepys's, and the biographies, like Boswell's *Johnson,* which bring together the supplementary thoughts and casual statements of great or interesting men. The phase of the ancient tradition of symposia that has survived and grown strong in this tradition is found in the *Saturnalia,* with its love of private and otherwise unavailable data, useful in interpreting what is apparent and available to all. The information recorded in such collections is only occasionally and accidentally about love, usually in odd, paradoxical, or fearful forms, as when Luther interprets the Ten Commandments as reiterated injunctions to fear and love God, expresses his horror at the consequences of the contempt and persecution by men of God's grace and word, and his urgent conviction of the need to be reconciled to God.[33] If the heritage of symposia is sought, not in the literary form, but in the history of the term, "symposium" today means the discussion of any subject, particularly one concerning which there are urgent doubts and active apprehensions, preferably by experts but at least by representatives of divergent views; and we organize, as a consequence, symposia on cancer, the dangers threatening democracy, the predicament of poetry or the humanities, and the present status of the mind-body problem. Table talk and symposia, however, have no close connection with the dinner table, and, if the heritage of the ancient form is sought in the institutions surrounding dining, it is found in the after-dinner speech, in which serious topics are treated lightly or, following the formula of Hermogenes, the serious and the ridiculous are conjoined.

Each of these tenuous connections of present practices with a great tradition is a sign and symptom of the transformation of the subject matter which is relevant in the discussion of love. The widespread acceptance of a religious revelation during the Middle Ages transformed the ancient vocabulary and dialectic of love to the service and elucidation of a divine charity; the widespread applications of science in the modern period have transformed the analysis of love and the precepts of charity to the service of the communities of men. We preserve the notebooks as well as the published treatises of men of science and of wisdom lest any useful or suggestive item of information escape us; we institute discussions because we seek expert solutions of problems, although we also enjoy stumping and badgering the experts; and we cultivate the art of explaining lofty truths in common language and unforbidding contexts because we are convinced that knowledge should be popularized. But the new problems of love that have been created by science can be stated only in the transformed meanings attached to the old terms. Freud gives eloquent expression to one formulation of these problems in the final paragraph of his *Civilization and Its Discontents:*

The fateful question of the human species seems to me to be whether and to what extent the cultural process developed in it will succeed in mastering the derangements of communal life caused by the human instinct of aggression and self-destruction. In this connection, perhaps the phase through which we are at this moment passing deserves special interest. Men have brought their powers of subduing the forces of nature to such a pitch that by using them they could now very easily exterminate one another to the last man. They know this—hence arises a great part of their current unrest, their dejection, their mood of apprehension. And now it may be expected that the other of the two "heavenly forces," eternal Eros, will put forth his strength so as to maintain himself alongside of his equally immortal adversary.[34]

These eternal powers—death and love—have been opposed in other accounts that men have constructed to explain the career of man and of human society, but the struggle of those powers has taken on a new scope for destruction or for realization as a result of the advance of science.

All the analyses of our present frustrations and discontents express or apply theories of love, and all the past constructions of love have been adapted to the problems of a society transformed by science and technology. Two loves are sometimes contrasted, and in recent statements of that opposition they have been called again *eros* and *agape*. Denis de Rougemont, in *L'Amour et l'occident*, which appeared in England as *Passion and Society* and in the United States as *Love in the Western World*, distinguishes *eros*, a lawless passion, engaged in the pursuit of endless becoming, from Christian love, which returns to life from beyond death, obeys God, and brings forth our neighbor. Anders Nygren, in his *Agape and Eros*, contrasts egocentric *eros* to theocentric *agape* which Luther first established with the formula "Fellowship with God on the basis of sin, not of holiness."[35] M. C. D'Arcy, in *The Mind and Heart of Love: Lion and Unicorn, a Study in Eros and Agape* finds a new law of love which joins the self-centered and the disinterested love—the love of taking and the love of giving—in the relations of persons.[36] Much of modern theology and much of the new mysticism are stated in terms of two loves or more, and the solution to contemporary problems is then found in the transformation of one love by another or the abandonment of one for another in mysticisms such as Aldous Huxley preaches. On the other hand, love is sometimes sought beneath the appearances presented in conscious, or rational, or expressed intentions, and love is then pitted against an antagonist: idea overlays will, Apollonian is opposed by Dionysiac, love instincts run counter to death instincts, personalities are compounded of conscious egos and of the unconscious. The Romantic poetry and philosophy of the nineteenth century has been adapted to new uses in the twentieth century which concentrate attention almost exclusively on the term contrary to love: phenomenologists and existentialists study anxiety, historians study the deaths of civilizations, psychologists study guilt and fear, and sociologists study social tensions. In the third place, love is sometimes defined in minimum terms on which almost all philosophers and all the rest of mankind have agreed from Plato to the numerous schools of the present: "Now everyone sees that love is a desire," Socrates says at the beginning of his first speech about love in the *Phaedrus*, and Spinoza gives piquant mathematical precision to this common notion in his definition of love as "pleasure accompanied by the idea of an external cause." This common definition, which poets share with politicians, has been given a new extension in a technological civilization that has built the instruments by which most of the basic needs of men might be satisfied as well as the instruments by which men might be annihilated: most programs of international co-operation are expressions of this love—the Point IV program of the United States, the technical assistance program of the United Nations, the fundamental education program of UNESCO—and it is written into the Universal Declaration of Human Rights as "the right freely to participate in the cultural life of the community, to enjoy the arts, and to share in the scientific advancement and its benefits." But politicians encounter opposition to these programs, not only in other politicians who are corrupted by some narrower loyalty or by love of power or of money, but also in recipients who fear cultural imperialism; and poets are determined in the selection of themes of love by political decision in dictatorships and by force of economic circumstance and social preference in democracies. Love, finally, is sought sometimes, in a fourth way, in the bonds of communities and in the values which determine the patterns of cultures: this is perhaps the form of love which we have adapted to the most characteristic modern uses in our programs of international

Thought, Action, and Passion

understanding, our area and language courses, and our investigations of cultures and civilizations, for we have made the discussion of the love which binds men in communities, which the Greeks called φιλία, a battleground in which φιλία contends with passionate ἔρως, divine ἀγάπη, and scientific φιλότης.

This modern symposium, like many ancient symposia, might lead to a brawl, even without benefit of wine, if our problem required the resolution of the differences of these conceptions of loves. The question is not which is fundamental—subconscious drive, individual desire, community bond, or transcendent attraction—for they can all be explained on theories of sexual love or religious inspiration, of fundamental urges or social influences. Our experience with the intricacies of the earlier treatments of love suggests, therefore, that this discourse on love might best be brought to a useful or at least intelligible conclusion by abandoning the subject matter to consider the method and the circumstances of the discussion of love.

The methods which men have employed in the discussion of love through the ages have been carefully adapted to the subject matter. The dialectic method, as it was practiced in antiquity, whether by Plato in the whole of his philosophy or by Aristotle in the preliminaries to his scientific inquiries, was a method of resolving the differences of philosophers to discover a common truth which they all sensed or approximated. It was a method oriented to the requirements of the problem and to the nature of things, and its success depended, as Plato put it, on cutting at the joints. The scholastic method was likewise a method of resolving differences in the doctrines of philosophers and of the doctors of the church and in the decisions of popes and of councils. It, too, was adapted to the solution of problems and to the nature of things; but it was also adapted to treat the effects of a love first revealed in a scripture, and the interpretation of statements was therefore placed on a new level of importance in the interpretation of things. The scientific method, to which philosophers have been adjusting their inquiries for more than three hundred years, is also directed to resolving differences of doctrines that purport to state and explain what is the case. Great importance is still attached to the interpretation of symbols as well as to the interpretation of facts in the use of that method, but the new importance given to the consensus of scientists in the resolution of differences serves as a touchstone in interpreting the significance of the place assumed by φιλία in the modern period at the side of ἔρως and ἀγάπη.

It is a commonplace that philosophy, and indeed the whole of culture, has been a long dialogue in which old insights and old errors have been forgotten and revived, reinterpreted and refuted, and in which new insights and new errors have been supported by old and by new proofs. The scientific method, however, has made possible a new, more precise, and more practical form of the dialogue. When the implications of group thinking or team thinking in science are examined philosophically, however, they arrange themselves in a sequence that bears some analogies to the ladder of love which Diotima described to Socrates. We engage in group thinking, on its lowest level, whenever we use someone else's information or ideas; the group need not be assembled for such thinking—a book, a conversation, or a telephone call may provide the needed information. Group thinking assumes a second form when a problem requires for its solution many kinds of competence and many kinds of information: each member of the group then makes his contribution to the common task, and the solution is the composite result. There is a third kind of group thinking in which men of different backgrounds and different disciplines discuss a common problem, and the statement of a difficulty or a conjecture by an expert in one field, who is unaware of the implications of his statement and unable to develop them by the techniques he has mastered, may start in the mind of another expert a train of thought significant in his experience and adapted to the methods of his discipline which might not otherwise have occurred to him. Strictly speaking, none of these processes is *group* thinking, since in each an individual thinks in the varying contexts and influences of the group. There is a fourth stage of group thinking, however, in which the result exceeds, not only what any member of the group has thought, but also what emerges as the sum of their individual thoughts. There are not many clear examples of such thinking, but its nature may be seen in the contrast between philosophical dialogues in which one of the interlocutors is called "Master," or "Wisdom," or "Intelligence," and in which the truth is found exclusively in what he says, and philosophic dialogues, like Plato's and Hume's, in which the truth is expressed by no one speaker but is found in the total development of the discussion. This is a form of thinking that promises new achievements in two dimensions which are traditional paths of love: in the advancement of knowledge by common thinking in the service of the love of wisdom, and in the advancement of the community of men by common action based on the understanding rather than on the abandonment and destruction of the principles, ideals, and values which bind men by love in other or smaller groups.

We have only gradually become aware of the new philosophic problems presented by the possibility of this method and the complexity of its subject matter, and the discussion is still surrounded by circumstances over which the philosopher has no more control than Socrates had over the social tensions which Aristophanes symbolizes or the drunken frenzies embodied in Alcibiades. Plato enumerated four forms of divine madness—prophecy, poetry, love, and the mystic madness inspired by the god of wine—and his exploration of these madnesses shows that he was fully and subtly aware of the demoniac perversions to which each is susceptible. He could have had no inkling of the forms of power created by modern science which might remove the chief sources of man's insecurities and frustrations—disease, hunger, lack of shelter, and mutual fears —and he could not therefore have suspected the oppositions of power which hinder the use of those powers. These oppositions of divine and demoniac madness and these oppositions of disinterested and interested power are at the center of the philosophic problems to which the method of common or group thinking is adapted. If philosophers could construct some such method to explore the inter-relations of the many loves which divide them, as well as all other men, and which make them mutually unintelligible and mutually indifferent, our discussions, and those of the world, might return to circumstances in which the inspirations of poetry, wine, love, and religion inspire, confirm, and strengthen what reason is able to discover and establish, and in which the satisfaction of desires and the defense of traditional ideals does not automatically take the form of opposition to action for the common good.

II

Truth and the History of Ideas

Except for the works of Plato and Aristotle, no major body of ancient philosophical writings and, in particular, no work of any of the numerous philosophers who preceded them or were contemporary with them has been preserved, either complete or in more than fragmentary part. By the accident of survival the dialogues of Plato and the treatises of Aristotle have become our oldest, most reliable, and, in many cases, our chief sources of information concerning early Greek philosophy. But since, in addition to this use to which they have been put in later ages as meticulously worked sources for the philosophies of other men, they serve a primary purpose as expositions and demonstrations of philosophical principles and conclusions, the history they present and employ is involved in philosophical problems, and philosophical differences in the doctrines they develop often assume the guise of historical changes. In the long use to which the works of Plato and Aristotle have been put as historical sources, the influence of the ideas of the historian on the ideas whose history he treats—the interaction of history and philosophy which is common to all forms of the history of ideas—is made unusually clear by the partial vacuum in which history has placed their works. The relation is reciprocal, for not only are the form and content of historical statements affected by philosophy, but history is made to bolster up and illustrate philosophic conclusions.

History is used, in the most innocent of its applications to ideas, as well as in deliberate distortions, as a substitute for philosophic arguments and to support judgments of value and of truth. When the exposition of the history of developments in philosophy or science or institutions is imbedded in the statement of a philosophy, the doctrines of that philosophy, in whatever fashion they may be advanced—dogmatically or tentatively, dialectically or apodictically—must seem to occupy a favored place in the evolution as final culmination or balanced supplementation or needed corrective or, at least, as skeptical solvent. The philosophy of the author inevitably enters as a stage in the development when he writes of the history of philosophy; and when, as in the case of Plato and Aristotle, little early or independent evidence is available against which to check the history, there is no attractive alternative to acquiescing, as most scholars do, in the assumption that such implications are correct, that the processes of time have been selective, and that in the main it is the best that has survived. The most exhaustive statement of evidence to the contrary does little more than afford grounds for suspicions and inspire regrets concerning the paucity of even fragments of a writer as admired in antiquity as Democritus or the mystery that surrounds the origins, doctrines, and even the persons of the Pythagoreans or (to turn to writers about whom we have more information) the fragmentary state of the literary remains of writers like Heraclitus or the difficulties of interpretation which persist even when the broad lines of the organization of an argument are known, as in the case of Parmenides. There is little or no material available to the historian of philosophy with which to reduce—should he wish to—the enhancement which the historical statements of Plato and Aristotle give to their own philosophies or to combat the attendant impression that earlier movements reached their completion in the philosophy of the one or the other.

The effect of historical statements on the judgment of the value of a philosophy may, nonetheless, be separated from the related effects of a philosophy on historical statements, since there is no paucity of materials concerning the effects of the philosophies of Plato and Aristotle on their conceptions of history, and most of the research into the relations of both men to their predecessors turns, in fact, on that question. For philosophers quote the statements of other philosophers usually for philosophic purposes; and, since the impress of that purpose remains in the citation, what Plato and Aristotle say, for example, about a doctrine of Anaxagoras may serve as evidence either concerning the philosophy of Anaxagoras or equally well concerning the philosophies of Plato and Aristotle. Read as history, there are good reasons in the statements of Plato and Aristotle for refusing to accept unquestioningly their reports of prior tendencies of philosophic thought; and, even when the accuracy of the restatement is least doubtful, some readjustment is needed to re-establish from what is said the probable form or intention of the original statement. Read as philosophy, however, the whole bodies of their works serve as checks to the interpretation, for, in spite of the fact that the reports of Plato and Aristotle furnish us grounds for only tentative judgments concerning earlier philosophers, the manner in which they put the history of philosophy to philosophic uses bears the unmistakable mark of their own philosophic processes. The history of philosophy is itself a form of philosophic inquiry; and, when philosophy is the object of philosophic inquiry, questions of fact are inseparable from philosophic questions.

Philosophers appear in person and by report in the dialogues of Plato. They discuss problems themselves, listen to the development of their views by acknowledged pupils, and are represented in their absence by professed friends or disciples who state their views or by Socrates, who develops conjectural defenses and expansions of views attributed to them. The dialogues are constructed with a considerable apparatus, much admired by Platonic scholars, of dramatic indications bearing on historicity. Parmenides and Zeno speak in one dialogue and are referred to sympathetically in others; Heraclitus is represented by his pupil Cratylus and is quoted by Socrates, sometimes affectionately, sometimes satirically; Timaeus, Simmias, Cebes, and other speakers may be presumed to represent (or it may be argued that they do not represent) authentic Pythagorean doctrines; the Sophists stalk through a dozen dialogues: Protagoras and Hippias speak for themselves in dialogues called by their names, and both, no less than Gorgias and Prodicus, are represented by pupils or are cited with a respect—sometimes more, sometimes less, than half-ironic—by Socrates, while the younger Sophists and the men who espoused their teachings—men like Thrasymachus, Polus, and Callicles, Dionysodorus, Euthydemus, and Clinias debate riotously against Socrates and suffer crushing dialectical defeats at his hands. A milieu of philosophic and intellectual life is reconstructed, together with a sense of living thought and mellow understanding, and pertinence and insight are prominent in almost everything Plato says of the doctrines of other men. This is doubtless what is meant when Plato is commended, as he usually is, for his historical sense and historical accuracy.[1]

Whereas Plato conveys the impression of entering into the intentions of men and of determining, possibly even better than they, their true "meaning," nevertheless, he presents almost no precise information concerning early doctrines. There is very little direct quotation from philosophers in the dialogues, and those few citations are used primarily as excuses for dialectical expansions; so that, for example, when Theaetetus develops, on the prompting of Socrates, a relativistic doctrine of knowledge from Protagoras' statement, "Man is the measure of all things," insight into the thought of Protagoras is doubtless increased, but no clue is provided concerning its relation to what Protagoras said or meant: whether he himself derived these implications from the statement or whether he thought it expressed these doctrines. The interpretation of most of Plato's statements concerning the history of philosophy depends on nice adjustments, which provide abundant materials for scholarly disputes, between the recognition of his historical sense and the appreciation of his ironical humor; and, although the manner of thought of earlier philosophers may be learned in the dialogues, the doctrines conceived according to that manner are never specified.

Aristotle, on the other hand, seldom troubles to lay out the general lines or to establish the mood of a philosophy except as they help determine a particular doctrine, but he abounds in precise details, direct quotations, and schematic paraphrases. His treatment of earlier philosophers is dialectical, but not after the manner of Plato's dialectic or to the same end. When the discussion in a Platonic dialogue turns on the doctrines of a man, some pregnant statement (and a verse of a poet or a casual remark made by a friend in the market place will serve as well as the pondered conclusion of a philosopher) is usually quoted, then labored and refined in possible interpretations; when the statement is one made by a philosopher, it turns out to be—however inconsequential it may have seemed at first—the focus of a whole philosophic attitude. Aristotle usually opposes one philosopher's solution of a specific question to those of other philosophers and uses the divergences of past conclusions and methods of investigation as the dialectical starting point for his own solution. Whereas Plato's dialectic eventuates in what seems to be the determination in his own philosophy of what other philosophers must or should have meant, Aristotle's dialectic leads to the construction in his philosophy of a doctrine which he presents as a novel departure from all previous doctrines, which nonetheless combines all their virtues and avoids all their errors. One consequence of this treatment of earlier doctrines is that Aristotle is often criticized, particularly by modern philologists and philosophers, for failing to appreciate the work of his predecessors, for being "literal-minded" in interpreting statements which are often too technical or subtle or humorous for his comprehension and so distorting their significance, and, in a word, for lacking historical sense and historical accuracy.[2]

There is, in Plato's scheme, no difference between philosophy and the history of philosophy. Both are dialectical conversations, and the positions of past philosophers continue to exist, if at all, in the exposition of living disputants. The dialectic of Plato may be said to be directed (among other ends) to determining the meanings of statements, and there is no difference between the use of dialectic to interpret and develop the statement of other men's doctrines and their relations in the history of philosophy and its use to solve a philosophic question. The two enterprises are identical in method and are pursued simultaneously; but, although a dialogue may be concerned indifferently with the statements of generals, politicians, rhapsodes, young boys, sophists, or philosophers, from the point of view of history the treatment of the statements of the philosophers differs from all the rest and constitutes the history of philosophy adapted to Plato's dialectic.

If the difference between philosophy and history is accidental and slight for Plato, a rather more important difference appears in the conditions of truth and accuracy of philosophic and historical statements, inasmuch as the account of previous doctrines which results from Plato's dialectical approach to the history of philosophy has been accorded almost universal credence, whereas the results of his dialectical approach to philosophy have met on occasion with skepticism. In general, the dialectical interpretation of any statement will show it to have a vast number of meanings, all false except one, and a given statement may seem in different dialogues, or even in a single dialogue, to be refuted and in turn approved. This apparent instability in the meanings of statements is little to modern taste (to restrict the consideration of reactions hostile to Plato to this almost universal criticism),[3] and the Socrates of the dialogues has frequently in recent years been accused of sophistry and trickery in questions which are supposed to involve truth and falsity. The historical suggestion, however, that a philosopher contradicted himself or held obscure or absurd doctrines does not—naturally enough, if one considers the doctrines philosophers have held and have been admired for holding—stir the same reaction; and, since we do not have sufficient independent evidence to dispute conclusively any of Plato's interpretations, what Plato determines that a theory must have meant is taken as what its author in fact intended. Appeal from Plato's judgment can rely only on fragments which are seldom conclusive on a point concerning which Plato's exposition is detailed or on Aristotle's interpretation of the same philosophy, which when it differs from that of Plato (and, interpreted literally, Plato is often in contradiction to Aristotle) is, in the tradition of contemporary scholarship, almost always in error. Moreover, philosophers are seldom thought to be wrong in their interpretations of other philosophers when their treatment is sympathetic and favorable, and—with the exception of the Sophists—few named and identified philosophers are subjected to much harsh criticism by Plato. The rather considerable group of modern critics which has taken up the defense of the Sophists against Plato is therefore almost an isolated case in Platonic studies.[4]

For Aristotle, dialectic is not the method of science, and Aristotle's dialectical treatment of the opinions of other philosophers, whatever its utility to scientific inquiry, could never be confused with the actual collection of data or demonstration of conclusions which are essential to the constitution of a science. Aristotle distinguishes the dialectical method from the method of demonstration and indicates clearly that the treatment of philosophical opinions is dialectical, not demonstrative or scientific. Philosophers are set against philosophers or in support of philosophers; and their mutual relations and oppositions are frequently used as the first indication of the nature of a problem or the direction of possible solutions, preliminary to fitting the inquiry into its characteristically Aristotelian formulation of the problem or his scientific establishment of a hypothesis bearing on its solution. The treatment of philosophers, therefore, follows the technique of dialectic as presented in the *Topics*, that is, the method is one suited to the formulation of *problems* and the defense or refutation of *propositions* rather than a technique for establishing principles and definitions or for organizing demonstrations. "For our study of soul," Aristotle says before embarking on the investigation of psychological questions,

it is necessary, while formulating the problems of which in our further advance we are to find the solutions, to call into council the views of those of our predecessors who have declared any opinion on this subject, in order that we may profit by whatever is sound in their suggestions and avoid their errors.[5]

"Let us start," he says before investigating the question of the generation of the heavens,

with a review of the theories of other thinkers; for the proofs of a theory are difficulties for the contrary theory. Besides, those who have first heard the pleas of our adversaries will be more likely to credit the assertions which we are going to make. We shall be less open to the charge of procuring judgment by default. To give a satisfactory decision as to the truth it is necessary to be rather an arbitrator than a party to the dispute.[6]

He says in relation to metaphysics, in which his dialectical treatment of other views is most extended:

It is just that we should be grateful, not only to those whose opinion we may share, but also to those who have expressed more superficial views; for these also contributed something, by developing before us the powers of thought . . . for from the better thinkers we have inherited certain opinions, while the others have been responsible for the appearance of the better thinkers.[7]

Or again:

We must, with a view to the science which we are seeking, first recount the subjects that should be first discussed. These include both the other opinions that some have held on certain points, and any points besides these that happen to have been overlooked. For those who wish to get clear of difficulties it is advantageous to state the difficulties well; for the subsequent free play of thought implies the solution of the previous difficulties, and it is not possible to untie a knot of which one does not know. . . . Further, he who has heard all the contending arguments, as if they were the parties to a case, must be in a better position for judging.[8]

The treatment of earlier philosophers is still for Aristotle a dialectical conversation or debate, but the conversation is preliminary to the serious work of philosophy, no longer its whole task, and the dialectic by which the opinions of men are set before the judge differs from the logical processes by which definitions are related to facts and conclusions derived from premises.

The scientific method of Aristotle depends on the establishment of literal principles peculiar to each of the sciences as he classifies them and on the accumulation of a body of data proper to each science, derived ultimately from observation and organized in accordance with those principles. His citations of other men's doctrines and arguments are always in the context of one or the other of these processes—the clarification of principles or the explanation of phenomena—and they constitute a proper step in both. In any particular question relevant observations and even tentative classifications may be found before a scientific formulation of the question is discovered, and the first inklings of a theory may sometimes be traced beyond the earliest systematic exploration of the subject matter to which it is relevant. For the one purpose—for the examination of principles—the dialectical method is not merely propaedeutic but is the only method applicable, whereas for the other—for the formulation and testing of specific theories in a science—it is only preliminary to the use of the proper method of that science.

Aristotle explains in the *Metaphysics* as well as in the *Posterior Analytics* and the *Topics*[9] that first principles cannot be demonstrated directly (since an infinite regress would then be set up in inference and no demonstration would consequently be possible), but principles can be defended indirectly against a critic who will commit himself on any relevant point or who, in the case of such ultimate principles as the law of contradiction and the law of excluded middle, will venture so far as to make an utterance or a simple statement. One of the proper uses of the dialectical method, therefore, is for the establishment of principles. In the theoretic sciences, which he traces back to Thales, Aristotle frequently devotes an entire first book to the treatment which his predecessors gave the principles of that science—the first book of the *Metaphysics* to earlier treatments of causes, the first book of the *Physics* to what his predecessors conceived to be the principles of motion, the first book of the *De anima* to conceptions of the functions and definition of the soul. In the practical sciences, which he thought to have been no older than the work of Socrates and Plato, the dialectical introduction is briefer: in the *Politics* the first book is devoted to a statement and organization of the problem, and Aristotle is able to assemble only the theories of Socrates and Plato and the report of a few ideal states for dialectical treatment in Book ii, while the use of dialectic in the *Nicomachean Ethics* has little more scope than the occasional and periodical refutation of the doctrines of Socrates, Plato, and otherwise unidentified Platonists. In the case of logic, since Aristotle conceived himself to have invented the whole or important parts (depending on whether the concluding paragraph of *On Sophistical Refutations* is taken to refer to the whole *Organon* or only to the last two books) of the analysis, the doctrines of earlier writers (apart from Plato) are seldom referred to, and when philosophers are quoted their statement is used more often as a form to be analyzed than as a theory to be considered. In rhetoric Aristotle recognizes that much work had been done; but, since "the ordinary writers of text-books treat of non-essentials"[10] and overemphasize forensic, to the exclusion of political oratory, Aristotle's approach is novel and without relevant antecedent work to serve as guide, while the actual practice of poets in numerous citations and of orators in general (but apparently only one, Isocrates, in specific citation) is made to serve a function similar to that of the arguments of philosophers and sophists cited in the later books of the *Organon*. For similar reasons in the *Poetics* the analysis of tragedy is preceded by a brief history of poetry, and the points made in the analysis are illustrated by citation of actual practices in Greek drama.

In the more particular and more empirical branches of inquiry, where principles and theories are derived from prior sciences, Aristotle uses his predecessors as one way to assemble the materials of a problem preliminary to or after resolving it either by reference to his own principles or by more detailed inquiry into the data. Thus he states the problem of the eternity of motion with the aid of quotations from Anaxagoras and Empedocles and proceeds to the resolution of the problem with the simple remark: "Let us take our start from what we have already laid down in our course on Physics."[11] He quotes the conception of chance and spontaneity expressed by Democritus and others, without troubling to name the authors, and then proceeds to a simple solution which depends on the classification of kinds of events yielded by the principles of his physical analysis.[12] Sometimes, again, unanimity of opinion is taken, as in the doctrine of the primacy of local motion, to clinch a position which had earlier been established without aid of citation.[13] Or again, the doctrines of earlier writers may be assembled, as in the question of the movement of the earth, to show that "one may well wonder that the solutions offered are not seen to involve greater absurdities than the problem itself,"[14] before disposing of the problem together with the solutions to it. Or, again, all the philosophers who held any form of a theory at variance with that of Aristotle may be assembled, and their common doctrine may be shown to be inconsistent with observed phenomena or with reason, as the many forms of the doctrine of the void are brought into opposition to the phenomena of action and passion.[15] Or, finally, in the explanation of specific phenomena the analyses made by other scientists and philosophers may be cited in the context of, or preliminary to, his own statement of the problem and of its solution, as the problem of the origin of the sea is introduced by the statement of three anonymous theories[16] (whose authors have been the subject of conjecture by scholars since the time of Alexander of Aphrodisias) or as Aristotle's theory of the nature of earthquakes is preceded by refutation of three theories which he attributes explicitly to Anaxagoras, Anaximenes, and Democritus.[17] In the biological works data and the classification of data in good part take the place of theories and the refutation of theories much as they had in the *Poetics* and, to a lesser degree, in the *Rhetoric* and in the practical sciences. The reason, too, is doubtless the same, for apart from the writings of physicians, of which Aristotle makes repeated use, he seems to have found few predecessors to aid him with data or theories either in the voluminous assemblage of materials in the *History of Animals* or in the treatment of some of the problems to which he attached particular importance, such as those involved in the motion or in the generation of animals.

What Aristotle chose to quote, under the influence of these principles of selection, could seldom have furnished inspiration for a Platonic dialogue; and, therefore, the information of Aristotle only rarely and accidentally bears directly on what Plato had to say concerning the philosophy of the same man. Although both treat other men's doctrines dialectically, the manner of the dialectic has been seen to be different in the two cases, and the information given is a function of the dialectic. Aristotle's dialectic is directed to the discovery of principles, the formulation of problems, the amassing of materials, that is, it is heuristic. But, since truth and the ultimate resolution of questions depend not on what has been said but on the interpretation of observed facts in the light of tested principles, it is only heuristic and not also demonstrative. Consequently, philosophers, living and dead, are assembled in considerable numbers about a *single problem* for this preliminary dialectical inquiry and are quoted—almost casually and often without inquiry into what their statement could mean—even when their formulations of the problem are at variance with one another and with Aristotle's version. Plato's dialectic is demonstrative as well as heuristic and requires no nondialectical inquiry or proof to supplement it or to warrant the conformity of its conclusions to the conditions of truth and being, and therefore the two investigations, which are separate in the method of Aristotle—the determination of the truth and the determination of what a man has said—are a single inquiry in the Platonic dialectic to be accomplished by questioning one living philosopher about the implications of a *single statement*, even when it involves a number of problems.

There are problems of interpretation in either approach. Many philosophers are usually quoted verbatim or paraphrased from actual statements by Aristotle, while one philosopher is made to speak for himself by a dramatic artistry that conceals the extent to which the arguments are Plato's, or he is furnished other manners of defense in "living words" which he may never have uttered or heard. It is often apparent that the philosopher did not, in fact, say precisely what Plato puts into his mouth, but the statements are such as he might have made, and the doctrines are conformable to doctrines we have reason to believe he held; whereas, although there is often good evidence that the philosopher (or someone reporting his position) said precisely what Aristotle quotes as his statement, it is no less often clear that the interpretation Aristotle puts on the statement could not have been what was originally intended. It is apparently permissible as history to attribute to a man a statement he did not make, provided it is a statement which he might in the circumstances have made; and Plato, like Thucydides, suffers no loss in credibility because of his verbal inventions and developments. Even if one were disposed to be critical of the technique, there is little more to be said than that, for example, we have no evidence that Parmenides ever made such a statement or that it is unlikely that Protagoras would have given his doctrine such a development. But to misinterpret a statement and to leave evidence that its original meaning has been altered is a fault in historical method which can be much elaborated by ingenious scholars, and the catalogue of Aristotle's shortcomings as a historian, which has been assembled from such evidence, is long.[18] He will sometimes interpret the terms in which an earlier doctrine is stated as if they had technical significances which they acquired later, and he will frequently bolster the doctrine with facts which its author probably did not know and with theories to which he would probably not have subscribed. He will introduce into his paraphrases Aristotelian terms where they could not have been in the original, and he will interpret terms in his paraphrases and quotations as if they had senses which were first attached to them in his own works, so reducing the doctrines of his predecessors to lisping and partial anticipations of his own.

All these processes of translation would doubtless have passed unquestioned (since the mass of information Aristotle transmits is large and unique and the expert care he uses in citation and selection is apparent), and Aristotle's inadequacies might have been unsuspected, if his practices had not been brought to confrontation with Plato's alleged virtues as a historian. We possess in the case of Aristotle's testimony what we lack in the case of Plato's—a large body of writings against which to test the adequacy and accuracy of his representation of another philosophy—for what Aristotle says about Platonic doctrines may be checked against the dialogues of Plato. That comparison is involved in a great variety of problems. Aristotle sometimes discusses a Platonic doctrine which is treated in the dialogues, and in such discussions, as notably in his criticisms of the doctrine of forms, he is more usually than not held to have misunderstood and misrepresented the doctrine; he sometimes outlines, in a manner which only astounds scholars, portions of the arguments of a dialogue we possess, as in his summary in the *Politics* of the relevant points of Plato's political theories from the *Republic* and the *Laws*;[19] he sometimes tells of doctrines that cannot be found in the dialogues, and the critic may in that case decide whether they are malicious and mistaken inventions of Aristotle or doctrines expounded in the "lectures" of Plato (in the course of such speculations the lost "lecture on the Good" has grown into a possible repository of almost any doctrinal origins) to be reconstructed from the imperfect hints of Aristotle's statements. With respect both to the scope of Plato's philosophy and to the import of its particular doctrines such comparisons would seem to indicate inadequacies in Aristotle's appreciation of the Platonic philosophy. But, if he failed to understand the master he revered, it is probable that he suffered a like blindness, so it has been argued, in the case of all the philosophies concerning which Plato expresses an opinion. Aristotle's manner of treating his predecessors supplies materials for the pursuit of such an interpretation, for he usually quotes a specific doctrine, then comments on it, usually adversely, expressing at best only partial approval as occasional variant to his customary brief refutation. The critic has only to develop a rival interpretation of the quotation and argue for its greater insight and comprehensiveness. As a result of the opportunities presented to scholars by this method, there is scarcely a philosopher from whom Aristotle has quoted a doctrine who has not found a modern defender against the injustice and misunderstanding thought to be implicit in the citation or its interpretation.

The effects of these differences in dialectical method can be found conspicuously in all the historical data preserved by Plato and Aristotle, in the criteria they applied to information—as marked, for example, by their judgment of the point at which the history of philosophy and science began or the kind of detail which is relevant to the formulation of the views of other philosophers—or, when they both refer to the same philosopher, in the differences in the information they present concerning his position or, when they do not treat of the same men, in the reasons, stated or implied, for the exclusion of men prominent in one account from treatment in the other. Once the philosophic differences which are reflected in these conceptions of history are recognized, it is seen that questions which seem at first purely factual are determined by dialectical distinctions, and oppositions which seem to require only reference to data or correction of misunderstandings or adjustment of perspectives are resolved by the redefinition of terms. Such translations of historical into philosophic and dialectical problems may be illustrated in each of the contrasts of historical data found in Plato and Aristotle that have been enumerated.

The question of the origin of philosophy, if one may judge from testimony of Diogenes Laertius, came early to be of interest to the Greeks. "There are some," he says, "who say that the study had its beginning among the barbarians," but after examining opinions on the subject he concludes, "And thus it was from Greeks that philosophy took its rise: its very name refuses to be translated into foreign speech."[20] On this question, as on many others, Aristotle and Plato would disagree; there is little doubt that Plato was among those who supported the conclusion Diogenes himself chooses, and Diogenes informs us that Aristotle was among those who said that the study of philosophy began among the barbarians.

Although they received rules for mensuration from Egypt, it was the Greeks, according to Plato, who first generalized them into geometry; and, although they received from the Babylonians observations of the stars and their cyclic recurrences, the Greeks first set the rational foundations of astronomy. Neither science nor philosophy was of oriental derivation. The Egyptians (except those of the legendary past whose wisdom is set forth on the authority of Solon in the *Timaeus*) are referred to in the dialogues as businessmen rather than as philosophers—possessed of nothing more lofty than practical knowledge—and this judgment is reinforced by scientific reasons supplied from a theory of climates and races. States and cities have characteristics like those of individuals: in Thracians, Scythians, and northern natures the quality of spirit or passion predominates, "and the same may be said of the love of knowledge, which is the special characteristic of our part of the world, or the love of money, which may, with equal truth, be attributed to the Phoenicians and Egyptians."[21] In line with the same conviction, Plato or the unknown Platonic author of the *Epinomis* maintains that, since the nature of Greece, unlike that of Egypt or Syria, is medium between winter and summer, whatever is taken from the barbarians must be modified. "Let us hold," he urges, "that the Greeks carry to a more beautiful perfection whatever they take from the barbarians."[22] Doubtless, much of this social science is playful and half-humorous and might easily, as Platonic critics are soberly fond of pointing out, be taken too literally, particularly if the admiration expressed by Critias[23] for the age-old wisdom of the Egyptians—in comparison with whom the Greeks seem children— is forgotten. Yet, without holding the statements to literal account, it is within the spirit of the Platonic discussion to observe that philosophy and science are not constituted by occupation with problems of a given kind or by investigation of a given subject matter, but they are constituted by a given kind of consideration—that is, a dialectical consideration—of any question or subject matter.

Apart from the statement by Diogenes Laertius that Aristotle sought the beginnings of philosophy among the barbarians, there is good ancient authority (as well as fragments from his works) to show not only that he, unlike Plato, wrote works concerned with the history of philosophy as we understand it but that among those works was one on the Magi and (on somewhat less trustworthy authority) that Aristotle treated Zoroaster in that book as the discoverer of wisdom. This judgment might seem to be in flat contradiction to that of Plato, and the difference might seem to be subject to resolution only by consideration of the facts (with Aristotle, for once, coming from the contest with the palm of modern approval). But the statements need not be so interpreted. Aristotle does not differ from Plato in his judgment of the inferior character of the barbarians[24] or even of the nature and extent of their intellectual achievement, but such considerations do not enter the problem, for what has changed is the meaning he puts on the question of the origin of philosophy. Whereas Plato sought a kind of rational investigation and discussion and found no example of it earlier than the Greeks, Aristotle sought the origins of particular questions and found that many (or at least some) of even the more speculative problems which were later treated by Greek philosophers had been touched on by barbarians.

When it is a question of the philosophy of one man who is treated by both Plato and Aristotle, the differences in their testimony are usually so great that scholars take as their task the arbitration—by appeal whenever possible to "the facts," attested usually by interpretation of these texts and aided when possible by texts from other sources—of inconsistencies or downright contradictions. These are trials from which Plato almost always, at least in recent times, emerges victorious; but the historian's decision, for all the apparatus of history, is the product of dialectical, not of factual, considerations. If, to use Burnet's words, Aristotle is "distinctly unfair" to the Eleatics, his unfairness is apparent only when his statement is measured against the standards furnished by Plato, and interpretation in such terms may be shown to be distinctly unfair to Aristotle. To take a single example from the notorious case of the Eleatics, Plato's testimony has provided the means of correcting Aristotle's failure to understand the methods and arguments of Zeno of Elea: "If historians of philosophy had started," Burnet writes, "from this careful statement of Plato's (*Parmenides* 128 C), instead of from Aristotle's loose references, they would not have failed to understand his arguments, as they all did before Tannery."[25] It is relevant to add that if they had confined themselves to Plato's statement, they would have had no arguments to understand, for the arguments are all contained in Aristotle's "loose references" or in similarly organized references that go back to early Peripatetic sources.[26] Plato's careful statement is confined to brief indication of the purpose Zeno had in mind in writing his book—to supplement Parmenides' argument for the One by showing against those who opposed it "that their assumption of multiplicity will be involved in still more absurdities than the assumption of unity, if it is sufficiently worked out"; the organization and even the number of arguments in the book are specified, but not a single argument is stated. Aristotle's "references" do not, like Plato's statement, specify Zeno's intention to defend Parmenides, but they do indicate what cannot be gathered from the dialogues—the two lines of attack that were used against the Eleatic position.[27] If he does not, like Plato, explain the general relation of Zeno's arguments concerning the many to Parmenides' arguments concerning the One, Aristotle does, unlike Plato, give and refute two specific applications of the arguments—to the unit and to space[28]—and his careful statement (in his own terms and accompanied by refutation) of the four paradoxes of motion has been influential (even without the aid of Plato and Tannery) to such an extent that literature and common speech are dotted with references to the flying arrow and to Achilles and the tortoise, and philosophic speculation has repeatedly been centered on the solution of these paradoxes, as in the mathematical theories of the late Middle Ages, the physical theories of Spinoza and his contemporaries, the metaphysical doctrines of Bergson and his emulators, or the logical theories that stem from Lewis Carroll and Bertrand Russell. The question of fairness to Zeno is more difficult to judge. It may be true that Aristotle distorts his arguments by stating them in the context of another physical theory and by answering them with the aid of other distinctions concerning unity, continuity, and infinity; but Aristotle has sketched the principles and the purposes of the Eleatics in other places in his works, and it should be possible to reconstruct the original intention of the arguments (a purpose somewhat at variance with Aristotle's) without need of appeal beyond the principles and the arguments. It might be argued that Plato's failure to supply the arguments is, for all the insight he conveys concerning their purpose, a serious defect as far as the historical value of his exposition is concerned; but he does state the purpose and he does give examples of the Eleatic dialectic, and that should be sufficient to aid in constructing the arguments (a purpose more in conformity with Plato's conception of philosophy than the repetition of what a man happened to have said).

For the most part no direct comparison is possible between the historical information supplied by Plato and that of Aristotle. Aristotle's most detailed historical data are often relevant to points which are not treated by Plato; he quotes philosophers who are not mentioned in the dialogues; and he interprets to utterly different purpose, and estimates at quite different value, many of the philosophers who are mentioned there. Yet even these differences may be made commensurate by consideration of the respective methods of the two philosophers.

As is frequently the case in the relation of the two philosophers, it is possible to suggest a schematism in Plato's citation of philosophers which would hardly be apparent before Aristotle's treatment of them has been examined. The reason for this is not far to seek, since Aristotle usually distinguishes several concepts where Plato's dialectic is used to reduce distinctions to a single concept. The manner of Aristotle's use of earlier doctrine and opinion varies with the purpose for which he cites them, and his purpose is determined by his problem and the scientific method appropriate to it, while these are, in turn, suited to the respective subject matters of the sciences. For Plato, on the other hand, there is ultimately only one method and, therefore, only one valid basis for agreement with, or refutation of, another man's philosophy.

Plato, the Pythagoreans, and the Eleatics are cited by Aristotle primarily for their doctrine of being or for their inability to account satisfactorily for change; their doctrine is prominent, therefore, in the *Metaphysics* and contributes positively and negatively to Aristotle's conclusions most frequently in problems such as those treated there. The early physicists, as well as Leucippus and Democritus, are, naturally enough, thought to be sounder on questions of change, and they are cited with favor and partial approval more frequently as one proceeds down the list of the particular scientific problems treated in series in the *De caelo*, the *De genera-*

tione et corruptione, and the *Meteorologica,* and they receive only slight approbation in the *Metaphysics* for their primitive and crude insights into the material aspects of the problems of being. In terms of Aristotle's fundamental metaphysical distinctions this is an opposition between philosophers who sought explanations by means of formal causes and those who made use of material causes: neither group was able to account satisfactorily for generation and motion, and Aristotle, therefore, thought his own peculiar contribution to the general discussion of philosophic problems was the analysis of efficient causes.[29] Both Plato and Democritus are criticized for doctrinal and methodological defects which follow from failure to recognize efficient and final causes or to use them properly, while Empedocles and Anaxagoras attain prominence, despite much deprecation of the expression they gave the doctrine, because of their anticipation, after a fashion, of the doctrine of efficient causes.

In terms of this classification it is accurate to say that Plato dwells at greatest length on the doctrines of the philosophers with whom Aristotle classifies him as anticipating the conception of formal causes, that he scarcely mentions the philosophers who treated of the material causes, and that he makes use of the doctrine of philosophers who conceived of a kind of efficient cause primarily as casual and playful analogies for his own treatment of problems of becoming. Of the early Ionian philosophers, Thales is the only one who slips, by reference, into the dialogues, and even he does not appear in the guise of a natural philosopher. The ordering principles of the long sequence of philosophers (some of whom are mentioned by Plato for the same or other doctrines) familiar to readers of the history of philosophy—water, air, the Infinite, fire, a collection of all four elements or some like principle—no less than the rearrangement of the same philosophers in other similar sequences in terms of other principles are derived wholly from reiterated statements of Aristotle and from doxographical reports that go back to the Peripatetic tradition. Democritus, at the other end of the historical development, who appears frequently in the pages of Aristotle and is one of the few philosophers (among them Socrates

and Plato) credited by Aristotle with important methodological in-
novations,[30] is passed over by Plato without a single mention or
even an indirect reference, unless passages generally descriptive of
materialistic philosophers be taken, as they have usually been interpreted, to apply to the followers of Democritus.[31] Empedocles
and Anaxagoras, the exponents of the efficient cause according to
Aristotle, are typical scientists in the dialogues: two of the doctrines of Empedocles are used,[32] and Anaxagoras appears as the
scientist who was the preceptor of Pericles and whose method
Socrates criticized and abandoned.[33]

The Sophists, who are treated by both Plato and Aristotle, are an
excellent example of philosophers to whom are ascribed different
functions and degrees of importance in the two interpretations. The
statement, doctrine, and example of the Sophists are recurrent in the
dialogues of Plato, and their errors or arguments might be introduced in any branch of inquiry in which he engages. Plato shows, indeed, no little sympathy and respect for doctrines attributed to the
elder generation of Sophists, particularly for those of Protagoras;
and his constant concern with their teachings and claims might
argue a consciousness that their method approached close to the
Platonic dialectic and might result from a brooding memory that
Socrates had seemed to his fellow-Athenians a Sophist. Plato is fond
of repeating that knowledge must be differentiated from verbal substitutes for knowledge and that dialectic must penetrate to the nature of things, whereas sophistic technique succeeds only in trick-
ing men's minds. Moreover, there is no third possibility, no science
over and above sophistic and dialectic, no division of the universe
other than being and becoming. Aristotle, on the other hand, almost
never quotes the Sophists as philosophers or for points of doctrine,
not even in the *Politics* and the *Nicomachean Ethics*;[34] yet he makes
frequent use of Plato in those works, and he could not have been
ignorant of the fact that the Sophists were an important foil to the
Platonic Socrates in the investigation of moral and political questions. The Sophists are quoted frequently by Aristotle but almost
exclusively for examples of fallacious arguments, and they suffer

purely formal refutation, in which there is no need for reference to the subject matter of their argument. This is the manner of their appearances in the *On Sophistical Refutations*, and even the citations of Protagoras and the refutation of his disavowal of the principle of contradiction in the *Metaphysics* depart from formal considerations only to relate, still dialectically, his doctrines and arguments to his belief that man is the measure of all things. But for Aristotle there is a third possibility—in addition to dialectic (which argues from the opinions of men according to Aristotle) and sophistic (which makes appearance reality and holds all opinions to be equally true), a "scientific" method which shares with sophistic a direct relevance to observation of the sensible world and with dialectic a concern with changeless truth.

The treatment of earlier philosophers by Plato and Aristotle is a use of the history of philosophy for philosophic purposes in the schematism and to the ends of their respective philosophies. Such use is not calculated, in either case, to do full justice to the intentions or to the scope of the philosophies cited. But the manner of the injustices committed by Plato and Aristotle is opposite; therefore, one has usually been taken as standard when the other is criticized as inaccurate, and the history of our histories of early Greek philosophy has been a cyclical flux of defense and criticism in which now Plato and now Aristotle furnishes the criteria. Yet, much as subsequent histories reflect an abortive or fully developed philosophy, since even the charge of injustice or the silent rectification of error involves recognition, if not of a philosophic standard for judgment, at least of the philosophic principles impugned, each of the two treatments of the history of thought can be justified not only as stages in that flux but as proper interpretations defensible on grounds to be found in the two philosophies. To judge between the histories of thought envisaged in the philosophies of Plato and Aristotle is to judge between their philosophies; and, conversely, to enumerate and compare their peculiarities is to set forth basic problems which are still crucial in the writing of history in general and of intellectual history in particular. The two questions—how change is accounted for in the philosophy and how changes are narrated—are inseparably connected and should be treated in that order in any philosophic consideration of history.

Both Plato and Aristotle treat the phenomena of change in terms of the concepts of Reason and Necessity, and the differences between the philosophic bases of their treatments of history may therefore be displayed in their different uses of those concepts. In Plato the two are opposed as Being is opposed to Becoming, as the intelligible to the sensible, for the universe was made and is governed and piloted according to a pattern discernible by reason, while the order of reason is resisted and broken by the materials in which that order is embodied.[35] The account of the processes of the universe, no less than of its creation, requires account both of the unchanging rational basis which is the cause of the universe and also of the interrelations of the myriad subordinate and concomitant causes which are brought into opposition and co-operation in the things controlled in that order.[36] The evolution of man and of human institutions is influenced by the same forces as cosmic evolution, and the account of that evolution is in terms of conflicts of opposed powers and recurrent destructions and generations, in which the invention or the god-given gift of the arts and sciences is one factor of one phase.[37] The explanation of the processes of change is sought by Aristotle in the science of physics where the causes of motion and change are found to be two: *necessity*, which is in the matter of the thing or animal, and the *end*, which is in the form.[38] Notwithstanding the similarity of the terms in which the basic conditions of change are discussed (and Aristotle sometimes calls his end or final cause "Reason"), the relation of Reason and Necessity is not necessarily one of conflict for Aristotle, for they are no longer related as Being to Becoming but as different directions in which the processes of Becoming may be considered—Necessity being involved in the treatment of an event in terms of its antecedents, Reason in terms of its consequences. There are still cycles in the historical prospectus of Aristotle, but they are cycles of the seasons and of the corresponding phases of the lives of animals and men, not cycles of cataclysmic reversals in cosmic processes or destructions of civilization.

History as it is used by Plato may be contrasted to history as it appears in the works of Aristotle by means of characteristics suggested by their opposed philosophies of change. For Plato history traces the interrelations of the innumerable concomitant causes which operate only occasionally under the persuasion of Reason, and the proper form which it takes, therefore, is the "myth" in which Plato so frequently sums up in narrative the consequences of his dialectical examination of the nature of things. It need not take a single form, and the various versions of the periodic catastrophes which civilization undergoes need not be harmonized too literally with, say, the opposition of the age of Cronus to the age of Zeus. Yet history is not less true for being a myth, and the likely stories which treat of subordinate causes frequently supplement the dialectic which treats of the single cause of things or even supply an explanation inaccessible to it. It is not a loose use of language, therefore, when the story of Critias is contrasted as statement of fact to the "myth" which Socrates related in his account of a perfect city, in the very dialogue in which Timaeus' account of the cosmological and physical nature of things also is called only a likely story.[39] Or, conversely, the dialectical development of the state from simple beginnings to its final complete complexity may be conducted in stages which resemble, and have frequently been mistaken for, history.[40] The mark of that conception of history may be seen in the use which Plato obviously makes of the myths and stories of poets and historians, adapting and selecting them to suit the pattern of his dialectic; and his citation of earlier philosophers becomes history in the same fashion, not by faithful repetition of details (which would be to follow Necessity) but by examination of significances (under the guidance of Reason). The dialectic is fitted to the history, and the history to the dialectic.[41] History, for Aristotle, is sharply differentiated from myth, on the one hand, and philosophy, on the other; for, unlike myth, it attempts a literal account of actual processes and, unlike philosophy, it is concerned with particulars, not universals, and therefore is at best probable, not true. History, as an account of what actually happened, has much the relation to philosophy that "natural history" or the "history of animals" has to biology: in both cases history assembles the factual data that are organized systematically through an inquiry into causes. The evolution of man and of human institutions, moreover, is not analogized to cosmological and physical processes, but rather the cosmological and physical changes figure among the causes operating in the development of human institutions. But, in addition to the general or seasonal influences exercised by the movements of the heavenly bodies, the specific causes sought by history are to be found in individual persons, institutions, and events. As a result Aristotle not infrequently, as in the *Constitution of Athens*, writes history as we understand history, and his use of historical materials from the historians and mythographers conforms more nearly to our standards, for he will question the historicity of statements and will use myths only as evidence of what men once thought or, when the myth has been long or widely repeated, as evidence of a common belief or experience of mankind, while Plato uses the myths to account for processes and rarely distinguishes fictional reconstruction from historical fact, or myth from history.

When the history is concerned with the development of ideas, as it often is in Plato and Aristotle, these differences can be discerned more readily precisely because the facts treated in the history are theories. For Plato myth supplements dialectic and may be interpreted dialectically, and the stage of dialectical consciousness of truth is the highest achievement of mankind, whereas for Aristotle the equivalent of those two influences, of facts and of theories, in human achievements, can be discerned within history itself. It is possible to find both the elements of a theory of history and instances of historical narrative in Aristotle, whereas, strictly speaking, there is no history (as differentiated from myth) or theory of history (as differentiated from dialectic) in Plato. Viewed as history, the sequence of men's inquiries and speculations partakes, according to Aristotle, in part of the cyclic return that governs the seasons and lives of all sublunary things and in part of the progressive character of an enterprise that has a beginning whose record survives only in the form of myths, stages of improvement to which all men have contributed in their respective ways, but no end within the view of any man. One may, therefore, expect, on the one hand, doctrinal recurrences, and one may hope, on the other hand, for doctrinal advance. As necessity guides, the arts and sciences may have been invented a number of times, and with the disappearance of the need they may have been forgotten as many times; and "the same opinions appear in cycles among men not once nor twice but infinitely often,"[42] yet beyond necessity an important truth may persist through the ages, embodied first in myth and continuing subsequently unmodified except for the addition of extraneous details of doctrinal development or institutional device.[43] The exigencies of life and the needs of political institutions, the common features and recurrences of the world of nature, and the basic conditions encountered even in the first thought and speculation that grows from wonder—these will leave a common fund in myth, in language, in art, and in the remembered experiences of the race, and the same environing conditions will, as they recede and return, set the need for comparable techniques, arts, and sciences. The similarity of the various forms which the recognition of common or recurrent features takes is sufficient; it is not necessary—indeed, it would be false to argue—that the distinctions embodied in myth, in linguistic usages, and in customs are identical with those later worked out by the sciences. Finally, across such persistent or recurrent cognitions as might be expected in man's long experience of a common environment is traced the advancement of man in the adornment and enrichment of life after the necessities of life have been secured. The end of man in all his activities and in his most perfect institutions is not merely to live but to live well, and not the least important part of the good life, as Aristotle views it, is the satisfaction of the desire which all men have by nature, beyond the mere requirements of utility, to know.[44]

The pursuit of truth is not governed by utilitarian considerations or subject to cyclic recurrences. Within the limits of man's ingenuity, appreciation, and memory it is progressive to an end no one man could hope to achieve, and in that pursuit preceding doctrines—those that have recurred again and again as well as those that have had their first statement during any given generation in the philosophies of men still living—are used according to criteria suggested by the truth. It is a delicate enterprise, and in it, as in the comparison of doctrines by means of the common conditions and necessities that led to their formulation, there is need neither for the sensitive preservation of an author's original intention nor the arrogant assumption that the restatement one proposes is the last step in the search.

The investigation of truth is in one way hard, in another easy. An indication of this is found in the fact that no one is able to attain the truth adequately, while, on the other hand, no one fails entirely, but every one says something true about the nature of things, and while individually they contribute little or nothing to the truth, by the union of all a considerable amount is amassed. Therefore, since the truth seems to be like the proverbial door, which no one can fail to hit, in this way it is easy, but the fact that we can have a whole truth and not the particular part we aim at shows the difficulty of it. Perhaps, as difficulties are of two kinds, the cause of the present difficulty is not in the facts but in us. For as the eyes of bats are to the blaze of the day, so is the reason in our souls to the things which are by nature most evident of all. It is just that we should be grateful, not only to those whose opinions we may share, but also to those who have expressed more superficial views; for these also contributed something, by developing before us the powers of thought. It is true that if there had been no Timotheus we should have been without much of our lyric poetry; but if there had been no Phrygnis there would have been no Timotheus. The same holds good of those who have expressed views about the truth; for from the better thinkers we have inherited certain opinions, while the others have been responsible for the appearance of the better thinkers.[45]

No simple statement of the differences between Plato's and Aristotle's conceptions of history could be unambiguous. Perhaps it is most just to observe that for Plato all difficulties are ultimately dialectical and therefore history cannot be treated except in a dialectical context, whereas for Aristotle a theory of history is possible precisely because in history, no less than in philosophy itself, the difficulties are of two kinds. In intellectual history, in particular, the difficulties of the subject matter, that is, the difficulties which the doctrines were designed to solve, are seldom coincident with the difficulties of the history, that is, the difficulties envisaged in the development constructed by the juxtaposition of men's doctrines at any given time and in any given place, and it is the rare and happy historian who finds his thesis strengthened automatically by each new accretion of data. For Plato, to discuss another man's doctrine, if the discussion is significant, is to seek the truth; for Aristotle, to discuss another man's doctrine is, in part, to explain its occurrence by its circumstances and, in part, to use what is still true and useful in it in the further pursuit of the truth.

Neither Plato nor Aristotle wrote as historians, and neither of them is a source of strictly historical information. Both, as philosophers, tried to relate the philosophers they quoted, not simply to times and circumstances, but ultimately to the truth; and the numerous differences in the information they supply concerning what other men had said and their use of it in the statement of their own philosophies result from differences in their conceptions of truth and the means by which to attain it. For Plato there is one truth, arrived at dialectically from any beginning, to which all philosophers approximate more or less closely and from which, since it is inexpressible, all deviate. As a result Plato (to the confusion of later scholars) did not think it necessary to differentiate in his dialogues a doctrine stated in his own way from the ways in which Pythagoreans, Eleatics, and Sophists express themselves concerning the truth, and for the same reason he finds it possible and desirable to refute or to modify in one place almost every important doctrine enunciated in other places. For Aristotle truths, like goods, are relative to subject matters, and the doctrines of philosophers must be related and aligned as they bear on the problems treated. Each philosopher makes a specific contribution, however unsuccessful his total discussion of the problem, toward its solution. The approach to truth, which in Plato is a dialectical approximation in adequacy of analysis as it proceeds from appearances to being, is in Aristotle a literal approximation to the statement of the most adequate and latest analysis of a specifically conceived problem. As philosophic statements, the accuracy of Plato's or Aristotle's reports of philosophic positions cannot be judged apart from their own philosophic principles and methods. As historical statements, their virtues are contrary to one another, for Plato's treatment of his predecessors, when accurate, enables one to recover the spirit of a philosopher and to understand him in the sense of appreciating his intentions, while Aristotle's treatment, when accurate, enables one to recover the statements of a philosopher and to understand him in the sense of knowing what he said.

It would be invidious, not to say futile, to try to determine whether concern with insight or concern with detailed precision of statement is more important for historical accuracy. Whatever the relation of these virtues in historical writings, insight into the spirit of a philosophy is seldom accompanied in the writings of philosophers by detailed documentation and exposition of the doctrines of the philosophy, and the philosopher who quotes the statements of other men notoriously uses them for his own purposes with little effective concern, whatever his professions of sympathy or his display of precision, for their original intentions. By the accident of history, however, the quotations of Plato and Aristotle are our chief source of information for early Greek philosophy, and the use that has been made of this *matter* is indicative of the continuation of philosophic principles of selection in the *methods* of historical organization. Even when we praise the historical accuracy of Plato, we seldom try, in the use we make of historical statements derived from his writings, to relate, after his manner, the doctrines which he develops dialectically to the truth which they approximated. In the place of the truth we construct a momentary substitute for it— the spirit of an age or the character of a time—and relate the doctrines of philosophers to it. The dialectic becomes historical by breaking the changeless truth into self-consistent, dated stages, sometimes following in a strict dialectic progressively toward truth

as in the dialectical histories of Augustine or Hegel or Marx, sometimes following no less strictly but to no final truth as in the cyclic
history of Spengler. Sometimes the history becomes dialectical in
the organic interrelation among political, social, economic, and intellectual phases of life, and a man's doctrine may be shown to be
irrelevant to our problems by relating it to the circumstances in
which it was developed and which are different from ours, as in the
historical philosophizing of John Dewey; sometimes the dialectic
and the philosophy themselves are reduced to historiography and
the dialectic of truth to the history of development, as in the practical philosophy of Croce. The transformation of Aristotle's treatment of his predecessors to a method for intellectual history is very
similar and, like the transformation of Plato's method, follows the
lines of older philosophic disputation. The alteration worked in the
Platonic dialectic when reference to Being and the Truth is omitted,
is saved from being sophistic (for Plato's description of the methods
of the Sophists is stated almost in those terms) by being referred to
ages or to classes or to stages of Spirit or Matter or to advancements
of science, and the dialectic by that device becomes historical. Aristotle's statements about his predecessors are made historical by a
similar separation from all reference, not to a transcendental truth
but to the subject matter appropriate to the science in which the
statements are made; thereafter they cannot be arranged as stages
toward a true doctrine, and they are saved from being dialectical by
being referred, without explication or refutation, to specific names
and particular times. The whole apparatus and scheme of divisions
of causal relations and influences which Aristotle devised have en-
tered almost unquestioned into our histories of philosophy, but,
whereas the "collections" of Aristotle and the Peripatetics were
always of doctrines on specific problems, the devices have been
generalized in Platonic fashion to cover entire philosophies and
entire schools or even ages. Where questions have been raised, they
have been relative to Aristotle's appreciation of a statement he
quotes or to the justification for assigning the author the place he
gives him in the development; but the tables and successions of the

philosophers, most of the details concerning their positions and interrelations, the sequence of the Milesians in their shuffling choice of basic elements and their ultimate influence on Socrates, the interdependence of the Pythagoreans and the Eleatics and the dependence of the Atomists on both, the relation of Plato to the Heracliteans, to Socrates, the Pythagoreans, and the Eleatics—these and many like questions are found discussed by Aristotle and in need only of alterations which are philosophic in nature to be adapted to historical purposes. The historian has only to omit all distinctions of subject matter and quote indifferently from any work in which Aristotle mentions the doctrines of philosophers. When reference to subject matter is removed in Aristotle's philosophy, the result, viewed in philosophic terms, would be the reduction of all method to one dialectical method, and Aristotle's assembled statements about a philosopher or a group of philosophers, without the benefit of dialectical development, would have significance only as history.

The "philosophy of history"—which took on many forms from Augustine to Machiavelli before it came to its voluminous and characteristic development in the nineteenth and twentieth centuries, in Herder and Hegel, Marx and Dilthey, Croce, Spengler, and Toynbee—is built on assumptions and antecedents that go back to the dialectic of Plato. The "history of philosophy"—which was put to many uses from Diogenes Laertius to Leibniz before it acquired scholarly methods and apparatus in the nineteenth and twentieth centuries in Ritter and Tennemann, Zeller, Windelband, and Ueberweg, Diels, Robin, Gilson, and Bréhier—is built on distinctions and data that go back to the doxographies and citations of Aristotle. The differences that separate thought about history from history of thought reappear in the broader fields of history and in the more inclusive forms of human activity as controversies concerning facts and oppositions of preferences. By recent standards Thucydides is thought to be more "scientific" than Herodotus; what is admired in Thucydides is reflected in historical research directed to the determination of facts and their interrelations, yet the composition of histories tends to large sweeps, broad characterizations, and overarching concepts that should, but seldom do, make the reportorial methods of Herodotus intelligible and congenial to modern writers of the various forms of *Geistesgeschichte*. Historians would doubtless prefer to revise Aristotle's statement that history is less philosophic than poetry rather than call histories "myths" with Plato or find historical myths illustrative of philosophic truths; yet a remnant of the difference is found in the continuing discussion of whether history is or can be scientific or whether it should or must be primarily an art.

The controversies of historians and their differences in interpreting data, however, are usually between similar methods and related interpretations, not between the extremes which scarcely meet in the materials they employ to treat the same periods and places. There are two grand types of history determined by two antithetical sets of philosophic criteria; some of the differences that separate the two types are reproduced, in turn, within each type. The problems of history and its uses may be conceived to be primarily the construction of patterns and schemes—ages, peoples, civilizations, modes of production, basic convictions—within which to order and interpret facts and events viewed from the vantage point of those wholes; such histories may therefore be called "holoscopic." The problems of history and its uses may be conceived to be primarily the study of documents and remains and the establishment of facts from which interrelations and causes—the sequence of events, the occurrence, complication, and resolution of problems, the success or failure of programs, the growth of power, the development of knowledge—can be inferred and used to construct patterns determined by the parts from which they result; such histories may therefore be called "meroscopic."

Holoscopic history is sometimes conceived on a theoretic base, constructing its patterns by the methods of philosophy, anthropology, or the "science of the history of society"; the result is some form of *dialectical* history, which yields insight into a time or a society as an organic whole and suggests analogies among all contemporaneous fields of human activity—science, religion, economic conceptions and practices, political institutions, artistic forms, social customs, and psychological attitudes. Distrust of theory need not result in the abandonment of holoscopic history, since patterns are also found to result from the influence of great men, the spread of their ideas, and the consequences of the actions they initiate or inspire; the result is some form of *exemplary* history. The transition from Plato's use of history in the service of his dialectic to Cicero's use of history to illustrate the variety of ways in which orators have spoken and statesmen have acted and to estimate the success or failure of those ways, like the transition from Herodotus' reconstruction of the civilizations underlying a basic conflict to Plutarch's analogies of the great men of rival forms of culture, are variant uses of patterns to explain events and to guide action. The uses of the two variants of holoscopic history are as different as Carlyle's appeal to heroes and Marx's application of periods determined by modes and relations of production.

Meroscopic history sometimes makes use of a theoretic base— political science, economics, military theory and tactics—on which to select, assemble, and arrange, in sequence and in narration, events that can be shown to be related according to the principles of that theory; the result is some form of *causal* history in which human associations and human actions are interpreted as caused or influenced by basic changes in political and social institutions, in economic circumstances and practices, in military dominance and dynastic structure, or in any other structure or relation in which scientific theory or practical generalization can distinguish cause and effect, antecedent and consequent. Or, as an alternative to using the discipline to guide the selection of historical facts and the specification of relations among them, history may be used to trace the development of the discipline. The problems treated in theory, practice, and art, the manners in which they are stated, the analyses and hypotheses proposed, the programs and experiments put into operation, the forms invented, the contents expressed, and the new problems presented by the success or failure of analyses and actions, may thus themselves be made the content of meroscopic history; the result is some form of *disciplinary* history. Causal history traces the sequence of events determined, in the complex of human actions, by political, economic, military, diplomatic, geographic, and other changes; disciplinary history traces the sequence of problems and resolutions in the history of art, literature, philosophy, religion, and science.

Opposition within the two grand types of history differs from opposition between them. In the holoscopic tradition the question of whether history is a science or an art faces an opposition between "science" found in the dialectical establishment of the character of ages and the law of their succession and "art" found in the interpretation of a genius, a hero, or a great man and insight into the spirit that moved him and the nature of his achievements. The possible answers to the question are not simple, for the science which determines the characters of ages also determines dialectically the qualities valued in art, and dialectic in turn is an art; and the art which expresses adequately the values achieved by men also supplies exemplarily the true criteria of what is practically successful and what is significant in theory, and without that art action is arbitrary and science pedantic. In the meroscopic tradition the same question faces an opposition between the use of "scientific method" in research and the "application" of "scientific laws" in ordering materials newly uncovered, on the one hand, and the use of "art" in formulating problems and in tracing the interrelations among interpretations and among solutions, on the other. The possible answers to the question are not simple, for the science which is applied to uncover the causes of action is not itself a cause of action but an intellectual explanation of causes which are for the most part nonintellectual, whereas the art which is employed in the statement of problems does not exclude the use of the scientific method and is one of the causes of action and production. In the opposition of the two grand types of history, neither seems from the point of view of the other to be scientific—holoscopic history because it neglects or distorts facts, meroscopic history because it abstracts from the context of the whole and the organic movements that give significance to facts—and both, from the viewpoint of the other, fail as arts in the practical function of relating knowledge to effective action and in the aesthetic function of giving knowledge pregnant expression.

These differences seem in the oppositions of controversies and histories to be differences concerning facts and their interpretations, or concerning the discoverable causes of actions and their discernible consequences, but in one branch of history, the history of ideas, the oppositions of philosophic principles appear among the facts that are treated as well as among the influences that determine the modes in which they are to be treated. Historians of ancient philosophy, when they treat the relation of Aristotle to Plato and when they combine the insights of Plato concerning their predecessors with the information of Aristotle, encounter not only historical questions which can be resolved by appeal to historical data but also philosophical questions which have been debated, ever since Aristotle first stated the dialectic of his opposition to his master, by Platonists and Aristotelians, by dialectical and problematic philosophers, who take little cognizance of the historical traditions by which they are influenced. Philosophy determines the history, since the philosophic assumptions of the historian enter into his choice of facts and his use of contexts, and the truth of the history is dependent on the principles to which it has recourse; but history in turn transforms philosophy and, by the simple process of treating philosophy in the plural and of arranging philosophies in temporal sequence, relates the statements of philosophers, not to the principles of their truth, but to the conditions of their formulation, and reduces what is presented as true, and therefore changeless, to the changing form of its presentation; and, in that historical sequence, the doctrine which is last in the development or the doctrine by which the historian orders the development is true and supplies the criteria by which to judge the truth of earlier theories and opinions.

III

Freedom and Disputation

Aristotle argued, in the course of his analysis of the elements which go into the construction of a tragedy, that the "perfect plot" is one which has a single issue, the change in the hero's fortunes from happiness to misery. The cause of the change must lie, not in any depravity, but in some great error on the part of the hero. Confirmation for this theory is found in fact, according to Aristotle, for although in the beginning poets had taken any tragic tale that came to their hands, in more recent times the finest tragedies were all based on the stories of some few houses. The family of Alcmaeon leads the list which Aristotle drew up to illustrate his thesis,[1] and the fate of that family continued to play a dominant part in the larger perfect plot which has its issue in the history of the decline of the fortunes of Athens. The Lacedaemonian embassy to Athens during the year before the outbreak of the Peloponnesian War emphasized strongly Pericles' connection on his mother's side with the Alcmaeonidae by suggesting that the war might be prevented if the Athenians drove out the "curse of the Goddess" and banished Pericles.[2] The issues of the war can be related to the actions of the family of Alcmaeon, however, only in so far as those actions were themselves determined by the contending factions in Greece which arose out of the efforts of men to promote a democratic way of life. The great artistic, moral, and intellectual achievements of Greece have left their mark on the aspirations, statements, and actions of every later generation of men in the West, but they have also reminded men recurrently of the tragic error which brought to an end the way of life that produced those great achievements. Historians, philosophers, poets, and statesmen have continued to tell the story, to rephrase the basic ideas, and to renew the effort to achieve the ideals of those few men who in a few generations in Athens illustrated both the high purposes which men may pursue in life and the disasters, anticipated and yet unavoidable, which may ensue.

The Funeral Oration of Pericles, delivered at the end of the first year of the war, is at once the statement of an ideal and the formulation of a problem. The speech is reported by Thucydides, who explains his use of speeches by his custom of making the speakers say what in his opinion is demanded of them by various occasions, while adhering as closely as possible to the general sense of what they really said.[3] There is no reason to doubt the historical accuracy of the sentiments attributed to Pericles in the speech; but, whatever its accuracy as an account of what Pericles said or, at a further remove, as a report of how Athenians lived, it is one of the most lucid statements that has ever been made of the idea of liberty in operation in the lives of a community of men. The significance of Pericles' oration is not exhausted, however, by consideration of the democratic ideal of liberty which it expresses. Thucydides' interest in the study of this war, without parallel in the misfortunes which it brought on Hellas, is based on his purpose to determine its real cause, in the expectation that exact knowledge of the past might aid in the interpretation of the future. The grounds alleged by either side, though they are relevant to the immediate causes of the war, do not touch the real issue.[4] The Funeral Oration, therefore, takes on additional dimensions of significance from consideration of the circumstances under which it was pronounced and of the forces that threatened the ideal it expressed, as well as from consideration of the problems with which the pursuit of freedom has been encumbered since the time of the misfortunes recorded by Thucydides as a guide to future action.

The lengthy description of the character of Athens is an essential part, as Pericles makes clear in the course of his speech, of the panegyric of those who had fallen in the war, inasmuch as the Athens that he celebrates is what the heroism of such men had made her. The training, the political institutions, and the manner of life that brought Athens to greatness are the fitting prelude to the praises of those who died. The city Pericles describes is the people, for the laws and institutions, even the military policy and foreign relations, are based less on system and power than on the native spirit of the citizens. The life of the city is animated by freedom of the spirit, and the operation and success of its institutions depend on this freedom.

The freedom of the spirit manifests itself first in the political and social institutions of Athens, for those institutions were the creation of Athenian statesmen, a pattern imitated by others, not a copy borrowed from another original. It is a democracy, since the administration of the city is in the hands of the people, and there is a single law for rich and poor. On the other hand, recognition is provided for excellence, not of birth or of wealth, but of merit; and whoever can serve the state is given the opportunity to do so. Moreover, the freedom which characterizes the political life extends also to social relations. Everyone does what he pleases without suspicion or offense, yet this unrestrained freedom in private relations and this tolerant absence of impulse to interfere in the lives of others do not lead to lawlessness. Instead, a reverent fear teaches obedience to magistrates and the laws, especially laws, written or unwritten, concerning the protection of the injured. This mingling of political and social freedom, in which intelligent obedience is rendered freely to political regulation and law, in which merit is recognized freely and permitted to contribute to the political structure and operation, and in which private preferences and eccentricities are developed freely without disapproval or even notice, can result only from the attitude of mind and the training that animate institutions and regulations; it is not the product of the restraints or the guaranties provided by those regulations. The same springs of action provided, in the Athens of Pericles, relaxation from toil and satisfaction of want—games and sacrifices, homes fitted with taste and elegance, and luxuries from all over the world drawn to the harbor of Athens by the magnitude of the city. Moreover, the military and foreign policies of Athens reflect the same spirit. There are no alien acts ex-

foreigners from observing and learning whatever they wish
confidence is put in the native spirit of the citizens rather
than in prearranged devices to test and enforce loyalty, and the educational system avoids the restraints of a strictly military training.
Yet with these habits of ease rather than labor, and with this courage born of nature rather than art, the Athenian citizens have been
willing and able to meet every danger to the state.

Pericles finds the foundations of these freedoms—political freedom, civil freedom, freedom from toil and want, and freedom from
fear—in the spirit of the Athenians. Lovers of beauty without ex-
travagance, lovers of wisdom without weakness, they find means to
bring thought to bear on action. Citizens and statesmen are not
sharply separated, but public men are able to attend to their private
affairs as well as to politics; and ordinary citizens, though occupied
with details of business, are good judges of public matters. Even
when they are unable to set a policy in operation, they are able to
form a good judgment of it; and, instead of considering discussion a
stumbling block in the way of action, they look upon it as an indispensable preliminary to wise conduct. The courage of the Athenians is therefore not due to ignorance or stupidity, nor is the policy
of Athens a mere calculation of self-interest, for Athenians can be
fearless of consequences and can confer benefits on their friends in
the confidence of freedom. This is the city which as a whole, in the
opinion of Pericles, is the school of Hellas. Each of her citizens
could with grace and versatility prove himself self-sufficient in the
most varied forms of activity. This is the city—whether it ever
existed in fact and in detail or whether it took on this form and
freedom only in the eloquence of Pericles interpreting his contemporaries—which has been the teacher of the world for over two
thousand years.

The Funeral Oration of Pericles is a moving and clear statement
of the dependence of institutions and actions on the character of the
people and, therefore, of the dependence of all kinds of freedom—
political, civil, economic, and social—on the training and judgment
of those on whom the freedoms are conferred. Yet it contains in its

statement the elements of the problems which the Athenians were unable to solve. These are isolated easily by considering the speech in its context. It is the statement of a way of life placed in opposition to another way of life. One of the problems of the Athenians in the opening year of the Peloponnesian War was to clarify the grounds and implications of that opposition. It is the statement of the way of life of a people engaged in a long and desperate war, addressed to that people itself. Like Lincoln's Gettysburg Address, with which it has frequently been compared, it is at once praise of those who have fallen and rededication of the living in a spirit of confidence in government by the people. The second problem of the Athenians was to find the means to make the rededication to the purposes of democracy effective in times which try the courage of the people.

Pericles' statement of the ideal of freedom of the spirit is in explicit contrast to the opposed ideal of the Spartan way of life. Yet it was a Spartan who had told the Persian King, when Spartans and Athenians were allies in an earlier war, that the Greeks are free men, but not free in every respect, since law is their master, and they fear that master more than the Great King's subjects fear him.[5] In the face of a common danger the Athenians could profess constant awareness of the bonds of common blood, language, religion, and culture,[6] yet, once the threat of that common danger had been removed, opposed interests and fears led to the discovery of differences in the common roots and purposes and to the elaboration of ambiguities in the common statements about freedom and law. Pericles contrasts Athenian liberality to the painful military discipline, to the narrow life, and to the restrictions and secrecy of the Lacedaemonians. The rivals of Athens agreed that the two ways of life and the two national characters were sharply contrasted, and they even granted the superiority of the Athenians in science and technology. But they saw in the actions of the Athenians not virtue to be imitated but expansive imperialism and acts of overt aggression.

In the first of the two Lacedaemonian congresses that preceded the outbreak of the war, the Corinthian ambassadors reproached their Lacedaemonian allies with the isolationism which they saw as a consequence of confidence in their own constitution and social order, for that confidence was the source both of the Spartans' moderation and of their rather limited knowledge of foreign politics. The Corinthians found the difference between the two national characters in the spirit of innovation of the Athenians and their swiftness in conception and execution of designs as contrasted to the genius of the Spartans for keeping what they had, accompanied by a total want of invention and a tendency not to go far enough even when forced to act. At each point the Athenians are found to be the opposite of the Lacedaemonians: adventurous beyond their power, daring beyond their judgment, sanguine in danger, prompt in action, quick to follow up a success and slow to recoil from a reverse, devoted in every effort of body and mind to their country's cause, and, in brief, born into the world to take no rest themselves and to give none to others.[7] This is a recognizable statement of the qualities that inspired the panegyric of Pericles, and it serves, therefore, at once as a control to his interpretation and as a formulation of the oppositions and tensions which were the immediate occasion of the war. At the second Lacedaemonian Congress, after the Corinthians had succeeded in arousing their allies and had persuaded them to vote for war, these differences appear in a different light. The Corinthians now give two reasons for expecting success: first, superiority of numbers and, second, general and unvarying obedience in the execution of orders. One naval victory will suffice to ruin the Athenians and provide time for the allies to train themselves in seamanship; and, as soon as they have brought their skill to a level with that of the Athenians, they will of course be their superiors in courage. For, the Corinthians argue, the advantages that the allies have by nature, the Athenians cannot acquire by education; while the Athenians' superiority in science will be removed by the practice and experience of the allies.[8] The characteristically brief Lacedaemonian ultimatum to the Athenians turns on the familiar ambiguities of aggression and independence: "Lacedaemon

wishes the peace to continue, and there is no reason why it should
not, if you would leave the Hellenes independent."

Thucydides succeeds in conveying the oppositions in what men
said, the differences in their complaints, and the equivocations in
their estimations of the threats and dangers contained in the situation. Yet under the succession and opposition of statements the same
circumstances are recognizable. In both interpretations the signs of
an inevitable clash are found in the circumstances of the opposed
states; and, in both, grounds are sought for their conviction of right
and their expectation of ultimate victory. Pericles could see in the
Spartan ultimatum evidence of long-term designs against Athens.
Instead of the legal negotiations of differences which the treaty between the two states called for, the ultimatum takes the tone of a
command and appeals to war. He balances the complaint concerning
the aggressive actions of Athens with a criticism of the alien exclusion acts of the Lacedaemonians and their allies against Athens and
her allies, and he answers the charge of action imperiling the independence of the Hellenes by the countercharge that the Lacedaemonians have made their allies subservient to the Lacedaemonian
interests. Athens, he concludes, will not commence hostilities but
will resist those who do. Where Pericles saw freedom of the spirit
in the Athenians as a source of the institutions emulated by all the
Greeks, the Corinthians saw a restlessness which was a source of
unprovoked aggression. The wealth which, according to Pericles,
resulted from the activity of that spirit was the one advantage of the
Athenians, according to the Corinthians, which they used to de-
prive other states of their independence. Even their naval skill and
knowledge could be reduced to the same terms of opposition and
could be traced to wealth as opposed to nature. The marks of the
laborious life are then found, not in the military state of the Spartans
which is characterized by orderly obedience to authority, but in the
ceaseless plotting and intrigues of the Athenians. In the lines that
were drawn by both courses of argument, the war became, as
Pericles recognized, a necessity.

The way of life which Pericles sets forth in the Funeral Oration

is hedged in, not only by the opposed way of life by which its enemies judged and criticized it, but also by the circumstances of the
war which endangered and curtailed it. The speech may be read as
the statement of an ideal that transcends time and circumstances,
but the judgment of even that statement of an ideal depends for its
interpretation on its circumstances, not merely those presented in
the opposed statements of other speeches, but those apparent in the
further career of Athens and the life of her citizens. Moreover, the
consideration of such circumstances cannot be far from the mind of
the modern reader, for the final disasters of the Peloponnesian War
form the denouement of the actions consequent on the energy attributed so differently to the spirit of the Athenians. That freedom
of spirit which is characterized by ready obedience to authority
combined with tolerance of differences, by artistic taste and intellectual curiosity combined with promptitude of action and ready
endurance, by enjoyment of spectacles and luxuries combined with
an application to practical problems and the resolution of difficulties, by the combination of reason and courage which enables men to
discuss and calculate dangers beforehand and to encounter them
willingly, by the combination of private industry and public interest
which keeps awake the concern of both rich and poor and permits
both to bring competence and judgment to public discussion and
public action—that spirit, if it existed in Athens, did not endure long
after the time of Pericles and his contemporaries. During the
Persian War, fifty years earlier, arts, letters, and philosophy had
not yet made their appearance as forceful expressions of the growing democratic spirit. During the time of Demosthenes, seventy
years later, the intellectual vigor of Athens continued strong, but
the personal enterprise and spirit of the citizens had lost the independence described by Pericles. Three generations were sufficient
to complete the cycle of political decline. Socrates lived during the
period of growth that culminated in the Age of Pericles and during
the struggles of the Peloponnesian War, which saw the defeat of
Athens. Plato was born during the Peloponnesian War and died
almost ten years before the hegemony of Macedon in Greece was

finally established at the Battle of Chaeronea in 338 B.C. The teaching of Aristotle in Athens coincided with the rule of Alexander the Great, and he died within a few months of the deaths of Alexander and Demosthenes.

Moreover, even the short period of Pericles' influence does not reflect unmistakably the freedom of spirit expressed in his eloquent words, and the context of that period leaves it doubtful whether those words should be read as objective description of the situation or as stimulus to change and improvement. The testimony of the spirit of the age is found in the material remains of the art which resulted from Pericles' patronage of Phidias, Callicrates, and Ictinus, in the literature that came to maturity in the work of a group of writers among whom Sophocles and probably Herodotus were personal friends of Pericles, and, finally, in the philosophic speculations which had begun to center in Athens and which are reflected in the dialogues of Plato. Yet Phidias was arrested on charges of peculation and sacrilege in representing himself and Pericles on the shield of Athene, and he died in prison. The philosopher Anaxagoras, who had been Pericles' teacher, was indicted and sentenced to death "for sacrilege and Persian leanings"; Pericles succeeded in securing his release, and he left Athens for Lampsacus, which was still under Persian rule (thereby no doubt appearing to lend greater plausibility to the charges brought against him). Nor was the tolerance of Athenians for unconventional behavior great enough to permit Pericles' relations with Aspasia to pass without public notice and legal action: she was put on trial for sacrilege and for receiving freeborn women in a place of assignation for Pericles. Protagoras was expelled and his books burned in the marketplace, and Socrates was put to death for introducing new gods and corrupting the youth. In an earlier generation, after the Greek victory over the Persians, two of the men who contributed outstandingly to the preservation of Greece—Pausanias, the hero of Salamis, and Themistocles, the hero of Plataea—ended their lives in the service of the Persian court, and in a later generation Aristotle fled the city lest Athens sin a second time against philosophy by bringing him to trial during the excesses of anti-Macedonian agitations that followed the death of Alexander the Great. The list of statesmen, philosophers, and poets denounced and condemned in Athens is testimony of the genius that flourished in the city but not to its spirit of tolerance for novelty or its discriminating self-expression.[9]

The political career of Pericles is no less ambiguous in its possible interpretations than his account of the character of his fellow-Athenians, for his successes and setbacks may be judged to be stages by which the Athenian people became aware of the wisdom of his policies or to be stages by which he learned to use public funds to balance the vast private fortune by which Cimon could purchase public favor. Thucydides was convinced that the failure of the Athenians to carry out the strategy of Pericles was the basic cause of all their later misfortunes. Pericles was for him the outstanding moral example of the time: himself incorruptible, he could restrain the multitude without infringing on their liberties; he could lead them, because he would not flatter them; he could frighten them from their insolent self-confidence and restore their confidence when they were frightened without reason. Athens became a democracy in name under Pericles, according to Thucydides, but in fact a government by its foremost citizen.[10] Plato and Aristotle, on the other hand, judge the actions of Pericles to have contributed to democracy, but by demagogic devices. Plato represents Socrates shocking the cynically practical-minded Callicles by raising the question whether the Athenians were made better or corrupted by Pericles, since he had heard that Pericles had been the first to give the people pay, and to make them idle and cowardly, and to encourage them in the love of talk and of money. Callicles can retort only that Socrates has been listening to Spartan sympathizers.[11] Aristotle reports more soberly that Pericles curtailed the Areopagus and instituted the payment of juries, a demagogic measure which increased the power of the democracy and which led eventually to the deterioration of juries.[12] These questions of the influence of Pericles on the forms of government, however, are less important than his influence on the spirit and freedom, which are fundamental to the associations of men, to their co-operation, and to their institutions. Plato presents that problem in the *Meno* and the *Protagoras* as a paradox as poignant as the plot of any Greek tragedy, for although it is easy to teach any man almost any subject— even an uneducated slave can readily be taught an obscure theorem in mathematics—the wisest teachers may dispute whether virtue can be taught, and even the sons of Pericles, who had every educational advantage, did not learn that lesson.[13]

The discussion of freedom has proceeded into many elaborations and subtleties since the time of Pericles. The application of freedoms has been extended to include, in formulation at least, all the peoples of the world; institutions have been established for the promotion and extension of freedoms; and the word itself has been defined to include many meanings only vaguely adumbrated in earlier discussions. Yet the basic problem underlying all forms of freedom, and conditioning the operation of all regulations and rights, is still in the freedom of the spirit which animates institutions and gives employment to rights in the lives of men capable of freedom. In the debates of philosophers concerning the nature of freedom, foundations have been sought for it in human nature, in natural law, in the conventions of men, and in the utilities of life. Philosophers have, at one extreme, found intimate connections between freedom and wisdom and have argued that knowledge makes one free; and, at the other extreme, they have placed the foundations of freedom in the regions of indifference where a man may do as he pleases because his actions have no effect on the rights of another. Instruments of government, which make provision for political freedom in the exercise of progressively more widely extended rights of self-government, have been framed by statesmen, usually in the language of some one of the schools of philosophy. Bills of rights have been drawn up to afford judicial protection of civil rights, usually in the form of abstention from action or guaranties of noninterference. Within the framework of extended and diversified political and civil rights, the development of economic and social rights, designed to provide freedom from fear and from want, has required other devices of implementation, for, whereas political rights consist in freedom to exercise proper functions in self-government, and civil rights consist in freedom from restraint in thought, expression, worship, and assembly, the freedom from fear, and the freedom to participate in the benefits of the progress of man depend, not on one's own privilege to act, or on the abstention from action of others, but on positive and co-operative action on the part of the communities of men.

Freedom of the spirit is basic to all the manifold array of modern freedoms which have been assembled in the long struggles of men, as it was basic in the democracy which Pericles saw come to maturity in Athens. In one sense the problem has become easier, for democracy exists in the world today as an inescapable ingredient in the resolution of problems, because of the modern means of communication which make it necessary even for dictators to appeal to the sentiments of their people in radio, press, and film. But the problem is also, for the same reason, more difficult, since these means of communication have made the community of men the whole of mankind, and that community can be based on freedom of actions agreed on in discussion, only if the confidence born of courage and judgment, which Pericles found among Athenians, is extended to all men. The form of the debate is still the same. All the diversified freedoms to which men have aspired can be attained and can be widely extended only by that confidence, co-operation, and judgment which are the expressions of freedom of the spirit. But any statement of that ideal, even one which has been undiminished in eloquence by the changing circumstances and idioms of ages of men, is involved in the double debate which conditioned and defined the meaning of Pericles' Funeral Oration, the opposition of another way of life to the ideal it portrays, and the opposition of facts which fall short of the ideal to the statement of the essentials of a free life. The debate still continues between freedom and the charge of aggression; and the opposition between the advantages of discipline and wealth, of nature and skill, is still in progress in a form in which each side can still claim, despite all the changes in inciden-

tal argument, the greater benefit to mankind as a whole, as well as
all the virtues. The resolution of this debate will not be on the level
of the opposed statements of position, for in the formulation of
political propaganda and in the march of unified political action the
advantages are with the disciplined narrower life. Such a concentra-
tion of force and fear must reduce its opponents to a like form and a
like use of like instruments, unless respect for authority can coexist
with free tolerance of the preferences of others, and unless political
judgment and determination can flourish together with intellectual
and artistic vigor. The accusations against democracy have in the
past been justified when freedom of the spirit declined. The ideals
of democracy have then been degraded to a censorious and inquisi-
torial control of thought, expression, and action; its freedoms have
been subordinated to self-interest and the accumulation of wealth;
and its individual determination has been leveled to the purveying
wholesale of articles of common taste. This great error, transforming freedom to its contrary, constitutes the "perfect plot" of the
tragedy of human history. Ultimately the advance of mankind in
freedom must reflect the growth of freedom of the spirit, for freedom in this sense is the prerequisite, as well as the end, of democratic institutions.

IV

Imitation and Poetry

The ancient quarrel between philosophy and poetry, to which
Socrates appeals for extenuation of his treatment of poets,[1] has
broken out frequently and in many forms since the distant beginnings Socrates recalls. The quarrel is ancient and recurrent, but it is
not universal or continuous. Hostilities are resumed when critics—
philosophers or poets—think the enterprises of philosophy and poetry to be identical or comparable. Philosophic reasons can then be
used to instruct poets by truths, or to restrain them by prescriptions, which have moral, political, or religious grounds and consequences; and poets can give expression to philosophic truths which
exceed the reach of pedestrian reason, or which deal with mysterious and irrational forces of love, passion, or compulsion, or which,
at least, are more effectively expressed than they could be in precise cognitive language or in rigid syllogistic deduction. It is a
quarrel in which philosophers and poets are frequently joined by
statesmen, politicians, and priests who find reasons in the common
assumptions or in the differences of philosophy and poetry to justify them in their censure, restraint, modification, and employment
of art and inquiry. The quarrel is interrupted, however, whenever
critics separate the themes and techniques of poetry from those of
science. Philosophers and poets then coexist in amicable mutual
understanding or indifference, for it is apparent to philosophers who
follow the way of science that poets do not think or use language
cognitively and that philosophers who make statements incapable
of empirical verification are poets; while it is no less apparent to
poets who enrich meaning by ambiguity, or adornments of meta-
phor, or evocations of emotion, or concealments of unintelligibility,

that the truths of philosophers are not important and that poets whose lines could be thought to be true or false are philosophers.

The relation between philosophy and poetry or art is involved in a complex circularity. Speculation cannot begin with poetry as a neutral phenomenon concerning which theories might be formed, since the data—the character of poetry and the values embodied and expressed in it—are affected by the acceptance or abandonment of theories of poetry. It cannot begin with philosophy as a neutral method by which to examine the nature of poetry, since the processes of forming theories and constructing cogent arguments are identified with, or opposed to, the processes of poetic creation or lyric statement. Nor can the difficulty be resolved on the supposition that speculation concerning art—and indeed, following the recollection of Greek distinctions, concerning the actions of men as well as their productions—differs essentially, because of its subject matter, from speculation concerning the nature of things, for to suppose such a difference would be to exclude without examination, not only philosophies in which nature is the work of a divine artist and in which philosophy itself as well as morals are arts, but also philosophies in which science and art are explained by practical processes and external determinations—moral, social, economic, or political.

Philosophers have borrowed forms and devices from literature to express philosophic arguments, and the ideas of philosophers frequently have poetic or practical origins, interpretations, or counterparts. Xenophanes, Parmenides, and Empedocles expounded their philosophies in poems. Plato borrowed the dramatic devices of the mime and the fable to construct the dialectic of his dialogues, and he found arguments and examples in Homer, Hesiod, Pindar, and Aeschylus. Lucretius used the charm of poetry as "honey" to sweeten the rim of the wormwood cup of scientific and moral truths. Augustine added the soliloquy and the autobiographical confessions to the dialogue as philosophic forms of exposition. Boethius alternated prose and verse in his adaptation of the satura form. Twelfth-century philosophers gave lyric expression to cosmology, theology, and philosophy. Machiavelli used biography, Montaigne essay and apology, Pascal and Montesquieu aphorism and letter, Voltaire *conte* and *roman*, Diderot drama, Kierkegaard and Nietzsche aphorism, parable, and fiction. Greek philosophers, moreover, were not the last to seek philosophic truths in poetry, and the opponents to excessive reliance on reason allege as motivation, sometimes recognition of the practical exigencies of life which determine what is significant in thought and which reduce the differences of experts to idle verbalisms, sometimes sensitivity to the dark forces and attractions which operate as ineffable mysteries beyond the reach of reason and which even control reason's conscious searching for clarity. The Sophists substituted opinion for philosophic reason but gave common opinion a philosophic turn in the quest for a wisdom and an art that are practical and efficacious and a virtue that can be taught. Orphism, Gnosticism, and Manichaeism explored fateful, passionate, subconscious, and irrational emotions from which are derived the loves and frustrations celebrated in medieval romances and Provençal poetry and systematized in romantic oppositions to philosophy or in romantic philosophies and arts developed in opposition to the clarities of purely rational systems. The dialogues of Lucian exhibited the chicaneries and rivalries of philosophic sects against a norm symbolized by the substitution in the place of Plato's stonecutter Socrates, whose wisdom consisted in his ignorance, of Lucian's ignorant cobbler Mycillus, humorous and shrewd in his untutored instincts, pathetic and naïve in his expectations, but usually vindicated in the outcome by qualities not unlike the virtues Victor Hugo and Dickens later discovered in humble circumstances where wisdom is craft or insubstantial pretension. Rabelais's Doctors of Law, Erasmus' philosophers and theologians, and Molière's physicians evolve their pedantries and deceptions in a corner of a world they share with Sancho Panza, Bottom, Becky Sharp, and Huckleberry Finn, and they would experience comparable confusions and frustrations if they were transported to a romantic world in which nature expresses and intensifies human moods and passions and in which men go to their inexorable dark dooms impelled by forces at once unintelligible and deeply familiar.

Poets, on the other hand, have made poetic use of philosophic differences, sometimes setting forth the circumstances and the means for their literal resolution, sometimes merging philosophy and poetry in analogies that have no simple interpretation or literal verification. The differences of philosophers are identifiable in Dante's Heaven and in the long approaches to Goethe's Hell, and philosophers and critics have renewed their disputes in the interpretation of the proposed reconciliations. Poets and novelists have also told stories, which are apparently comprehensible, but in which the plot, the *mythos*, extends beyond literal interpretations to a mythological significance; in which characters have verisimilitude, although the simplicities and complexities of their qualities do not attach plausibly to men; in which thoughts influence action and character without issuing from the ratiocinations or the subconscious impulses of protagonists and without appearing in their statements; and in which the language used by the characters in conversation has no plausible literal content or cultural provenance. Melville often uses ideas as context and environment for the development of action in his novels; Dostoevski constructs in the narrative the several dimensions in which different characters view their own actions and those of others, as well as act; Kafka permits characters, situations, and thoughts to emerge alike from a dream context and sets actions in frames that shift and alter literal meanings; the structure of what men think, do, and are develops from the intricacies of James's involuted prose; the history of mankind and of human thought and language are concentrated in a few hours in Dublin by the linguistic devices of Joyce; Sartre and Queneau permit their characters to create their circumstances and themselves. Ideas operate and are used, and poetic and rhetorical devices are transformed and transposed, in these mergings and clashings of philosophy and poetry, yet no simple opposition or literal relation of philosophic analogies and poetic arguments is achieved or enunciated. Nonetheless, there are also systems of literal or scientific philosophy which are sharply differentiated from poetry, even in the case of philosophers who, like Aristotle, Peter Abailard, and Thomas Aquinas, also wrote excellent poetry; and there are literary masterpieces which can be made expressions of moral convictions, social significance, or theoretic truths only through devices which are ingenious and extraneous.

The range and richness of poetry present a problem to be resolved rather than a fortunate diversity to be explored, because the nature of poetry is affected by the instabilities of what men conceive it to be and by the oppositions of contexts in which they place it. Many of the problems of poetry and of criticism result from opacities induced by critical and aesthetic theories formed to clarify the nature and consequences of art. The range of poetry is limited by theories of what poetry is, and criteria become prescriptions in the manifestoes of schools, in the varied and changing tastes of peoples and periods, or in the principles and assumptions of aesthetic systems. The discussion of critics is then deflected from the task of directing attention to the poetic qualities of literary works and of facilitating their discovery, to the fascinations of sectarian dispute and to the revelation or invention of absurdities in opposed theories. It is not plausible, a priori or on historical grounds, to suppose that there is a single way in which great literature should be read and interpreted or a single set of causes by which to account for its occurrence and operation. The long histories of the interpretation of Homer, of the Bible, and of Shakespeare—and like histories can be traced for any poet, historian, or tale-teller who has been much read or interpreted—run the full range of literal, analogical, moral, and anagogic, of historical, psychological, rhetorical, formal, and social interpretations. Sophocles, who provided Aristotle with his most satisfactory examples of art imitating the actions of men, has also been the source of speculation concerning profound truths and basic conflicts that have moved from literary criticism to political and moral theory, the sociology of myth and ritual, and the psychology of complexes and subconscious compulsions; and Virgil's poetry may be read for precise lines and images as well as for theoretic and practical analogies, and it may inculcate patriotism in young Romans or inspire Christians to mystic, moral, or poetic visions. Some interpretations of poetry are manifestly fantastic; many, however, are relevant, plausible, and suggestive, and it is likely that the nature of poetry will be better understood if we observe the qualities of a poem brought out by different theories than if we oppose what are alleged to be the assumptions of theories concerning the nature of poetry.

Similarly it is not plausible, a priori or on historical grounds, to suppose that a single correct theory of the nature of poetry will be discovered. The interrelations of aesthetic theories are more difficult to explore than the coexistences of aesthetic qualities to which they direct attention in poetry, when they are not used to exhibit the corpses of strange and implausible doctrines as the errors of other philosophers and critics. The nature of poetry, nonetheless, cannot be treated directly without the opacities and deflections of attention caused by the conflicts of critical schools and philosophic sects, for even the poetic quality chosen for attention or discussion is a sign or reflection of a preference that must be based on critical or philosophic principles when it is stated explicitly or defended. Yet there is an alternative to the empiric decision that poetry is simply what the taste and the critical preferences of a time or a place make it and to the fruitless opposition of critical theories that explain what poetry and criticism are and explain away as simple divergences from what they are whatever else they might have been supposed to be. That alternative to relativism and dogmatism is to examine the relations of doctrines on the supposition that all critical views of poetry and systems of poetics deal in some sense with an identifiable common object—poetry—and that the philosophies on which they are based can therefore be brought into relevance to common or at least related questions. Criticism and philosophy, when they come into opposition without the preliminary precaution of determining whether or not the opposed views are pertinent to the same problems and data, employ a variety of techniques to treat a variety of aesthetic, scientific, and practical themes: the themes assume fixed forms as concepts in the statement of doctrines and philosophies, but they may also receive various doctrinal formulation, and they wander from field to field to be developed in different sciences sometimes by the same, sometimes by different, techniques.

I

"Imitation" is a theme discussed in many contexts and applied to many subjects. It assumes many meanings when it is transformed from a theme, a commonplace, a question (often without a decent pause to examine the definition that has been imposed) into a concept; and the technique by which the concept is justified, developed, and employed is often elaborated as a method of practical control or of scientific proof. During one period of antiquity, when art and sensitivity to art, as well as philosophy, had reached a high development, "imitation" was a central term in the discussion of art, and it was given many meanings and put to many uses in the systems of philosophers. In the evolution of later theories these meanings were modified and applied to different subjects—to history and philosophy, to nature and science, to society and social theory, as well as to poetry—discovering in each application new distinctions and novel objects of imitation. The technique of analysis moved from poetic and criticism to rhetoric, morals, politics, sociology, and psychology, and the treatment of new questions was grounded by the method in the examination of new subject matters. Finally, under the influence of idealism and romanticism, some critics and historians of philosophy have found the concept of "imitation" unsuited to the treatment of art and have labored to resolve the problem, created by this discovery, of how a man of Plato's sensibilities (Aristotle was a literal-minded scientist and therefore presents no problem) could be insensitive to poetry or misconceive its nature, producing by that labor scholarly philosophical demonstrations that Plato did not criticize poetry or propose to banish poets, as well as scholarly historical explanations of his criticisms, which show that his times and circumstances were deficient in the art or science, the mysticism or social awareness, the respect for manual work and human dignity later to be developed. In the course of the history of the evolution of "imitation" the constellation of terms that surrounded it in ancient discussion—"imagination," "enthusiasm," "perception," "understanding," "making," "expression," "composition," "pleasure," "passion," "virtue," "sublimity," "beauty," "nature," "order," "harmony," "proportion"—has shifted, and the terms have changed their meanings, applications, and relative importance. The various uses of "imitation"—including the specification of what is in each case imitated, what results from the imitation, and what meaning is assigned to the concepts by which it is defined— suggest that poetic and critical problems might be treated with greater clarity and profit if critics examined the meanings of terms before transforming the clashes of critical theories into questions of fact—that is, if they raised the question, "What is meant by imitation?" before disputing the question, "Is art imitation?" Differences of approach revealed by reconstructing those meanings might, then, be used as a means to diversify the experience of poetry instead of as an instrument to extirpate the heresies committed against an embattled orthodoxy of interpretation whose credo finds expression in a critical theory.

For Plato, imitation ($\mu\ell\mu\eta\sigma\iota s$) is a term of universal scope used to express many shades and sharp differences of meaning and many degrees of approbation or censure.[2] The universe itself is created by a process of imitation. The artificer or demiurge of any object finds his model in what is uniform, and the model of the universe is the Eternal.[3] The principles of the universe are three: the model form or the Father ($\pi\alpha\rho\alpha\delta\epsilon\ell\gamma\mu\alpha\tau\sigma s$ $\epsilon\ell\delta\sigma s$), the imitation of the model or the Offspring ($\mu\ell\mu\eta\mu\alpha$ $\pi\alpha\rho\alpha\delta\epsilon\ell\gamma\mu\alpha\tau\sigma s$), and the Space or Receptacle or Mother in which Becoming takes place.[4] Accounts of the nature of the universe share the qualities exhibited in the construction of the universe itself. Statements based on what is abiding will have a like solidity and will be discernible by thought, while those which faithfully copy the likeness ($\epsilon\ell\kappa\omega\nu$) are themselves copies and at best likely and credible, for as Being is to Becoming, so is Truth to Belief.[5] The sciences and philosophy, the virtues and social and political institutions, no less than the arts and discourse, or communication in general, are all imitations. The problem of "imitation," whether it is a question of discovering truths or learning sciences, of forming virtues or making laws, or of creating beauty or interpreting art, is a problem of distinguishing good and bad "imitations," and the same distinctions apply in each case. Beauty cannot be separated from specious pleasures without distinguishing truth from falsities, knowledge from opinions, reality from appearances, good from expedient utilities. Poetry is therefore corrected by dialectic, and the philosopher and the lawgiver are both poets who attain a loftier beauty than is accessible to the Muses.

Nonetheless poets do attain truth and beauty by inspiration and a kind of divine possession. Poetry is a madness comparable to the madness induced by and manifest in love, prophecy, and drink.[6] Even when it is a question of inspiration and beauty, however, the poet's inspiration is less certain than the philosopher's, and the beauty the poet grasps and sets forth suffers defects comparable to his deviations from truth and from morality. The madness which comes from the Muses differs both from the madness that is of human origin and the madness which comes from God. The poetry of sane men is nothing, but poetry cannot be inspired by the Muses or created successfully without the divine madness.[7] In the hierarchy of such perceptions and in the sequence of modes of expression adapted to them the philosopher occupies the first rank with the lover of beauty and men of musical and loving natures, while the poet and imitative artists fall to a lower rank, inferior to the prophet and performer of mystic rites and only slightly superior to the tyrant.[8] The poet does express beauty, attain truth, and teach virtue; the dialectician can attain these values more surely and avoid the unpredictable vagaries of the poet, but, in the absence of philosophy, madness or right opinion must suffice. Poetry is a link in the chain of inspiration constructed in the *Ion*,[9] yet poets should be banished from the second best as well as from the best state. Ideal states, whether perfect or second best, are dependent either on wise legislators or on philosopher-kings, whereas actual statesmen, even those who rule well, follow at best true opinion and make no more use of knowledge or wisdom than do soothsayers or diviners.[10] The basic problems in all branches of human experience turn on the distinction between reality and appearance. Imitation is the making of images (εἴδωλον). Imitative art may either produce copies (εἰκών), which are like their objects, or phantasms (φάντασμα), which are not. Correctness in a copy does not mean the reproduction of all the qualities of what is copied. Plato is one of the first of the philosophers to distinguish imagination and fancy and to prefer the imaginative or likeness-making (εἰκαστική) to the fanciful or fantastic (φανταστική) image-making art (εἰδωλοποιική),[11] for the difference between them is the difference between truth or being and falsehood or seeming. Even philosophic arguments are copies, and dialectic possesses only three instruments of discovery and demonstration: word or name (ὄνομα), discourse or argument (λόγος), and instance or image (εἴδωλον).

The opponents of the philosophy in which imitation takes on this meaning and use are portrayed by Plato, engaged in discussing the problems of art, beauty, love, rhetoric, and virtue with Socrates. The Sophists, old and young, teachers and wealthy connoisseurs of art, swarm in the early dialogues. They lack, or deny, the upper half of the Socratic distinction between being and becoming, knowledge and opinion; yet it is only on that upper level that knowledge and virtue are joined to art. Socrates builds his numerous refutations of the doctrines of the Sophists on admissions he elicits from them of a distinction between true and false or better and worse, reducing their problem to the paradox, embodied dramatically in the dramatis personae of the dialogues, of deeds and words, of men who know the arts and virtues in the sense of practicing them without the ability to explain them and men who talk about the arts and virtues without the ability to relate their statements to effective practice. Isocrates also wrote in opposition to the "Sophists," but he included the philosophers in his conception of Sophists and gave systematic exposition to the doctrine that opinion alone is possible, not truth, and that its criteria are practical and aesthetic. Men who are well endowed by nature and prepared by practical experience can be made more skilful by formal training. Such training and knowledge is concerned with words and discourse, and it is the master who is the object of imitation.[12] In this tradition art is conceived, not as a process of making judged by the degrees of its fidelity in imitation to the true nature of things, but as a skill in using language acquired by imitation of great models, and nature is found in the natural abilities developed by art rather than in the eternal ideas or natural things represented in art.

Aristotle, the greatest of Plato's disciples, professes continued attachment to the philosophy of forms but not to the supposition that they exist as models separated from their occurrences in matter. His doctrine of imitation is part of his systematic effort to follow through the consequences of recognizing that virtue, for all its dependence on knowledge, is not a science and that the arts, although they have analogies to the sciences and the virtues, are developed by different processes than those that govern practical act or scientific proof and are related to different criteria than the purposes of morality or the grounds of knowledge. Man's activities are of three kinds—knowing, doing, and making—which are distinguished from each other by their ends, their subject matters, and their methods. Knowledge is acquired by learning through one's own inquiry or from a teacher, and it is based on the discovery of the causes of things; virtue is acquired through habituation by actions adapted to the nature and situation of the agent; art is acquired by practice imitating and completing natural processes and is judged by the qualities of the object made.[13]

The term "imitation" is therefore limited in Aristotle's use to human arts and to artificial things; it is not applied to the natural processes of natural things or to the moral and political actions of men. There are connections and analogies among the three. Virtues are dispositions to act which reinforce natural powers, and they are acquired by action as are the arts. Art imitates nature and has political and moral consequences. When speculation is extended to the order of the universe as a whole, order, beauty, and goodness are relevant even in science. The motion of the elements "imitates" the order and continuous motions of the spheres,[14] and the universe must be ruled by a single principle, not many, and by the good.[15] Nonetheless, despite these influences and analogies, a poem is "made," and it possesses, therefore, a unity and an order which are not dependent on the truth or falsity of any statement it contains or on the moral consequences to which it may lead; for its form, if it is a poem, is self-contained, and its "likeness" is not a repetition or copy of a natural object, such as the actions of man, but their presentation in the distinct and heightened necessity and probability achieved by use of the poetic medium. The doctrine of imitation in Aristotle is the foundation of an independent analysis of poetry as contrasted both to the common analysis of knowledge, virtue, and art in the Platonic imitation of the eternal exemplars of all things and to the reduction of theory and art to the analysis of practical experience and rhetorical discourse in the Isocratean imitation of the example of masters.

Ancient commentators attributed Plato's silence concerning Democritus to a deep-seated antipathy between the two philosophers[16] and yet found a fundamental similarity in their doctrines.[17] Aristotle set forth the identity and the opposition paradoxically: Plato sought to explain the nature of things by the ideas they embody or imitate, while Democritus sought to explain the nature of thought by the motion of bodies. Aristotle was therefore able to characterize their philosophies, from his point of view, by marks that are still used when "idealisms" are distinguished from "materialisms," for Plato made things basically or essentially ideas, and Democritus made ideas things. Long before Marx inverted the dialectic of Hegel by substituting matter for spirit the possibilities of such interchanges were subtly and thoroughly explored. Even the basic terms took on radically opposed meanings which go beyond the literal meanings given to them in Aristotle's statement: Democritus used the same term as Plato to refer to the basic realities of his philosophy, but for him the "shapes" or "ideas" (ἰδέα) are the atoms,[18] and nature, art, and knowledge are closely associated in both philosophies—the universe is a product of divine art, and nature, art, and knowledge are all imitations for Plato, while art is natural, since all things, natural as well as artificial, are the result of the motion of bodies, and nature and instruction are similar in their operation for Democritus. Nature transforms man and, in transforming him, creates his nature; and men imitate animals as well as the virtues of men.[19] The fundamental terms of Plato's dialectic—image, word, and argument—are all employed in meanings appropriate to this orientation and serve as bases for theories that were to have long histories of development in later philosophy. *Image* becomes a basic term in the explanation of knowledge, for sight, and, in general, sensation and thought, are produced by "images" or "idols" (εἴδωλον, δείκελον),[20] but it becomes important to differentiate among the qualities perceived, for sweet, bitter, warm, cold, and colors exist only by convention and usage (νόμος).[21] *Words* or names (ὄνομα) are "signs," "symbols," or "speaking images" (ἄγαλμα, σύμβολον, εἰκὼν ἐν φωνῆι) imposed arbitrarily or by chance on things.[22] *Argument* or discourse (λόγος) is the shadow of action.[23] Art and wisdom are attained through learning,[24] but the poet is characterized by enthusiasm and divine inspiration,[25] and the great pleasures are derived from contemplation of beautiful works.[26]

The relation which poetry is assumed to have to philosophy reflects the differences of these conceptions of imitation. For Plato all things are imitations at greater or less remove from the reality they reflect: the philosopher censures such poetry as is untrue or degrading in its imitations, and he employs the devices and forms of poetry in exposition of his truths. For the Sophists and Isocrates men imitate other men both in their deeds and in their words: the study of poetry teaches them to imitate the actions of good men,[27] and the art of rhetoric is comparable to the best in sculpture, painting, and poetry.[28] For Aristotle poetry is an imitation of the actions of men. Poetry is more philosophic than history; philosophic doctrines are quoted from poets; and educational and moral effects are found to follow from poetry; yet the quality of art does not depend on scientific truth, historical accuracy, or moral edification, nor is

philosophy transformed into poetry by being given versified statement. For Democritus, sensation and even knowledge are results of
images, while only the atoms and the void are truly, and art is natural in its occurrence, although it depends on images : he can agree
with part of Plato's description of poetry, that it is inspiration; he
can give priority to one of the rhetorical pair—words and deeds—
since discourse is a shadow of action; and the aesthetic effects of actions and of poetic accounts of actions can be treated as fundamentally the same, since beautiful actions, however known, cause pleasure. In this tradition it would be appropriate therefore to expound
philosophy in verse, as Lucretius did, in order to supplement truth
with charm.

Four fundamentally different views of the relation of "nature"
and "art" are reflected in these four conceptions of "imitation."
Nature may be viewed dialectically by Plato as a product of divine
art; or art may be viewed logistically by Democritus as a natural human process. Natural objects and moral habits may be distinguished
by Aristotle from artificial products according to the problems they
present; or sciences and virtues may be conceived as species or productions of art according to the operationalism of the Sophists in
which man is the measure of all things. Both "nature" and "art"
have different meanings in these different statements of their relations. In the dialectical and the logistic statements art and nature
are in some sense the same, but for Plato nature is the product of a
wise maker, and all processes in nature, animate or inanimate,
beautiful or ugly, wise or foolish, are imitations of being or imitations of imitations, while for Democritus nature is the motion of
atoms in the void, and art operates likewise by the motion and
combination of material objects. In the problematic and the operational statements nature and art are distinct, but for Aristotle the
distinction is between the natural object which operates by internal
causes and the artificial object which is the result of the operation
of external causes, while Isocrates finds his distinction between the
nature which man possesses and the arts which he acquires.

These differences have profound consequences in the ways in

which art is conceived and discussed. In the operational approach words and the manner of expression provide the "form," and orator, historian, poet, and philosopher are directly comparable in their treatment of problems of form or expression. The analysis of art has to do with content and "form" and with their interrelations: content is treated by the commonplaces designed to give the marks of sublime or beautiful thoughts or to identify the thought in poetry with common thoughts expressed either with uncommon wit or in the language of the ordinary man, while style is treated according to standards of what is appropriate—lofty, mean, or medium—or by analysis of figures, tropes, and larger forms of verbal organization. In the problematic approach the "form" is related to the object of imitation rather than to the means: the plot of a tragedy is its "form," language or diction is its matter, and the problems of art turn on the best employment of parts in the construction of artificial wholes (σύνολον) which are different in each of the distinguishable forms of art. In counterdistinction to these problems, the problems of rhetoric turn on the use of the available means of persuasion, the problems of history on narrating and accounting for occurrences, and the problems of philosophy on the discovery and demonstration of truth. The analysis of art has to do with the potentialities of materials or parts and the unifying effect of the "form": the tragedy is an organic whole realizing the potentialities of its parts, using the resources of character and thought to develop by means of language and linguistic devices the unity and structure, the probability and necessity, of the plot. In the dialectical approach "forms" are separate and eternal and are at best imitated by the "forms" of expression or the "forms" of art objects. The analysis of art has to do either with the recollection and direct experience of forms which constitute the highest knowledge, virtue, and beauty (and therefore with the relation of art to truth or falsity and with the consequences of art in good or evil) or with enthusiasm, inspiration, imagination, and madness in which the vision of forms possesses the mind (and therefore with the irrational and supernatural basis of thought, action, and passion). In the logistic approach the "forms" are shapes, and the problems of art turn on the relation of emotion to knowledge, of appearance to nature. The analysis of art has to do with the psychological analysis of the perception of pleasure and its accompaniments or with the analysis of "forms" as structures of material parts and as causes of pleasure.

There is an important sense in which all these varieties of theories are engaged in the treatment of the same problems, described roughly as the problems of art. It is obvious that the analysis in which "form" and content are taken as basic will find some place to treat transcendent values, organic unities, and pleasures, as consequences of style and what is expressed. Eternal ideas likewise are embodied in language which is organized in unities, and, however adumbrated, they cause pleasure and pain; indeed, in the dialectical examination of the actual world pleasure and pain may take precedence as immediate signs of ultimate values, as they do in Plato's *Laws*. Plots, which are the soul of tragedy, are constructed by use of language as matter; they attain beauty in their organization and order; and they cause a "proper" pleasure peculiar to that art form, so that the analysis of drama affords data for the discrimination of kinds of emotions even though the occurrence of emotion or pleasure is not a mark by which to distinguish a work of art. Finally, experienced pleasure is expressed in media, heightened by artful organization; and, so conceived, pleasure is the unique sign of value.

Since philosophic theories share common terms in the treatment of these common problems, philosophers are attracted by the possibility of resolving differences by deciding which statement of form or matter, of inspiration or value, of expression or pleasure is aesthetically correct and factually verifiable in application to art. This is not a real problem, however, and only countersenses and verbal disputes result from the disingenuous effort to determine whether or not art is "imitation" and in what sense, without remarking that "art" and "nature," whose relations are involved in the definition of "imitation," range, like imitation and its attendant concepts, through many meanings, uses, and dimensions of application. If, on the other hand, the different conceptions of imitation are examined as hypotheses, they may serve to focus attention on different aspects of art in its relation to nature in its different aspects—as nature is manifested or envisaged in the actions and statements of men, in the motions of physical things environing men, and in the properties of eternal things which men, animals, and inanimate matter embody and reflect. Since each of these conceptions of the relation of nature and art is meaningful and defensible, and since each assumes basic identities or relevant analogies between nature and art, the resolution of the issues which separate the fundamental theories is in one sense easy (since any theory can on its own ground expose what is erroneous and adapt what is sound in the others) and in another sense hard (since these refutations and adjustments are not valid on the grounds assumed in the theories so adapted or refuted). Two significant questions can nonetheless be asked in which the diversity of meanings of "imitation" is an asset rather than an embarrassment. The first is the question of the interrelations of the aspects of art which are brought to light when the various definitions of "imitation" are considered as hypotheses: they should provide in conjunction with each other a more diversified and richer conception of art, free from doctrinaire and sectarian limitation, and the usefulness of that diversity, apart from the mutual improvement and correction of aesthetic theories that might follow, should be sought in their respective applications to the same problems of the arts as commonly conceived. The second is the question of the relation of theories of art to the creations of artists and the appreciations of audiences, for theory imitates art and art imitates theory, and, although it is plausible that there is more than one satisfactory theory of art, many theories that have wide acceptance are inadequate, and the interplay between theory and art is often far from happy in its consequences.

II

When art is considered in relation to nature, "imitation" in its many senses—or other terms which express the same relations— may be a basic concept in theories of art. It may be questioned, however, as it frequently has been in the history of thought, whether the characteristics of art are found in objects as such, for the sounds or the printed words do not constitute the poem, or the carved marble, the statue. The characteristics of art may then be sought, not by relating artificial to natural objects or acquired to natural abilities, but by seeking the marks of art in perception, imagination, emotion, or understanding. It may be questioned in turn whether the important characteristics of art or of the experience of art as expressed in terms of the processes of the mind employed in its creation and appreciation avoid the shortcomings of theories conceived in terms of the characteristics of the object made by man and operative on man, for ideas and emotions are not poems unless they are expressed and communicated. The characteristics of art are then sought in noncognitive uses of language, in emotional accompaniments of intelligent problem-solving, in adequate expression of intuitions, or in tropes and ambiguities.

These shifts in the fundamental assumptions employed in theories and criticism of art have occurred frequently, and the place of "imitation" among the concepts employed in statements about art and the relevance of imitation to art change with the change of orientation. When art is conceived as a product of human action, the distinction between objects made by man and natural objects is fundamental, and "imitation" is a fundamental term whose differences of meanings are determined by the object or value imitated by art or by the person or emotion imitated by the artist. When perceptions, emotions, imaginations, and judgments are the starting point, art is not different from nature in any fundamental sense, for whatever is perceived in art—beauty, sublimity, order, harmony, proportion, form, symmetry, the picturesque, the pleasing—is also found in nature, and art is distinguished from nature by "creation," which is antithetical in some of its senses to "imitation" in some of its senses. A genius does not imitate the work of other men, and his work cannot be imitated without degradation; "imitative arts" may then be distinguished from the nonimitative arts to which they are inferior. When, finally, philosophers argue that neither things nor thoughts can be made the beginnings of philosophy, since they are not known except as they are inferred from or produced by the actions and statements of men, neither the relations between the artificial and the natural, which make art an "imitation," nor the relations of beauty, truth, and goodness, which make art a "creation" distinct from imitation, are fundamental; for art, like science and society, depends on the "expression" of "values," and the nature and efficacy of values depend on circumstances and "communication." The basic problems in science, society, and art turn on what is expressed and how it is expressed, or on what can be communicated and the conditions that determine the form of statement in proof, agreement, and edification, in coercion, persuasion, and emotion. In this context "imitation" is no longer the contrary of "creation": the discoveries of science may be stated as imitations or "models" constructed to account for natural processes; social institutions and moral behavior are the result of imitation; and poets borrow well-known subjects to give them novel expression or imitate the language of ordinary life to achieve poetic effects.

"Imitation" is a derived term in the latter two frames of philosophic discussion. Not only does it assume a variety of meanings, when it is taken as a basic term, to contrast and to relate the artificial to the natural, but it also takes on a variety of meanings in the systems of philosophy constructed on analyses of the nature of understanding or of language and action. All the terms employed as fundamental in one frame of discussion are treated as secondary and derived in other frames: theories based on imitation account for genius, imagination, pleasure, emotion, expression, and communication as easily as theories based on creation or expression account for imitation. Theories of art as creation or expression, however, are constructed in a context of, and in reaction to, theories in which art is placed in a context of nature. It is testimony to the vitality of the Platonic dialectic that at three stages of the history of Western thought theories were constructed in which the universe—as unified under Roman rule, as created by God, and as known by science—participates in and images changeless structures and is in turn imitated by man. The senses which "imitation" acquires later, when philosophies are constructed in which theories of imagination and expression are fundamental, change with the qualities ascribed to these universes.

Cicero sought the bases for a philosophy suited to the problems and life of the Roman people in the dialectic of the New Academy, in which fidelity was professed to the principles of Plato, and only verbal differences were found among the schools of philosophy—except for the Epicurean doctrine, which was inadequate and false. Cicero's new philosophy would rejoin wisdom and eloquence which had been separated since the time of Socrates. In that enterprise nature was encountered by art in the orator and in his cases: the orator must develop his natural abilities by imitation, and the real issues with which the orator deals are imitated only in art.[29] Yet, although Cicero conceives imitation in terms of words and deeds, contrasting habit and practice to nature and truth, he is able to differentiate the operations of mind and imagination, of intellect, reason, and sense, because there lingers in his Academic philosophy reminiscences of the Platonic distinction between becoming and being, between the copying of sensible models and the imitation of intellectual beauty.

But I am firmly of the opinion that nothing of any kind is so beautiful as not to be excelled in beauty by that which it expresses as an image (*imago*) expressed in speech. This ideal cannot be perceived by the eye or the ear, nor by any of the senses, but we can nevertheless grasp it by the mind and the imagination. For example, in the case of the statues (*simulacrum*) of Phidias, the most perfect of their kind that we have ever seen, and again in the case of the paintings we have mentioned [*sc.* of Protogenes and Appelles] we can, in spite of their beauty, imagine something more beautiful. Surely the great sculptor while making the image (*forma*) of Jupiter or Minerva, did not look at any person from whom he derived the likeness (*similitudo*) but in his own mind there dwelt a surpassing vision (*species*) of beauty; at this he gazed and all intent he guided his art and hand to produce the likeness (*similitudo*) of the god. Accordingly, as there is something perfect and surpassing in forms (*forma*) and figures (*figura*) and those things which do not themselves appear to the eye are referred to the intellectual vision (*species*) of that perfection by imitation, so with our mind we see the perfect vision of perfect eloquence but our ears catch only the copy (*effigies*).[30]

The error of the Epicureans consisted precisely in reversing that relation and making the gods copies (*effigies*), images (*imago*), and figures of the form (*formae figura*) of men.[31] Cicero also reproduces the Stoic argument by which nature is analogized to art and becomes itself an artist.

> Some define "nature" as a non-rational force that causes necessary motions in material bodies; others as a rational and ordered force, proceeding by method and plainly displaying the means that she takes to produce each result and the end at which she aims and possessed of a skill (*sollertia*) that no art or hand or artisan can reproduce by imitation. . . . Some again denote by the term "nature" the whole of existence—for example, Epicurus, who divides the nature of all existing things into atoms, void, and attributes of these. When we on the other hand speak of nature as the sustaining and governing principle of the world, we do not mean that the world is like a clod of earth or lump of stone or something else of that sort, which possesses only the natural principle of cohesion, but like a tree or an animal, displaying no haphazard structure, but order and a certain likeness of art (*ordo apparet et artis quaedam similitudo*).[32]

According to Academic criticism, the Stoic arguments concerning the nature of the gods and the rationality of the universe go beyond the evidence of reason, but Academic and Stoic would agree that art imitates a perfection and beauty in nature that exceeds perception and sensible experience.

Augustine set forth a Christian conception of nature and the universe which continued to furnish an almost unquestioned frame of discussion throughout the Middle Ages and the Reformation. The basic distinctions which he employs to explore this universe of likenesses, images, and vestiges, which is created in imitation of God and in which artists likewise imitate, are borrowed from the rhetoric of Cicero, the ethics of the Stoics, and the dialectic of Plotinus. The adjustment of art to nature by imitation of ideal objects is expressed in all three theories, for Plotinus repeats the example of Cicero, constructing for it a metaphysical basis that accords with the rationality the Stoics found in nature.

If any one despises the arts because they create only imitations of nature, it should be pointed out first that natural things likewise are imitations of other things, secondly that the arts do not imitate visible objects directly but mount to the reasons from which nature derives, and finally that they create many things themselves and add that which is lacking to the perfection of the object because they possess in themselves beauty. Phidias made his Zeus without reference to any visible model, but rather imagined him as he would be if he consented to appear to our eyes.[33]

"All art is an imitation of nature," according to Seneca, and there is only one cause of all things—the maker.[34] For Marcus Aurelius, too, nature is an art and art an imitation: "Nature is never inferior to art; the arts are but imitations of nature. If so, nature in its most perfect and comprehensive form cannot fall short of true artistic workmanship. But all the arts use the lower for the higher; and so too does nature."[35] Whether man imitates man or nature, whether his actions are imitations of a model or his arts are imitations of an action, the imitation is good, practically and artistically, because what is imitated embodies values which are not themselves perceived by the senses.

The universe explored by Augustine consists of images which owe their likeness, their unity, and their being to the fact that God created them. God is an "immutable nature," superior to the rational soul and at once first life, first essence, and first wisdom, and "that immutable truth" is rightly called the law of all arts and the art of the omnipotent artificer.[36] The works of God and their beauty are testimony to the goodness and greatness of God, and creation is a spectacle made for man. The natural, the artistic, and the practical are separated by no fundamental distinction, since nature is both a work of art and a society. The whole of creation is attributed to God as its author, much as one would read a great book of the nature of things,[37] and the universe is an immense republic in which all that occurs in the ordered motions of corporeal and incorporeal things, of rational and irrational spirits, reflects the will of the supreme Emperor.[38] To distinguish the complex relations among created things and between creatures and God, Augustine assembled the Latin forms for the large vocabulary of analogizing terms which Greek Platonists and Stoics had constructed, and which were to be used and refined by centuries of Christian writers : created things are footprints or vestiges (*vestigium, ἴχνος*), beckonings (*nutus, νεῦμα*), and shadows (*umbra, σκιά*) of God; they are imprints (*signaculum, τύπος*), impressions (*impressio, ἐντύπωσις*), and seals (*sigilla, σφραγίς*); men recognize in nature, and in turn construct by art, signs (*signum, σημεῖον*), copies (*simulacrum, εἴδωλον*), and representations (*repraesentatio, ἀπεικασία*); nature and art are perceived by phantasms (*species, φάντασμα*), fancy (*phantasia, φαντασία*), and imagination (*imaginatio, εἰκασία*); they are examples (*exemplum, πρωτότυπον*) representing models (*exemplar, παράδειγμα*) and patterns (*figura, χαρακτήρ, σχῆμα*). But the order of things is hierarchical, and the major steps of the hierarchy are marked off by the distinction between likeness (*similitudo, ὁμοίωσις*) and image (*imago, εἰκών*), for in the Trinity the Son is the perfect Image of the Father, and in creation man is made in the image and likeness of God,[39] while the rest of the universe testifies to God's workmanship as footprints, shadows, and beckonings.

Every image is like that of which it is an image, but not everything which is like something else is an image of it, just as images in a mirror and a picture are also like, yet if the one is not derived from the other, none of them can be called the image of the other. For that is an image which is expressed of some thing.[40]

Augustine seems to restrict the use of the word "imitation" (*imitatio, μίμησις*) to the actions of men in this universe constructed of images and likenesses : the arts and the sciences, or at least many of them, consist of imitation joined to reason,[41] and salvation is possible only by imitation of God. In both cases, in the arts and in actions, imitation may be good or bad, for sin came into the world by imitation of the devil, and redemption is possible by imitation of Christ.[42]

Throughout the Middle Ages the basic characteristics of the universe of likenesses and images in which man achieves his greatest perfection by imitation of Christ remained unchanged even when changes in the terms of philosophic discussion turned attention from the distinction between artificial and natural object to beauty and imagination or to expression and emotion. St. Bonaventura, thus, like Alexander of Hales, analyzes the beauties of the world ingeniously and develops a subtle theory of the imagination from the observations of Augustine. In that theory the creation of the universe is a work of art, and God is the "cause of causes and the most pre-eminently originating art" (*causa causarum et ars praestantissime originans*). The creature does not proceed from the Creator by nature, since they are different in nature, but by art.[43] Two arts should be distinguished: the art whose operation is consequent on nature, and whose product is artificial, is posterior to the art whose operation is the foundation of nature, and whose product is natural.[44]

Three aids are available by which to rise to the exemplary reasons that underlie and govern all things: the sensible creature, the spiritual creature, and the sacramental Scripture. The sensible creature is a shadow (*umbra*) in which the refulgence of the divine exemplar is mixed with darkness, a way (*via*) leading to the exemplar, a vestige or footprint (*vestigium*) of the wisdom of God; hence in general the sensible world is a kind of semblance (*simulacrum*) or statue (*sculptile*) of the wisdom of God or a book written external to man (*liber scriptus foris*). The spiritual creature is a light (*lumen*), a mirror (*speculum*), and an image (*imago*); hence the interior of the soul is a book written within man (*liber scriptus intus*). The sacramental Scripture, finally, is the heart of God, his mouth, tongue, and pen, and hence a book written both externally (since it contains beautiful histories and teaches the properties of things) and internally (since it contains mysteries and has diverse interpretations).[45] After the fall of man the book of the world was dead and destroyed in its function of returning man from a knowledge of created things to God, and therefore another book was needed "to expound the likenesses, properties, and metaphors of things written in the book of the world."[46] Shadows, vestiges, and likenesses are to be distinguished according to their removal from God, the knowledge they afford, and the creatures who possess

he second person of the Trinity is the most perfect beauty
͟ ͟ ͟le relation to the Father, whom he expresses in a perfect
and express likeness, and to all created beauty (*pulcritudo exempla-*
ta), to which he provides the reason of intelligibility.

> For as Augustine says, "Beauty is nothing else than numbered equality."
> Consequently, since he has beauty of equality in relation to the Father,
> because he expresses the Father perfectly as a beautiful image, and since he
> has all reasons in relation to things, for as Augustine says, "he is the full
> art of all living reasons," therefore, it is apparent that the reason of all
> beauty is found in the Son.[48]

The new translations of Aristotle in the twelfth and thirteenth centuries had made familiar the definition of an "image" (εἰκών) as
something generated by imitation,[49] and this meaning was reinforced by a Latin etymology deriving *imago* from *imitago*.[50] All created images are imitations, and the beauty found in them is of two
sorts: they have beauty when they are well constructed and when
they represent well that of which they are an image.

The philosophers of the seventeenth century, who sought to
state and organize the principles disclosed by science and to formulate and use the method of science, shared the distaste for scholastic
distinctions and Aristotelian terminology which had been expressed
by Platonists and Ciceronians during the Renaissance. In their
philosophies "imitation" assumes many meanings. Scientific discoveries, civil institutions, moral actions, as well as arts are imitations in many senses. These meanings continued to reflect the contrasts between the imitation of eternal ideas and the imitation of
imitations, between the imitation of the expression of great artists
and the imitation of the content they express, between physical
reality and its appearances and effects, between artistic imitation of
actions and scientific knowledge of processes or moral habituation
of powers. In the contest of these philosophies the terms and distinctions of Aristotle's *Poetics* were adapted or criticized in many
shifting senses to provide the theoretic background for neoclassical
criticism.

Imitation and Poetry

Francis Bacon was convinced that "present sciences" were use-less for the discovery of effects and that "the present system of logic" was useless for the discovery of sciences.[51] Invention of the arts and sciences is either by "learned experience," which is not properly an art or any part of philosophy but a kind of sagacity, or by "the interpretation of nature, Novum Organum, or new machine for the mind."[52] Inventions, however, are not only new creations but also "imitations of divine works."[53] Poetry, as a branch of learn-ing, is distinguished from other branches by the faculty of the mind from which it results: history being a product of memory, poetry of imagination, and philosophy and the sciences of reason. There are three kinds of poetry: narrative poetry, which is an "exact imita-tion of history"; dramatic poetry, which is "a kind of visible his-tory, giving images of things as if they were present, whilst history presents them as past"; and allegorical poetry, which is "history with its type, which represents intellectual things to the senses."[54] Allegorical poetry excels the others, and has two uses, one as a method of instructing by fables, allegories, and similes, the other as a method of concealing and enveloping the secrets and mysteries of religion, policy, and philosophy in fables and parables. Bacon gives three examples of the interpretation of fables, one yielding truths in natural philosophy, a second in politics, and a third in morals. He remarks of the first, the fable of Pan, that it is pregnant with the mysteries and secrets of nature; of the second, the fable of Perseus, that it "seems invented to show the prudent method of choosing, undertaking, and conducting a war"; of the third, the fable of Bac-chus, that it "seems to contain a little system of morality, so that there is scarce any better invention in all ethics."[55]

Invention of arts and sciences by the interpretation of nature turns from authority and the idols of the human mind, which are idle dogmas, to discovery and the ideas of the divine mind, which are the real stamp and impression of created objects as they are found in nature;[56] invention is an imitation of nature. Ethics, which has the human will for its subject, is divided into two parts: the Doctrine of Models and the Georgics or Culture of the Mind. The

Doctrine of Models provides no more than an image or beautiful statue without life or motion, to which the Georgics adds a knowledge of the different natures or dispositions of men, of the affections and perturbations which are the diseases of the mind, and of the means to remedy and cure them, such as custom, exercise, habit, education, example, imitation, emulation, company, friendship, praise, reproof, exhortation, reputation, laws, books, and studies.[57]

Descartes employs the same terms in different senses and orients the lines of imitation differently in his effort to improve the method of philosophy and the sciences. He says that the *Discourse on Method* is put forth "as a history, or if you prefer a fable, in which, among some examples that can be imitated, there will be found, perhaps, as many more which one would be well advised not to follow."[58] The sequence of events which he recounts in that history runs through three stages: one in which he studied literature and the books written by men, a second in which he studied the book of the world, and a third in which he made himself the object of study.[59] The effect of the first two stages, which acquainted him, respectively, with the contradictions among the opinions of the philosophers and the differences among the manners of men, was to free him from unconsidered attachment to his own preconceptions and habits and to open the way to a search for true principles. Descartes refers to himself, during the second of these periods, as a spectator rather than an actor in the comedies of the world, since his purpose was to discover the sources of error and to root them out.[60] He found the principles of true philosophy in himself. Consequently, he decided not to publish the principles of his physics, because they would be involved in the oppositions of doctrines in spite of the fact that they are so evident that assent to them requires nothing more than to understand them,[61] but instead published his method to aid those who chose to follow a course similar to his (*suivre un dessein semblable au mien*) to make like discoveries.[62] Method and the imitation of method serve to circumvent the oppositions of doctrine.

The method which Descartes proposes for imitation to the end of making inventions accessible even to men of mediocre genius (such as Descartes professes himself to be) depends on nature, since good sense, or the ability to distinguish truth from falsity, is by nature equal in all men. The method requires the differentiation of the sciences which are one and adapted to a single rational method from the arts which are many and dependent on bodily skills.[63] The discovery of the method and the foundations of science, on the other hand, was itself a consequence of enthusiasm,[64] which likewise depends on nature, since the seeds of wisdom are found in all men. Descartes explains his choice of a collection of poetry in preference to a dictionary in his dream by interpreting the Dictionary to signify all the sciences brought together and the Collection of Poetry to signify philosophy and wisdom joined together.

> For he did not think that one should be very much surprised to see that the poets, even those who only trifle, were full of sentences solider, more sensible, and better expressed than those which are found in the writings of philosophers. He attributed this marvel to the divinity of enthusiasm and to the force of the imagination, which cause to spring up the seeds of wisdom (which are found in the spirit of all men like sparks of fire in flint) with much more facility and indeed with much more brilliance than can reason in the philosophers.[65]

The discovery of method depends, like poetry, on enthusiasm, and method in turn may lead to discoveries by rules of intuition and deduction. However, when something is encountered in the series of things to be investigated which the understanding is not able to intuit sufficiently well, recourse must be had to enumeration, or comparison, or imitation,[66] and the method itself imitates the devices of the mechanical arts which construct their own instruments.[67] Extension, figure, motion, and the like are known by the same ideas in different subjects, and the process by which something unknown is deduced from something previously known consists in the extension of knowledge by the perception that the thing sought participates in this or that manner in the things previously given. The common idea is transferred from one subject to another by simple comparison by which it is known to be like something given or identical with it, or equal to it, for in all ratiocination we know truth only by comparison.[68] Principles of physics are discovered by examining what would happen in a new world if God created sufficient matter in the imaginary spaces to compose one, for nothing is observed in the phenomena of the actual world which must not, or at least may not, appear similar (*semblable*) to the phenomena of the world so described.[69] The laws of nature are the same as the rules of mechanics, and even the phenomena of human behavior, except only speech and reason, can be explained on the analogy of automata or machines which bear the image (*ressemblance*) of our bodies and are capable of imitating our actions (*imitassent ... nos actions*).[70] The power of nature is so ample and vast, and the principles of physics so simple and general, that particular observed effects can be deduced in many different modes from the principles, and experiments are needed to choose among them.

There is no place for verbal arts apart from the gifts of spirit or the arrangements of method. Descartes professed great esteem for eloquence and poetry but none for rhetoric or poetic, for those who have the most powerful reasoning and who direct their thought best to render them clear and intelligible are always the best able to be persuasive concerning what they propose, even if they have never learned rhetoric; and those who have the most pleasing inventions and who know how to express them with the greatest embellishment and harmony would not fail to be the best poets even if they were ignorant of poetic.[71] The natural bases of science and poetry in the spirit of man, as revealed in their joint derivation from imagination and enthusiasm, provide no useful place for the verbal arts of the syllogisms of logic, the commonplaces of rhetoric, and the tropes of the *Arts poétiques*. But science proceeds by reason, and method equalizes the differences of genius in the use of reason for the discovery of truth: the practice of the method can be imitated, the application of natural laws to particular instances requires the construction of models and machines whose products correspond to observed phenomena, and the enumerations of induction depend on comparison and imitation. The inventions of poetry, on the other hand, depend on imagination, and the problem of the poet is to set such inventions forth in appropriate language. Purity of expression (*elocutio*) is in literature what health is in the human body. Neither is perceived when it is perfect, but both are noticed by their absence.[72] Truth as well as style are likened by Descartes to health: "knowledge of the truth is, as it were, the health of the soul; when one possess it one thinks no more of it."[73]

Other qualities of style follow on purity of expression.

Elegance and charm are over and above purity of expression like beauty in a perfectly formed woman, which does not consist in any one thing but in such an accord (*consensus*) and due proportion (*temperamentum*) of all parts that none of them can be designated as more important than the others lest the fact that the proportion of the other parts has been poorly preserved be taken as mark of imperfection.[74]

Descartes enumerates four types of literary imperfection: elegant discourse which expresses insignificant thoughts; richness and sublimity of thought expressed in concise and obscure style; between these two extremes, language employed in its true usage to express pure things too rigidly, and therefore so austerely as to offend delicate sensibility; and, finally, tricks and plays of word, ridiculous equivocations, poetic fictions, sophistic argumentations and puerile subtilities comparable to the absurdities of buffoons and the gesticulations of apes.[75] What Descartes praises is a happy concord of things with discourse, in which thoughts far removed from the ordinary are expressed accurately in ordinary language. For Descartes, as for Bacon, poetry is the work of imagination as distinguished from science, which is the work of reason. But Bacon's analysis leads him to treat poetry as an imitation and an invention and to concentrate his attention on the analysis of content, while Descartes's analysis leads him to treat poetry as a gift of the spirit to which nothing is beautiful except the true and to concentrate on purity and beauty of expression as its natural manifestation. His *Compendium of Music* is primarily a mathematical analysis of musical relations, pursued with due attention to the fact that music has its effect by setting up passions or affections in the soul comparable to those of the music itself. Although Descartes wrote little on aesthetics or criticism, this view was to have a profound influence on poetry and critical theory and was to find systematic expression, despite Descartes's distaste for poetics, in the *Art poétique* of Boileau.[76]

According to Hobbes, nature is an art, imitated in human arts and in human society, and the characteristics of poetry are found in the kinds of imitation, not in truth of content or in use of verse. "Nature, the art whereby God hath made and governs the world, is by the *art* of man, as in many other things, so also in this imitated, that it can make an artificial animal."[77] Automata and machines imitate the motions of the body, but art goes further still and imitates that rational and most excellent work of nature, man, in the great Leviathan or Commonwealth. The political philosophy of Hobbes is an elaboration of the matter, form, and power of the commonwealth conceived as an imitation of man, and the treatise *On Man*, which lays the model for that imitation, in turn begins with the recognition that the thoughts of man are all "representations" or "appearances," caused by the motion of an object, but consisting of an "image" or "seeming" or "fancy."[78] An image, in the most strict significance of the word, is the resemblance of something visible. Images are originally and most properly called *ideas* and *idols;* they are also called *phantasms* or *apparitions;* and from them one of the faculties of man's nature is called the *imagination.*[79]

In the context of this philosophy in which nature is an art developed in the motions of bodies and man is a body whose response to motion is imagination and whose arts imitate nature, poetry approximates philosophy in imitation and in practical purpose.

As philosophers divided the universe, their subject, into three regions, *celestial*, *aerial*, and *terrestrial;* so the poets, whose work it is, by imitating human life, in delightful and measured lines, to avert men from vice, and incline them to virtuous and honourable actions, have lodged themselves in the three regions of mankind, *court*, *city*, and *country*, correspondent, in some proportion, to those three regions of the world. For there is in princes, and men of conspicuous power, anciently called *heroes*, a lustre and influence upon the rest of men, resembling that of the heavens; and an insin-

cereness, inconstancy, and troublesome humour in those that
populous cities, like the mobility, blustering, and impurity of the air, ...
plainness, and, though dull, yet a nutritive faculty in rural people, that en-
dures a comparison with the earth they labour.[80]

There are, corresponding to these three regions, three sorts of
poesy: heroic, scommatic, and pastoral. Each of these kinds is in
turn distinguished into two varieties according to the manner of
representation, dramatic and narrative. Heroic poems are either
epics or tragedies; scommatic poems are satires or comedies; pas-
torals are bucolics or pastoral comedies. Poetry does not signify
whatever is written in verse: sonnets, epigrams, eclogues, and like
pieces are essays and parts of a poem, and Empedocles, Lucretius,
Phocyclides, Theognis, Pybrach, and Lucan are philosophers and
historians and not poets in spite of the fact that they wrote in verse.
Poetry imitates actions; it does not recount their natural causes,
moral prescriptions, or actual sequence. "The subject of a poem is
the manners of men, not natural causes; manners presented, not
dictated; and manners feigned, as the name of poesy imports, not
found in men."[81] On the other hand, if verse is not the mark of
poetry and if much that is written in verse must be excluded from
poetry, fictions and presentations in prose are at a disadvantage
when they contend with those expressed in verse, for poetry depends on the delightfulness not only of fiction but of style.

Content and expression are related as soul and body, or, in another figure which Hobbes uses, expression provides the countenance and color of a beautiful Muse. Content is the work of judgment and fancy; expression depends on how well and how much
the poet knows.

Time and education beget experience; experience begets memory;
memory begets judgment and fancy; judgment begets the strength and
structure, and fancy begets the ornaments of a poem. The ancients therefore fabled not absurdly, in making Memory the mother of the Muses. For
memory is the world, though not really, yet so as in a looking-glass, in
which the judgment, the severer sister, busieth herself in a grave and rigid
examination of all the parts of nature, and in registering by letters their
order, causes, uses, differences, and resemblances; whereby the fancy,

⟦ 133 ⟧

when any work of art is to be performed, finds her materials at hand and prepared for use, and needs no more than a swift motion over them, that what she wants and is there to be had, may not lie too long unespied. . . . But so far forth as the fancy of man has traced the ways of true philosophy, so far it hath produced very marvellous effects to the benefit of mankind. All that is beautiful or defensible in building; or marvellous in engines and instruments of motion; whatsoever commodity men receive from the observations of the heavens, from the descriptions of the earth, from the account of time, from walking on the seas; and whatsoever distinguisheth the civility of Europe from the barbarity of the American savages; is the workmanship of fancy, but guided by the precepts of true philosophy. But where these precepts fail, as they have hitherto failed in the doctrine of moral virtue, there the architect Fancy must take the philosopher's part upon herself. He, therefore, who undertakes an heroic poem, which is to exhibit a venerable and amiable image of heroic virtue, must not only be the poet, to place and connect, but also the philosopher, to furnish and square his matter; that is, to make both body and soul, colour and shadow of his poem out of his own store.[82]

Descriptions of great men and great actions are the constant design of the poet; descriptions of worthy circumstances are the necessary accessions and ornaments of a poem. Expression, finally, should give the poem true and natural color.

That which giveth a poem the true and natural colour, consisteth in two things; which are, *to know well*, that is, to have images of nature in the memory distinct and clear; and *to know much*. A sign of the first is perspicuity, propriety, and decency; which delight all sorts of men either by instructing the ignorant, or soothing the learned in their knowledge. A sign of the latter is novelty of expression, and pleaseth by excitation of the mind; for novelty causeth admiration, and admiration curiosity, which is a delightful appetite of knowledge.[83]

All the virtues of a heroic poem, and indeed of any writing, can be reduced to a single word—*discretion*. Discretion consists in every part of the poem conducing, in good order, to the end and design of the poet, that is, to the profit and delight of the reader. The virtue of discretion is found in seven virtues: (1) the choice of words, (2) the construction, (3) the contrivance of the story or fiction, (4) the elevation of the fancy, (5) the justice and impartiality of the poet, (6) the clearness of the descriptions, and (7) the amplitude of the subject.[84]

According to Malebranche, imitation has a natural basis in the universe and in man, and its operation is apparent both in the communities of men and in letters, but the meaning and the problems of both kinds of imitation are different from those explored by Hobbes. The universe is a structure of truths and beauties which the human spirit traces back to their source in the Creator, and the imagination, though necessary to community and communication, presents problems primarily of derangement and error.

Why do you think that all men love beauty naturally? It is because beauty, at least the beauty which is the object of the spirit, is visibly an imitation of order. If a painter, able in his art, has disposed all the figures of a painting in such a way that the principal personnage is most in view, that the colors of his clothing are liveliest, that the air of the countenance and the posture of the body of all those who surround him turn to consider him and indicate the movement of soul by which they ought to be agitated in respect to him; everything will please in the work of this painter because of the order which is encountered in it. . . . Order and truth are encountered even in sensible beauties, although it is extremely difficult for man to discover them there. For these sorts of beauties are only proportions, that is to say, ordered truths and just and regular relations. . . . However, take good care not to love sensible beauties nor to make your taste too fine and too delicate in discerning them. There is nothing which weakens the spirit and corrupts the heart so much. As sensible beauties are discovered with pleasure, you would soon neglect the search for intelligible relations, which alone can enlighten your spirit. When one loves a beauty which touches the senses, do not believe that it is loved because of the order which can be encountered in it, for most often it is not encountered there. It is oneself that one loves: it is one's own pleasure. Or, if one did love something distinct from oneself, it would not be God that one loved, but the sensible object: it would not be the true cause of one's pleasure, but only that which is the occasion of it. However, the movement of love which God impresses in man is not given to him in order that man stop at loving himself. Man is not himself his own good: he can not make himself either more happy or more perfect: God impresses movement in man in order that he raise himself above himself and sensible objects, in order that he search for truth and that he love the beauty of order.[85]

God has placed in us three fundamental inclinations: the love of God, the love of self, and the love of creatures. We are bound to the universe as a whole, but particularly to creatures like ourselves and to the men with whom we live. Society is based on this natural love of one's neighbor and is itself natural. These invisible bonds which unite men in society take their origin from psychophysiological dispositions which push us to imitation and compassion.

There are certainly in our brain springs which push us naturally to imitation, for that is necessary to a civil society. Not only is it necessary that children believe their parents, disciples their masters, inferiors those who are above them, it is also necessary that all men have some disposition to assume the same manners and to perform the same actions as those with whom they wish to live. For in order that men bind themselves together it is necessary that they resemble each other both in body and in spirit. This is the principle of an infinity of things of which we will speak in what follows.[86]

The same kind of communication between the natural dispositions of the brain and other parts of the body accounts for compassion.

This natural disposition to imitate, although it is essential to society, is also a serious impediment to reason and to rational life. "Man is a machine which goes where it is pushed. He is directed much more by chance than by reason. Everyone lives according to opinion. Everyone acts by imitation."[87] The disposition to imitate certain of those among whom we live is sustained and augmented by two principal causes, one in the soul, the other in the body. The first consists principally in the inclination of all men to grandeur and elevation, to obtaining an honorable place in the spirit of others. It is this inclination which incites us secretly to speak, walk, dress, and assume the air of people of quality. It is also the source of new fashions, of the instability of living languages, and even of certain corruptions of morals. Finally, it is the principal origin of all the extravagant and bizarre novelties, which are not based on reason but only on the fantasy of men. The other, bodily, cause—which augments the disposition we have to imitate others—consists in a certain impression which persons of a strong imagination make on weak spirits and on tender delicate brains. "I understand by a strong and vigorous imagination that constitution of the brain which renders it capable of extremely profound vestiges and traces, which so fill the capacity of the soul that they prevent it from applying any attention to other things than those which these images represent."[88] Persons of imagination are able to please, touch, and persuade because they form lively and sensible images of their thoughts, and also because they usually speak of easy subjects well within the grasp of most spirits. Malebranche illustrates the force of the imagination and the absurdities which it can render plausible by detailed analyses of the prose styles of Tertullian, Seneca, and Montaigne.[89] Tertullian was a man of profound erudition, but he had more memory than judgment and more penetration and extension of imagination than penetration and extension of spirit. Seneca illustrates the need to distinguish the force and beauty of words from the force and evidence of reason. Montaigne's *Essays* are a tissue of bits of history, little stories, *bons mots*, distichs, and apothegms which, by affecting a negligent, natural, and lively air, persuade without adducing reasons for the things they advance. In the case of Tertullian obscurity is affected as one of the principal rules of rhetoric, and his art of persuasion consists in part in rendering himself unintelligible. Experience shows that most men esteem what they do not understand and are dazzled by a language of imagination in which reason has no part. The good which is alone capable of satisfying us is wholly infinite and inaccessible; grand and obscure expressions have the same character. Obscurity therefore excites our desires as grandeur excites our admiration and our esteem, and these expressions win us by the movements they produce in us.[90]

Philosophers of the seventeenth century sought the foundations of their philosophies in "nature," and they described their philosophic method as scientific or contrasted it to the methods of scientific inquiry. "Imitation" is employed to relate art to nature, and the meaning of the term varies with the varying meanings of the "nature" which art imitates. Plato had analogized art, politics, and science; the Stoics had conceived the universe not only as rational but as a poem and as a city of gods and men ruled by reason; Christian Platonists saw creation itself as a vast poem in which the city of God is established; and Platonizing scientists looked upon the universe as a work of God's art imitated in human arts that achieve truth, beauty, and goodness. The impulse to find the basis for art, virtue, and political associations in nature by making nature a poem or a city did not begin with Christianity, nor did it disappear with Renaissance attacks on scholasticism. Yet important differences separate the various uses of the common analogy, depending on whether science, art, or politics supplies the fundamental terms: seventeenth-century philosophers explained the nature of things by a theory, and, in the context of that theory, the art of God tended to be mathematical and politics to be scientific; medieval theologians adapted their accounts of nature to the story of creation, and the Scriptures facilitated the interpretation of the book of nature and were indispensable to discovering the ends of men; the Stoic law of nature was political in character, and the analysis of means and ends, of the useful and the good, determined the pursuit and uses of science and art. Moreover, in each of these periods there were numerous philosophers who denied the truth or the utility of the analogy in its political, aesthetic, or scientific forms.

The different meanings of "imitation" and "art" correspond to different meanings attached to "nature" within, or in opposition to, this analogizing tendency. "Imitation" may be defined relative to the objects imitated or to the persons involved in the imitation, and four fundamentally different meanings are found for it in these relations. If imitation is defined relative to an object of imitation, the proper object of imitation may be conceived to be a transcendent value which determines and controls all things including actions and arts. This is the mark of the Platonizing dialectical concept of imitation, in which two kinds must be distinguished, a better which is the imitation of reality and a worse which is an imitation of imitations, that is, changing sensible things. If, on the other hand, nature is conceived to consist of particular finite things exercising natural

functions, such as motion or, in the case of animate things, reproduction, nutrition, growth, sensibility, but not to include among
existences transcendent values or separated forms, the proper object of imitation in art is found in things and particularly in the actions of men. An artificial thing, as conceived according to a problematic concept of imitation, is different from a natural thing precisely because the principle which determines it is external, in the
artist, rather than internal, in the nature of the object, and its quality as a product of art depends, not on the quality of the object it
reproduces (for beautiful art may be produced by imitating ugly
natural things), but on its form and on the interrelation of its proper
parts by which it achieves a necessity, a probability, and a unity
distinct from those found in nature. The commonplaces of dispute
suggested by these two conceptions of imitation have been developed in many terminologies: whether beautiful art must imitate
beautiful objects, or whether the imitation of the ugly may be
beautiful; whether or not beauty can be separated in the consideration of art from the good; whether the unity of a poem is to be
found in the unity of action in the plot or in the unities of action,
time, and place in the deeds imitated; and these differences appear
in Platonic interpretations of Aristotle's *Poetics* and in literal-
minded attempts to mitigate Plato's censure of imitative poets as
well as in the discovery of creative processes in nature and in the
vindication of art for art's sake.

If imitation is defined relative to the persons involved in the imitation, the emphasis may fall on the skill of the artist or on the
nature and sensibility of the audience. In the rhetorical tradition the
concept of imitation is operational: the natural abilities are en-
hanced by art which the artist acquires by imitating other artists
and their art. By so doing, he achieves beauty and sublimity and
pleases a variety of audiences, young and old, court and country,
proletariat and bourgeois. Audiences may, in turn, be guided in
their taste and appreciation by a similar use of the touchstones of
great art, or they may simply denominate art that which in fact
pleases, and the history of art then becomes the history of tastes.

According to the logistic concept of imitation, art deals in appearances, while science penetrates to realities, and the pleasures produced by art may be examined in scientific analyses of the nature of man or of his mind or of his language. The pleasures of art imitate the pleasures of nature. The commonplaces of dispute suggested by these two conceptions of imitation have likewise had many developments: whether what pleases or what ought to please is the mark by which art is recognized; whether the objective basis of aesthetic quality is found in the skill of the artist, which may make any subject pleasing and instructive or in the sensibility of the audience which relates the pleasure of art to organic well-being; whether beauty is perceived by an aesthetic sense or a sense of beauty, and what is so perceived pleases, or whether pleasure is the very nature of beauty, and what pleases is for that reason called "beautiful."

The concepts of imitation which appear in the philosophies of the seventeenth century bear striking resemblances—particularly in the structure of relations and oppositions which appears among them—to the concepts of imitation developed by ancient and medieval philosophers. Yet the methods by which the concepts were developed and the principles on which they were based are different from those which the ancients and medievals employed for the comparable concepts. The new method which Bacon outlined was problematic, and his purpose to improve the method of Aristotle is apparent in the title he gave to his book on method, the *Novum organum.* Yet principles are found in action and derived from the tradition of rhetoric rather than of logic: they are principles for interpreting nature, distinct from the commonplaces of rhetoric which are applicable to things rather than words, even when knowledge of nature and precepts for action are derived from interpretation of literature. Imitation is of agents for the purpose of acquiring arts, and the criteria for knowledge and statement are found in action. The new method of Hobbes, on the contrary, was operational: if knowledge was power for Bacon, power is the ultimate determinant of practical values and criteria for Hobbes, while ratiocination is computation, and first principles are discovered by

analysis. Yet Hobbes's conception of imitation in literature is problematic—imitation is of human life for the purpose of delighting
and improving—and the distinctions of Aristotle reappear in his
analysis of poetry. The scientific method of Descartes is logistic in
the search for simple ideas from which to construct in long chains
of reasoning the interdependent truths of science, yet his use and
development of the method lead to the dialectical discovery of two
kinds of imitation, one—which is verbal, dogmatic, and disputa-
tive—to be avoided, the other—which is dependent on method—to
be cultivated, and the method of uncovering truth is intricately in-
terwoven with imagination and enthusiasm, dependent on them and
endangered by them. Imitation is of truth and of the methods by
which it may be discovered or concealed. Malebranche, on the contrary, adapted the Cartesian philosophy to a dialectical development, yet his conception of imitation is logistic, dependent on the
nature of man and the movements of his brain, and analyzed most
pertinently in the pleasures and admiration it excites. Imitation is
an appearance which pleases. These conceptions of imitation are
closely interrelated, for the methods according to which they are
employed are applied to the same problems and data, yet different
aspects of poetry assume prominence as one is replaced by the
others and different modes of interpretation become pertinent in
criticism—an allegorical interpretation to lead to the discovery of
new truths and insights, a structural analysis to differentiate aesthetic qualities of poems, and examination of accord and proportion
in which style is adapted to truths expressed, and a study of the
effects of style on the motions of the brain.

III

Both the variety of the conceptions of "imitation" and the variety of the modes of analysis in which the term was used in the
seventeenth century were familiar in antiquity and the Middle
Ages. Differences in contemporary theory based on science were
therefore reinforced and complicated by quotations from ancient
doctrines which were approved and by refutations of ancient and
medieval doctrines which were found to be inadequate on the as-

sumptions accepted. Scholars have, consequently, found good tex-
tual reasons for calling each of the major philosophers of the seventeenth century "Platonic" and for identifying in the doctrines of
each traces of Stoicism and Epicureanism, and for isolating devices
derived from rhetoric and for discovering rules based on the Aristotelian tradition. In the transition from age to age, however, the
dialectical and the operational traditions are more adaptable, since
the Platonic analogies can survive no matter which term of the
analogy—Being or Becoming, Knowledge or Opinion, Spirit or
Matter—is taken as fundamental, and the rhetorical tradition can
find practical and theoretic as well as artistic criteria for the employments of words and for the consequences of action. On the contrary, the Aristotelian analysis of a work of art as a whole depends
on principles of knowledge grounded in the nature of things, and
logistic philosophies, which find principles in elements and their
combinations, are altered radically when material atoms and local
motions are abandoned for simple ideas and their associations or for
simple signs and their syntax. It is this difference that gives the
Platonic and the rhetorical traditions the appearance of greater continuity in the history of thought, in spite of the fact that the changes
in doctrinal content and practical consequences which the same
phrases and statements undergo in these analogical traditions are as
great as those sought expressly in the literal traditions. During each
of the periods in which dialecticians and rhetoricians discussed
whether, or in what sense, the universe is a poem or a city or both
or neither, philosophers in the literal traditions either denied the
analogy or questioned its utility in relating science to politics and
art. Frequently philosophers turn from these questions to what
seems in the circumstances the prior question of the grounds on
which we might be said to know that the universe is a poem or a city
or that poems and cities are made by men in a universe which is an
organization of substances, a congeries of atoms, or beyond the
scope, as a whole, of possible experience and knowledge and the
subject therefore of conjecture and probability. Metaphysical principles are mediated or prepared by epistemological principles, and

"imitation" ceases to be a fundamental term relating kinds of things and becomes instead a derivative term whose meanings are determined by relations discovered among the operations of human faculties. The differences that were found in the kinds of "imitation" reappear, however, in the kinds of "perception" or imagination required in the creation and appreciation of art.

Late in the eighteenth century, Kant undertook to "imitate" in metaphysics the revolution in mathematics and natural science and likened his construction of a "critical" philosophy to the revolution instituted by Copernicus. The experiment was to consist in examining how objects conform to the constitution of our faculty of intuition rather than how our intuition conforms to the constitution of objects.[91] In this broad sense, however, there have been many Copernican revolutions in philosophy. Stoics, Epicureans, Academics, and Peripatetics of the Hellenistic period sought a "criterion" or "criticism" of knowledge by which to judge the principles of their ethics and physics. Boethius, in the fifth century A.D., does not depart in his *De Trinitate* from the doctrines of Augustine, but he orients his discussion to the problem of how knowledge of God is accessible to the perception of human reason (*humanae rationis intuitus*), and he investigates the relations of the sciences and the uses of the categories. His *Consolation of Philosophy* illustrates the human as well as the epistemological development of the experiment of making objects conform to our faculties of perception, for the consolation which philosophy affords Boethius through teaching him to control his passions by reason depends on recognizing that whatever is known is not comprehended according to the power of the object known but according to the faculty of the knower, and the criterion by which sense, imagination, and reason are judged is found in the understanding.[92] Duns Scotus begins the *Oxford Commentary on Sentences of Peter Lombard* with a series of questions concerning the relation of God to human knowledge and the relation of the final end to the human will, and he resumes, after a lapse of centuries, the arguments by which the skepticism of the Academics is refuted.

In the various forms of the critical philosophy and in the various forms of idealism, empiricism, skepticism, and instrumentalism in which it eventuates, "imagination" becomes a central term. The problem of art and its relation to nature is subordinate to the problem of beauty, natural or artistic, and its relation to truth. Problems of the perception of beauty, its effects, and its relation to the good take precedence over the problems of "poetic" or making, its products, and its relation to virtue. The term "imagination," however, took on a series of meanings which serve as principles for the continuation, in theories of beauty, of the fundamental positions marked off by the different interpretations of "imitation." For the Stoics, "imagination" was a broad term embracing whatever is perceived in any mode of presentation, rational or irrational, active or passive, and the criterion of truth was the "apprehensive imagination" (καταληπτικὴ φαντασία).[93] The Stoics accordingly continued the Platonic tradition of equating the beautiful and the good, and they divided beauty into four kinds: the just, the courageous, the orderly, and the wise.[94] The perception of beauty is one of the marks setting man apart from other animals.[95] Beauty, finally, is found in body and soul: "And as in the body a certain symmetrical shape of limbs combined with a certain charm of coloring is described as beauty, so in the soul the name of beauty is given to an equipoise and consistency of beliefs and judgments, combined with a certain steadiness and stability, following upon virtue and comprising the true essence of virtue."[96] The Epicureans, on the contrary, applied "imagination" to motions originating in the sense or comparable to sense, and all imaginations are true, including the "imaginative presentations of the understanding" (φανταστικὴ ἐπιβολὴ τῆς διανοίας).[97] The good is defined in terms of pleasure: "As for myself, I am unable to conceive the good apart from the pleasurable motions derived from taste, from sexual intercourse, from hearing and from forms perceived by sight."[98] Any other view seemed to Epicurus ridiculous: "I spit upon the beautiful and upon those who vainly admire, when it does not produce any pleasure."[99]

The Academics were among those who denied that there was any absolute or certain criterion; according to the Carneades, probability was criterion enough for the conduct of life, and the Academics called the apparently true "appearance" ($\check{\epsilon}\mu\phi\alpha\sigma\iota\varsigma$), "probability," and "probable imagination" ($\pi\iota\theta\alpha\nu\dot{\eta}\ \phi\alpha\nu\tau\alpha\sigma\iota\alpha$).[100] Imagination is defined as a passion, and the "criterion" is sought therefore in the passions caused by sense.

For since the living creature differs from lifeless things by its faculty of sense, it will certainly become perceptive both of itself and of external things by means of this faculty. But when the sense is unmoved and impassive and undisturbed, neither is it sense nor perceptive of things; but when it is disturbed and somehow affected owing to the impact of things evident, then it indicates the objects. Therefore the criterion must be sought in the passion of the soul caused by sensible evidence. This passion must be indicative both of itself and of the appearance that caused it, and this passion is nothing other than the imagination. Hence we must say that the imagination is a passion of the living creature capable of presenting both itself and the other object.[101]

Both the Stoics and the Epicureans were given to analyzing myths and incidents recounted in poetry, the Stoics to explore the nature of things which is adumbrated in the analogies of ancient fables and poetic tales, the Epicureans to illustrate the influence of pleasure and pain in human action. The Academics, on the other hand, tended to employ the analytical devices of the rhetoricians who had begun to examine the characteristics of language and style in their bearing on thought and the passions. The Peripatetics after Theophrastus apparently had two criteria, sensible and intelligible, irrational and rational, which they reduced to a single criterion common to both, the "evident" or the "clear" ($\tau\dot{o}\ \dot{\epsilon}\nu\alpha\rho\gamma\dot{\epsilon}\varsigma$). Sense is affected by the sensible object. The motion caused by sensation, which is clear or evident, leads in higher animals, who are capable of moving themselves, to a further motion which is called "memory" (when it is directed to the "passion" felt by the sense) and "imagination" (when it is directed to the sensible object which produced the passion in the sense). This second passion the Peripatetics likened to a footprint ($\check{\iota}\chi\nu\varsigma$). As a motion, it possesses within itself, in turn, a

third and supervenient motion, that of the "rational imagination"
(λογικὴ φαντασία), "which is an after-result consequent on our judgment and preference; and this motion is called mind and thought."[102]
Since the sources of human action are desire and imagination, the
Peripatetics apparently also considered the imagination productive
(ποιητικός) and a cause as well as passive.[103] In their studies of
literature Hellenistic Peripatetics tended to be scholars, librarians,
historians of literature, and critics.

All the characteristic terms employed in the development of theories of "imitation"—"image," "mirror," "impression," "footprint," "seal," "likeness"—reappear in the construction of theories
of "imagination." In the discussion of art and literature, moreover,
"imagination" takes on two meanings which set it in definite relation to "imitation"—as a creative faculty opposed to imitation and
as a means of developing or supplementing natural genius parallel to
imitation. The first meaning occurs in the dialectical tradition, in
which two kinds of imitation had customarily been contrasted, by
a simple substitution of imagination for the higher kind of imitation. Imagination, as a result, is creative, and imitation is a process
of copying. One of the earliest occurrences of "imagination" in this
sense emphasizes this derivation by using, in defining "imagination," the example of Phidias' statue of Zeus, which Cicero and
Plotinus employ to illustrate the higher imitation. While in Egypt
in the course of his travels, the mystic wonder-worker, Apollonius
of Tyana, criticized the Egyptian representation of the gods by
statues of animals. When Thespesion, the Egyptian sage, asked
Apollonius whether Phidias, Praxiteles, and other Greek artists
went up to heaven in order to copy the forms of the gods by their
art or whether they were guided in some other way in their sculpture, Apollonius replied that they were guided by another influence,
a way full of wisdom. Thespesion asked what that could be except
imitation.

"Imagination," said Apollonius, "wrought these works, a wiser and
subtler artist by far than imitation; for imitation can only create as its
handiwork what it has seen, but imagination equally what it has not seen;

for it will conceive of its ideal with reference to the reality (τὸ ὄν) and imitation is often baffled by terror, but imagination by nothing; for it marches undismayed to the goal which it has itself laid down. When you entertain a notion of Zeus, you must, I suppose envisage him along with heaven and the seasons and stars, as Phidias in his day endeavored to do, and if you would fashion an image of Athene you must image in your mind armies and cunning, and handicrafts, and how she leapt out of Zeus himself."[104]

The second meaning occurs in the rhetorical tradition, in which imitation of artists and their works is one of the means by which natural genius is developed and directed. In this tradition, and employing this meaning of "imitation," there is no conflict between imagination and imitation. Longinus treats three means by which natural genius may be trained to be sensitive to sublimity and to be impregnated with lofty inspiration: by contemplating great subjects, by imitation, and by imagination.[105]

Similar discussions of the criteria of knowledge—whether they should be sought in sense or reason or whether there is no certain criterion or whether criteria should be sought in the forms rather than the contents of perception and intuition—preceded and followed the Copernican revolution in which Kant inaugurated the critical philosophy again in the eighteenth century. The problem of how beauty and sublimity are perceived takes precedence again over the problem of the relation of art and nature, and the characteristic answers of the late eighteenth and the nineteenth century made appeal, in turn, to the senses, the emotions, the imagination, and the intellectual intuitions. The first of these answers provided a new name for the branch of philosophy devoted to the study of beauty, which has been called "aesthetics" since then, even in theories which attribute the perception of beauty to some faculty other than the senses. Leibniz had remarked that the area of sensuous perception had not been adequately or systematically explored, and to remedy that defect Baumgarten published the two volumes of his *Aesthetica* in 1750 and 1758. Aesthetics is identified with the "arts" and defined as the science of sensitive cognition.

"Aesthetics (theory of the liberal arts, inferior gnoseology, art of thinking beautifully, art of analogical reasoning) is the science of sensitive cognition."[106] Among its special uses Baumgarten enumerates seven: (1) philological, (2) hermeneutic, (3) exegetic, (4) rhetorical, (5) homiletic, (6) poetic, and (7) musical.[107] He also anticipates and answers ten objections to the science: (1) that it is extremely obvious; (2) that it is the same as rhetoric and poetic; (3) that it is the same as criticism; (4) that it is unworthy of philosophers, since sensitive knowledge, phantasms, fables, and the perturbations of the emotions are below their horizons; (5) that confusion is the mother of error; (6) that distinct knowledge is preferable; (7) that the cultivation of analogical reasoning might be detrimental to the realm of reason and solidity; (8) that aesthetics is an art, not a science; (9) that aestheticians, like poets, are born, not made; and (10) that the inferior faculties and the flesh should be combated rather than excited and confirmed.[108] Like its elder sister, logic, aesthetics is divided into two parts, Theoretic and Practical; and the Theoretic, in turn, is divided into three parts: Heuristic, Methodology, and Semiotic. Baumgarten, however, had not completed when he came to the end of his second volume the first part of *Theoretic Aesthetics*, his first chapter on "Heuristic." Since the foundation of the art or science of aesthetics is in the nature of the perceiver and his powers of cognition, the *Aesthetica* begins therefore with *Aesthetica Naturalis*, that is, with the character of the successful aesthetician (*character felicis aesthetici*). This character consists of an innate beautiful and elegant genius and an innate aesthetic temperament; the genius is determined by both inferior cognoscitive faculties and their dispositions and superior cognoscitive faculties. Imagination is the second of the eight faculties and dispositions discussed under the inferior faculties.

b) A natural disposition to imagining, by which the beautiful genius is ἐυφαντασίωτον (gifted with a vivid imagination), because 1) past things must often be thought beautifully, 2) present things often are past before thought detaches their beauties, 3) future things are known not only from the present, but from past things. In order that the imagination may combine sometimes with the other faculties, it is sufficiently great in the beautiful genius that it does not always and everywhere obscure with its phantasms other perceptions which are all by nature weaker individually than individual imaginations. If the faculty of making (*facultas fingendi*) is referred to the imagination, as it often is by the ancients, there is a double necessity that it be of greater importance in the beautiful genius.[109]

Natural genius is trained in thinking beautifully by imitation of examples of beautiful thought,[110] and since there is a proportion between the mind and the objects of thought, if thought is useful and delightful, "all devices (*artificium*) of beautiful thought seem to be contained in this one rule: *Imitate nature*."[111] "Imitation" is conceived in the sense, familiar in the rhetorical tradition, of imitation of great writers and of examples taken from their works,[112] and the analysis of sensitive cognition divides the modes of thinking into the three kinds—plain, medium, and sublime—which had been used to classify styles,[113] employing in the application of the distinctions arguments borrowed from Cicero and instances cited from poets.

Hume, like Baumgarten, played an important role in preparing Kant for his Copernican revolution, and, like many of his compatriots, he took the second position, identifying beauty and its perception with pleasure and the emotions. In this he agreed with Democritus and Epicurus.

If we consider all the hypotheses, which have been form'd either by philosophy or common reason, to explain the difference betwixt beauty and deformity, we shall find that all of them resolve into this, that beauty is such an order and construction of the parts, as either by the *primary constitution* of our nature, by *custom*, or by *caprice*, is fitted to give a pleasure and satisfaction to the soul. This is the distinguishing character of beauty, and forms all the difference betwixt it and deformity, whose natural tendency is to produce uneasiness. Pleasure and pain, therefore, are not only necessary attendants of beauty and deformity, but constitute their very essence.[114]

Beauty, whether moral or natural, is felt rather than perceived. It is an object of taste and sentiment. Some species of beauty, especially the natural kinds, move our affection and approbation immediately and are unaffected by reasoning. Other kinds of beauty, especially those of the finer arts, require reasoning as a preparation for feeling the proper sentiment.[115] Principles of a kind, based on the uniformity of the sentiments of the mind, are found in human tastes, but that uniformity is diversified by a variety of influences and circumstances.

> There is something approaching to principles in mental tastes; and critics can reason and dispute more plausibly than cooks or perfumers. We may observe, however, that this uniformity among human kind, hinders not, but that there is a considerable diversity in the sentiments of beauty and worth, and that education, custom, prejudice, caprice, and humour, frequently vary our taste of this kind. . . . Beauty and worth are merely of a relative nature, and consist in an agreeable sentiment, produced by an object in a particular mind, according to the peculiar structure and constitution of that mind.[116]

The study of beauty in the arts is in part a study of natural sentiments and sympathies and in part a study of actual standards of taste.[117]

In the analysis of the understanding, consideration of the operation of the "imagination" is fundamental to the derivation of ideas which are "copies" of "impressions" which in turn are copies of things. "The memory, senses, and understanding are . . . all of them founded on the imagination, on the vivacity of our ideas."[118] Contradictions and meaningless statements, such as those encountered in our inquiry into ultimate causes, result from an illusion of the imagination, whereas understanding consists of the general and more established properties of the imagination.[119] Memory and imagination mimic and copy the perceptions of the senses, and all thoughts and ideas may be resolved into simple ideas which were copied from precedent feelings or sentiments.[120] Unlike memory, imagination is not restrained to reproduce the order and form of the original impressions. The creative power of the mind amounts to no more than the faculty of compounding, transposing, augmenting, or diminishing the materials afforded us by the senses and experience. The beginning point is the impressions of sensation which arise in the soul originally from unknown causes, but truth about things discovered by reason consists in a conformity of ideas, considered as copies, with those subjects which they represent.[121]

According to Kant, who takes the third position concerning the perception of beauty, there are three fundamental faculties of the soul which contain the conditions of the possibility of all experience and which cannot themselves be derived from any other faculty: sense, imagination, and understanding.[122] He agrees with Baumgarten in viewing the judgments of the beautiful and the sublime as "aesthetical" judgments but denies that the aesthetic or the empirical provides principles for the criticism of taste.[123] He agrees with Hume that an objective principle of taste is impossible, but, although aesthetic judgments cannot be set forth in formulae that are universally applicable, the subjective principle of taste can be developed and justified as an a priori principle of the Judgment, and neither the beautiful nor the good is identified with pleasure.[124] In the *Critique of Judgment* the three faculties of the soul are enumerated as the *faculty of knowledge*, the *feeling of pleasure and pain*, and the *faculty of desire*. Corresponding to these, there are three higher cognitive faculties: Understanding (which legislates for the faculty of knowledge, if it is referred to nature as the faculty of theoretical understanding), Reason (which legislates for the faculty of desire according to the concept of freedom), and Judgment, which is the intermediate between Understanding and Reason.[125] Judgment in general is the faculty of thinking the particular as contained in the universal, and the aesthetic judgment of the beautiful differs from the aesthetic judgment of the sublime in that the imagination is related to intellectual cognition in the judgment of the beautiful, whereas it is related to practical reason and morality in the judgment of the sublime. Kant summarizes the important points of his treatment of the beautiful in the first section of the "Analytic of Aesthetical Judgment" by setting forth the relation between imagination and understanding in the judgment of taste:

If we seek the result of the preceding analysis we find that everything runs up into this concept of Taste, that it is a faculty for judging an object in reference to the Imagination's *free conformity to law*. Now if in the judgment of taste the Imagination must be considered in its freedom, it is in the first place not regarded as reproductive, as it is subject to the laws of association, but as productive and spontaneous (as the author of arbitrary forms of possible intuition). And although in the apprehension of a given object of sense it is tied to a definite form of this Object, and so far has no free play (such as that of poetry) yet it may readily be conceived that the object can furnish it with such a form containing a collection of the manifold, as the Imagination itself, if it were left free, would project in accordance with the *conformity to law of the Understanding* in general. . . . Hence it is a conformity to law without a law; and a subjective agreement of the Imagination and Understanding,—without such an objective agreement as there is when the representation is referred to a definite concept of an object,—can subsist along with the free conformity to law of the Understanding (which is also called purposiveness without purpose) and with the peculiar feature of a judgment of taste.[126]

The principle of taste is the subjective principle of judgment in general; and, since judgment requires the accordance of imagination and understanding, taste is the faculty of judging a priori of the communicability of feelings, that are bound up with a given representation, without the mediation of a concept.

"Imitation" is used in two senses in the course of the examination of beauty and taste: (1) the imitation of artists and their productions (which displays skill) is contrasted to the judgment of taste, and (2) the imitation of nature provides the rule for art and a principle of division among the arts. There can be no objective rule of taste which shall determine by means of concepts what is beautiful, but there is an empirical criterion in the universal communicability of sensation (satisfaction or dissatisfaction) without the aid of a concept, that is, the agreement, as far as is possible, of all times and peoples in this feeling associated with the representation of certain objects. "Hence, we consider some products of taste as *exemplary*. Not that taste can be acquired by imitating others; for it must be an original faculty. He who imitates a model shows, no doubt, in so far as he attains to it, skill; but only shows taste in so far as he can judge of this model itself."[127] We take an interest in beauty itself, however, only when it is Nature or regarded as nature, and art inspires such an interest only when it is an imitation of nature or an art obviously directed to our satisfaction.[128] Beautiful art is an art in so far as it seems like nature, and it is the nature of the genius of the artist which mediates between Nature and Art. "Genius is the talent (or natural gift) which gives the rule to Art. Since talent, as the innate productive faculty of the artist, belongs itself to Nature, we may express the matter thus: *Genius* is the innate mental disposition (*ingenium*) *through which* Nature gives the rule to Art."[129] The beautiful representation of an object is properly only the form of the presentation of a concept and the means by which the concept is communicated universally; to give this form to the product of beautiful art, mere taste is requisite. Taste is a faculty of judgment, not a productive faculty. Imagination is a productive cognitive faculty, by which another nature, as it were, is created out of the material that actual nature provides. Products that we expect to appear as beautiful art may lack spirit even when they exhibit taste.

Spirit, in an aesthetical sense, is the name given to the animating principle of the mind. . . . Now I maintain that this principle is no other than the faculty of presenting *aesthetical Ideas*. And by an aesthetical Idea I understand that representation of the Imagination which occasions much thought, without, however, any definite thought, *i.e.* any *concept*, being capable of being adequate to it; it consequently cannot be completely compassed and made intelligible by language.—We easily see that it is the counterpart (pendant) of a *rational Idea*, which conversely is a concept to which no *intuition* (or representation of the Imagination) can be adequate.[130]

Genius is the exemplary originality of natural gifts in the free employment of cognitive faculties, and the product of a genius is an example, not to be imitated, but to be followed, by another genius. Geniuses, however, are rare, and for other good heads, who follow the example of a Genius in a school, beautiful art is to that extent imitation, to which nature through the medium of a genius supplies the rule.[131] Among the formative arts, sculpture, as a corporeal representation, is a mere imitation of nature, but with reference to aesthetical Ideas.[132]

Various forms of the fourth answer concerning the perception of beauty and sublimity were developed in the highly variegated series of dialectical analyses which used the distinctions elaborated in Kant's critical philosophy to equate art to knowledge or knowledge to art. In the romantic reaction the characteristics which art and knowledge share tend to make philosophy poetic and poetry mysterious and passionate. For Novalis, both poetry and philosophy furnish a representation of the mind, the inner universe in its totality. Poetry is genuine absolute reality, and the distinction between poet and thinker is merely apparent. Romantic poetry, by his definition, is the art of estranging in a pleasant manner, of making an object appear alien and yet familiar and attractive.[133] "Our life is not a dream, but it should become one and it is likely to attain this end."[134] According to Schlegel, the characteristic of romantic poetry is irony, which never acquiesces in a definite shape but enjoys infinite freedom, ascending from one form to another and dissolving reality, making it over into an artistically arranged chaos, the charming symmetry of contradictions, the marvelous eternal alternation of enthusiasms and irony.[135]

Aesthetics assumes a fundamental place in systematic philosophic analysis of Absolute Idealism. For Hegel, art is the presentation of the Ideal, and philosophy must follow and interpret this presentation. The Ideal must be found in art rather than in nature—in an argument that employs reasons reminiscent of Plato's to invert the conclusion Plato derived from them—because art is nature twice-begotten, nature born again in the inventions of genius. Art has evolved through three phases: symbolic art, by which the ancient Egyptians and Hebrews sought to express a meaning without remainder and achieved ambiguity, uncanniness, and sublimity; classical art, which found its material in the perfections of the human body; and romantic art, which originated in subordination to the Christian religion, declined by becoming too self-conscious and subjective, and reached its eclipse in romantic irony. For Schelling aesthetic intuition is intellectual intuition turned objective. Beauty mediates between truth and goodness, for truth involves necessity, goodness involves liberty, and beauty is indifference of necessity and liberty contemplated in something real. The beautiful is a poem in which the highest freedom apprehends itself again in necessity. Art accordingly is an absolute synthesis and mutual interpenetration of freedom and necessity.[136] The universe is God in the form of the absolute work of art and in eternal beauty. Art, like philosophy, treats of Ideas, but the artist represents them not through prototypes but through reflected images, that is, art represents the ideal models of which things are defective images, and it provides therefore the illustration of philosophical truth. Schelling's philosophic ideas were expounded and interpreted by Coleridge in the *Biographia literaria* and provide the basis for his distinction between Imagination and Fancy. Coleridge sought in the Transcendental Philosophy grounds for the deduction of the Imagination, and the Imagination provided him with the principles of production and of "genial criticism" in the fine arts.[137] Imagination imitates the eternal act of divine creation. This is primary imagination which is the living power and prime agent of all human perception; secondary imagination is an echo of primary imagination, differing from it only in degree and coexisting with the conscious will. Fancy, on the other hand, is only a mode of memory emancipated from the order of time and space.[138] Human imagination imitates divine creation, and the composition of a poem is among the imitative arts. Imitation, as opposed to copying, consists either in the interfusion of the "same" throughout the radically "different" or of the "different" through a base radically the "same."[139]

IV

Kant's Copernican revolution, like earlier efforts to effect a similar reorientation of the world and our knowledge of the world to the standpoint of the knowing subject, arose from and led to oppositions of theories concerning human understanding and human nature. The methods and principles which had been employed in theories concerning the nature of things were put to new applications in theories concerning human understanding, and similar theo-

retic differences developed. The term "imagination" became basic
in differentiating the "beautiful" from the true and the good and
took on meanings comparable to those assumed by "imitation" in
differentiating "art" from nature and the virtues. The distinctions
between nature and art and the problems of their relations to each
other are no longer basic but emerge instead as consequences of
basic distinctions between apperception and desire, understanding
and will. To later critics the endeavor to make the character of the
known world depend on the constitution of the knowing mind
seems a return to an ultra-Ptolemaic system. They, in turn, sought
principles which make neither self nor world, neither soul nor nature, central but which bring out their interdependence and remove
the opposition between knowing and doing, theory and practice.[140]
In this new Copernican revolution (which has borrowed many of
its basic analogies from Einstein and Freud) action and passion are
brought into close relation or are identified with each other, and
conditions and contents of expression and communication are studied to discover the principles of science, action, and art.[141] "Expression" takes the place of "imitation" and "imagination" in the discussion of art, beauty, and experience,[142] and in the oppositions of
positivisms and relativisms, pragmatisms and systems of semantics,
the distinction between action and language, operation and meaning
takes the basic place vacated by the distinction of nature and art,
understanding and will.

In the transition worked in philosophy by this second revolution,
the terms and distinctions of rhetoric and the operational tradition
assume prominence much as the terms and distinctions of psychology and the dialectical tradition were employed and redefined in the
transition from philosophies based on metaphysics to those which
take their beginnings in epistemology. Among the Romans, Cicero
sought to re-establish philosophy by returning to a proper conjunction of eloquence and wisdom, words and deeds, while Sextus
Empiricus based his criticism of the dogmatists in all fields of
knowledge on a theory of signs and semiosis. Cicero inspired a like

nominalistic and practical trend in the twelfth century.[143] Logicians in the fourteenth century developed terministic logics and speculative grammars, and rhetoricians and political philosophers in the Renaissance studied examples of thought and style in literature and examples of character and action in history. During the twentieth century, reactions against idealism have taken the form of pragmatisms, naturalisms, realisms, phenomenologies, and existentialisms, which have explored experience and existence as structures of actions, or like reactions have taken the form of positivisms, symbolic philosophies, analytical philosophies, and semantics, which have explored expression and communication, denotation and connotation, synthesis and analysis, as structures of language. But words and deeds have dialectical, logistic, and problematic as well as linguistic or operational analyses; and the transition from the discussion of language and action to the discussion of things is usually mediated by the recognition that the universe is a poem and a commonwealth and that science consists of warranted statements about nature and of tested powers to modify nature. These major shifts from things to thoughts and from thoughts to statement or operation are of profound importance, for they affect what science, action, and art are thought to be. But no less important than the complexities of possible subjects of analysis that make it difficult to determine the nature of art—artificial object, beautiful art (i.e., *beaux arts*), or aesthetic experience—are the recurrent problems and the pattern of meanings that are encountered in the successive basic terms—imitation, imagination, and expression—for it is by these terms that the nature of art is defined and the aspects of art treated in criticism are determined.

As theories of imitation provide a subordinate place for imagination and as theories of imagination employ the concept of imitation, so too problems of expression are treated in the analysis of the imitations of art and of the creations of imagination, and theories of expression employ the concepts of imitation and imagination. A foretaste of the problems encountered in theories of expression is provided by the pattern of views concerning expression developed in theories of imitation and imagination. Four basic meanings of "imitation" and "imagination" have been distinguished; problems of "expression" are treated in four characteristic ways corresponding to these basic meanings expressed frequently in associated significances attached to familiar words, like "image," which is a reflection of a thing in imitation, a perception of the mind in imagination, and a figure of speech in expression. According to the dialectical method, questions of expression are inseparable from questions of truth. Plato, who uses "imitation" to construct a theory of language in the *Cratylus*, concludes that language is neither wholly arbitrary nor wholly natural. All the arts are reduced ultimately to dialectic, and the rightness of language, by which it achieves adequacy to thought and object, to intention and ideal end, is achieved dialectically. In dialectic the discovery of reality, the formulation of truths, and the education of minds are three phases of the same process. The three instruments of the dialectical method enumerated by Plato have symbolic names—word (ὄνομα), image (εἴδωλον), and statement or reason (λόγος), and the *logos* is the essence of the thing. Coleridge, who finds the prime agent of all human perception in "imagination," distinguishes the *poem* as a species of composition whose immediate object is pleasure from *poetry*, which is defined by reference to the *poet*, who "diffuses a tone and spirit of unity, that blends, and (as it were) *fuses*, each into each, by that synthetic and magical power, to which I would exclusively appropriate the name of Imagination."[144] No man was ever yet a great poet without being at the same time a profound philosopher, for poetry is the blossom and the fragrancy of all human knowledge, human thoughts, human passions, emotion, language.[145] This coincidence of philosophy and poetry in the poet provides the criteria for language. Coleridge states his differences from certain supposed parts of Wordsworth's theory "on the assumption, that his words had been rightly interpreted, as purporting that the proper diction for poetry in general consists altogether in a language taken, with due exceptions, from the mouths of men in real life, a language which actually constitutes the natural conversation of men under the influence of natural feelings."[146] The language of the rustic is not a model or "the best part of language."

> The best part of human language, properly so called, is derived from reflection on the acts of the mind itself. It is formed by a voluntary appropriation of fixed symbols to internal acts, to processes and results of imagination, the greater part of which have no place in the consciousness of uneducated man; though in civilized society, by imitation and passive remembrance of what they hear from their religious instructors and other superiors, the most uneducated share in the harvest which they neither sowed, nor reaped.[147]

As for Plato, there are two kinds of imitation for Coleridge, and both have their influence on language: imagination, primary and secondary, imitates in differing degrees the eternal act of creation, and the best part of language is adapted to imagination; fancy rearranges the fixities of experience according to the law of association, and ordinary language imitates the language of imagination. The best parts of language, which are employed by the poet, are the product of philosophers, not of clowns or shepherds.[148] Aristotle, who uses "imitation" primarily to characterize the object of art and to distinguish it from natural objects and habituated virtues, contrasts language as symbols (σύμβολον) or signs (σημεῖον) of the passions of the soul, sometimes calling them "internal discourse," to the passions themselves which are likenesses (ὁμοίωμα) of things. The languages of men, spoken and written, differ from each other, whereas the impressions of the soul and the objects of which they are likenesses are the same for all men, that is to say, they are natural.[149] Aristotle analyzes three fundamentally different uses of language, sketching the beginnings of what would today be called a "grammar" for each—logical uses in demonstration, rhetorical uses in persuasion, and poetic uses in imitation. The analysis of the fundamental "parts of speech" and their basic combinations in proposition, period, and verse, as given in the *De interpretatione*, the *Rhetoric*, and the *Poetic*, are consequently different. Language provides the matter of poetry. Kant places "imagination," conceived as a productive faculty of cognition which creates another "nature" out of the materials that actual "nature" gives it, between the principles of Reason, which are as natural to us as are the principles of understanding of empirical nature, and the materials which we borrow from nature to work up freely into something different which surpasses nature.[150]

Thus genius properly consists in the happy relation [*sc.* between the faculties of Imagination and Understanding] which no science can teach and no industry can learn, by which Ideas are found for a given concept; and on the other hand, we thus find for these Ideas the *expression*, by means of which the subjective state of mind brought about by them, as an accompaniment of the concept, can be communicated to others. The latter talent is properly speaking what is called spirit; for to express the ineffable element in the state of mind implied by a certain representation and to make it universally communicable—whether the expression be in speech or painting or statuary—this requires a faculty of seizing the quickly passing play of Imagination and of unifying it in a concept (which is even on that account original and discloses a new rule that could not have been inferred from any preceding principles or examples), that can be communicated without any restraint [of rules].[151]

Beauty in general is the expression of aesthetical Ideas, and the divisions of beautiful art are made on the analogy of modes of *expression* of which men avail themselves in speech.

We may describe beauty in general (whether natural or artificial) as the *expression* of aesthetical Ideas; only that in beautiful Art this Idea must be occasioned by a concept of the Object; whilst in beautiful Nature the mere reflection upon a given intuition, without any concept of what the object is to be, is sufficient for the awakening and communicating of the Idea of which that Object is regarded as the *expression*.

If, then, we wish to make a division of the beautiful arts, we cannot choose a more convenient principle, at least tentatively, than the analogy of art with the mode of expression of which men avail themselves in speech, in order to communicate to one another as perfectly as possible not merely their concepts but also their sensations.[152]

On the basis of this tentative division there are three kinds of beautiful arts: the arts of speech, which include rhetoric and poetry; the formative arts, which include sculpture, architecture, and paint-

ing; and the arts of the play of sensations, which include music and
the art of color.

Rhetoricians, who use "imitation" of literary models as a means
of acquiring proficiency in the art, often distinguished five things
which an orator must have: invention, disposition, expression
(*elocutio*), memory, and delivery. Invention is defined as "the ex-
cogitation of true or plausible things which render one's cause probable"; disposition as "the distribution of discovered things in an
order"; and expression as "the accommodation of suitable words to
the invented matter." All five can be pursued by three means: by
art, which consists of precepts; by imitation, by which we strive to
become similar in speaking to those we imitate; and by exercise,
which is the assiduous use and custom of speaking.[153] In general, the
criteria for expression in rhetoric are some form of appropriateness
to a subject matter in particular circumstances and for particular
purposes. Baumgarten, who uses "imagination" as the faculty of
conceiving past and future and of constructing artificial objects, divides the theory of aesthetics into three parts which recall the first
three parts of rhetoric (the remaining two parts also appear: memory is one of the dispositions of the aesthetician, and action is needed
when expression is by the spoken word): heuristic, methodology,
and semiotic. In the traditional scheme, invention has to do with
arguments relative to a subject matter, disposition with arrangements adapted to circumstances and audiences, and expression with
questions of appropriateness of language to thoughts and circumstances. Baumgarten distinguishes "beauty of sensitive thought"
from "beauty of order" and "beauty of signification." Beauty of
sensitive thought is an agreement (*consensus*) of thought abstracted
from the order of thoughts and signs, for ugly things can be thought
beautifully and beautiful things in an ugly manner. Beauty of order
and disposition is an agreement (*consensus*) of order by which we
meditate things thought beautifully and relate the internal thoughts
to things. Beauty of signification is an internal agreement (*consensus*) of signs with both order and things, such as "diction" and
"expression" when the sign is speech or word, and "action" as well

when the word is employed orally.[154] Baumgarten did not write his
semiotic, for which he gives the "customary" description—"elocu-
tion and action in beautiful speeches,"[155] but the proportions of
thoughts to objects, persons, and expressions underlie all five of the
major concerns (*curae*) which he treats in *Heuristic:* (1) aesthetic
richness is treated relative to matter (the aesthetic "horizon" being
distinguished from the logical as the sphere of analogical beautiful
reasoning) and to person (in which rules for the development of
genius are expounded); (2) aesthetic magnitude is treated relative
to matter (gravity of objects and thought proportioned to them)
and to person (subjective magnitude or magnanimity); (3) aesthetic
truth and verisimilitude is relative to things; (4) aesthetic clarity or
light is achieved by two special forms of argument: comparison or
figure, which is the substitution of one perception for another connected with it, and trope, which is the elegant substitution of one
perception for another by transfer of word, note, color, or any other
sign; and (5) aesthetic certitude or persuasion is concerned with
verisimilitude and probability.

Democritus, who identified sensation with the motion of physical
"idols," imagination with the resulting impressions, and beauty
with pleasure, considered language arbitrary in much the same
sense as appearances are, and he therefore called sensations *names*.
Hume, who treated ideas as copies and imagination as fundamental
to thought and who identified beauty with pleasure, held that language arises from convention without promise.[156] However, since
the sentiments which arise from humanity or benevolence, as contrasted to the sentiments produced by the selfish passions, are not
only the same in all human creatures, and produce the same approbation and censure, but also comprehend all human creatures, language must be molded upon these species of sentiment, and a peculiar set of terms must be invented to express the universal sentiments of censure and approbation. The nature of language is an
almost infallible guide in the formation of such judgments.[157]

When the terms "expression" and "operation," or "language"
and "action," assume a basic position in the definition of other

terms of philosophic explanation, they are used with meanings similar to those attached to them when they were derived from, and defined by, characteristics of things or faculties of thought. "Expression" and "communication" orient philosophic analysis in directions that emphasize dynamic processes and developments in which men are brought to common understanding and action. From the point of view of philosophies of process and action, as they were constructed during the late Roman Republic and early Empire, the twelfth century, the fourteenth century and Renaissance, and the twentieth century, earlier metaphysical and epistemological philosophies were committed to distinctions which were unreal and impractical; they were static, abstract, insensitive to organic processes, changing circumstances, and systemic interrelations. All these faults can be remedied by examining the structure of meanings in languages or by determining meanings by operations. "Expression" assumes particular importance in the analysis of art in semantic and pragmatic philosophies, and, depending on the meaning assumed by "expression," art is treated in relation to the values expressed, to the culture or the community in which the expression occurs, to the use of language and other symbolic forms appropriate to art as distinct from other uses of discourse or expression, or to the emotions which art expresses and communicates.

Croce's dialectic is a potent instrument for the reduction of disjunctions that had been justified by the assumptions of other philosophies. Once the basic distinction of human knowledge into its two forms—intuitive and logical—has been made, intuition is identified with expression, and expression makes further distinctions unnecessary and erroneous.

And yet there is a sure method of distinguishing true intuition, true representation, from that which is inferior to it: the spiritual fact from the mechanical, passive, natural fact. Every true intuition or representation is also *expression*. That which does not objectify itself in expression is not intuition or representation, but sensation and mere natural fact. The spirit only intuits in making, forming, expressing. He who separates intuition from expression never succeeds in reuniting them.

Intuitive activity *possesses intuitions to the extent that it expresses them.*[158]

Art is then identical with intuitive or expressive knowledge,[159] and the genius of the artist which expresses art is identical with the taste which appreciates it.[160] Expression cannot be divided into modes, kinds, or genres, since expressions are individual, and an intuition, unlike a concept, can be expressed in only one way.[161] Natural beauty, as contrasted to artificial beauty, is possible only when an observer contemplates nature with the eye of an artist, since without the aid of the imagination no part of nature is beautiful.[162] Aesthetic, finally, is identical with linguistic.[163]

In dialectical analyses two kinds of imitation are usually distinguished: one, which is usually approved, imitates ideal values or idealizes nature; the other, which is rejected, copies particular, contingent facts. Croce makes this distinction.

> The proposition that art is *imitation of nature* has also several meanings. Sometimes truths have been expressed or at least shadowed forth in these words, sometimes errors have been promulgated. More frequently, no definite thought has been expressed at all. One of the scientifically legitimate meanings occurs when "imitation" is understood as representation or intuition of nature, a form of knowledge. And when the phrase is used with this intention, and in order to emphasize the spiritual character of the process, another proposition becomes legitimate also: namely, that art is the *idealization* or *idealizing* imitation of nature. But if by imitation of nature be understood that art gives mechanical reproductions, more or less perfect duplicates of natural objects, in the presence of which is renewed the same tumult of impressions as that caused by natural objects, then the proposition is evidently false.[164]

In the dialectical tradition, reality, thought, and expression are identified in their upper ideal reaches, and it makes little difference in that elevated region whether the basic terms by which reality is treated apply, in their lower significances, primarily to Nature, Ideas, or Words. The operation of the dialectic as well as the doctrines justified dialectically may be profoundly altered by the consequences of that choice, but two forms of imitation usually continue, one of the ideal, the other of the contingent.

Dewey's instrumentalist or problematic method likewise employs the term "expression" to reduce distinctions, but they are

different distinctions from those of Croce, and the identities discovered to effect their reduction are different. The primary task of
the philosophy of the fine arts, according to Dewey, "is to restore
continuity between the refined and intensified forms of experience
that are works of art and the everyday events, doings, and sufferings that are universally recognized to constitute experience."[165]
Where Croce equates art and aesthetic experience with intuitive
knowledge, Dewey seeks the sources of aesthetic experience in
animal life below the human scale and finds art prefigured in the
very processes of living.[166] The use of art becomes at once the
ground of the distinction of man from the rest of nature and of the
bond that ties him to nature, and science itself is an art central to the
generation and utilization of other arts.[167] In the aesthetic experience there is a marked similarity between the experience by which
the appreciator perceives a work of art and that which the artist
underwent in producing it.[168] A work of art is the building-up of an
integral experience out of the interaction of organic and environmental conditions and energies. It is a result of the meeting of new
and old.

The junction of the new and the old is not a mere composition of forces,
but is a re-creation in which the present impulsion gets form and solidity
while the old, the "stored," material is literally revived, given new life and
soul through having to meet a new situation.

It is this double change which converts an activity into an act of expression. Things in the environment that would otherwise be mere smooth
channels or else blind obstructions become means, media. At the same time,
things retained from past experience that would grow stale from routine or
inert from lack of use, become coefficients in new adventures and put on
raiment of fresh meaning. Here are all the elements needed to define expression.[169]

The act of expression is unified: inspiration and expression are not
separate, nor are there two operations, one performed on outer materials and the other upon inner mental stuff.[170] There is no ground
in reality for the distinction between cognitive and emotive, by
which it is held that scientists and philosophers think while poets
and painters follow their feelings.[171] Aesthetic emotion is not sepa-

rable from expression.[172] Art is not nature, but it is nature transformed by entering into new relationships where it evokes a new emotional response.[173]

Croce's doctrine of expression led him to reduce everything related to the aesthetic experience to expression; Dewey's doctrine of expression led him to the "expressive object." "The expressiveness of the object is the report and celebration of the complete fusion of what we undergo and what our activity of attentive perception brings into what we receive by means of the senses."[174] Art is characterized by its object, its mode of communication, and the prior disposition of artist and appreciator. A work of art is representative, in that it presents the world in a new experience which those who enjoy the work of art undergo; it is an expression, which constitutes an experience, as opposed to a statement, which leads to one; it is dependent on antecedent motor dispositions.[175] The unity in which art is consummated is not the expression of an intuition but the building of a community. "In the degree in which art exercises its office, it is also a remaking of the experience of the community in the direction of greater order and unity."[176] The material of aesthetic experience is a manifestation, a record and celebration of the life of a civilization, a means of promoting its development, and it is also the ultimate judgment upon the quality of a civilization.[177]

Dewey's conception of expression and the expressive object determine his treatment of terms which are basic in other systems, such as "beauty," "imagination," and "imitation." If beauty is taken to be the total quality of an aesthetic experience, it can be treated better by examining experience itself and showing the origins and nature of beauty as a quality of experience.[178] Imagination shares the dubious place of beauty in aesthetic analysis: it is a way of seeing and feeling things as they compose an integral whole, an interaction of outer and inner vision.[179] The expressive object is, on the other hand, an imitation or a representation, and Dewey sets forth the Aristotelian conception of imitation in an unusually clear and persuasive fashion.

Aristotle, who gave the conception that art is representative its classic formation, at least avoided the dualism of this division [*sc.* between representative and non-representative art]. He took the concept of imitation more generously and more intelligently. Thus he declares that music is the *most* representative of all the arts—this being the very one that some modern theorists refer to the wholly non-representative class. Nor did he mean anything so silly as that music represents the twittering of birds, lowing of cows and gurgling of brooks. He meant that music reproduces by means of sounds the affections, the emotional impressions, that are produced by martial, sad, triumphant, sexually orgasmic, objects and scenes. Representation in the sense of expression covers all the qualities and values of any possible esthetic experience.[180]

Representation is one dimension of the continuity established by the expressive object. It supplements the continuity established between the experience of the artist and the experience of the appreciator by the continuity between aesthetic values that are intrinsic to things of ordinary experience and the aesthetic values with which the artist is concerned. Dewey therefore gives a profound analysis of representation in art, which states the Aristotelian insight concerning imitation admirably, in commenting on Roger Fry's effort to establish a radical difference between these two experiences.

Suppose the artist wishes to portray by means of his medium the emotional state or the enduring character of some person. By the compelling force of his medium, he will, if an artist—that is, if a painter, with disciplined respect for his medium—modify the object present to him. He will resee the object in terms of lines, colors, light, space—relations that form a pictorial whole, that is, that create an object immediately enjoyed in perception. In denying that the artist attempts to represent in the sense of literal reproduction of colors, lines, etc., as they already exist in the object, Mr. Fry is admirably right. But the inference that there is no re-presentation of any meanings of any subject matter whatever, no presentation that is of a subject matter having a meaning of its own which clarifies and concentrates the diffused and dulled meanings of other experiences does not follow.[181]

Art creates a new experience in the expressive object which is at once expression, communication, and representation.

Most semantic theories employ an operational method to construct or analyze languages, and three considerations usually enter at some point in those processes: consideration of the formal structure or of the relations of signs to each other, consideration of the relation of signs to the object to which they are applicable, and consideration of the relation of signs to speaker and hearer, writer and reader, in communication. In the *Semiosis* developed by the logical positivists or the logical empiricists, these three considerations are formalized into three dimensions: syntactics, semantics, and pragmatics. "Expression" is the term proper to the pragmatic dimension.

It will be convenient to have special terms to designate certain of the relations of signs to signs, to objects, and to interpreters. '*Implicates*' will be restricted to D_{syn}, '*designates*' and '*denotes*' to D_{sem}, and '*expresses*' to D_p. The word 'table' implicates (but does *not* designate) 'furniture with a horizontal top on which things may be placed,' designates a certain kind of object (furniture with a horizontal top on which things may be placed), denotes the objects to which it is applicable, and expresses its interpreter. In any given case certain of the dimensions may actually or practically vanish: a sign may not have syntactical relations to other signs and so its actual implication becomes null; or it may have implication and yet denote no object; or it may have implication and yet no actual interpreter and so no expression—as in the case of a word in a dead language.[182]

Once one enters into the analysis of signs, echoes and remnants of theories of imitation which reappear in the designations of semantics must be balanced against the formal structures of implication explored in syntactics and the structures of expression explained in pragmatics. "Thing-sentences," whose *designata* do not include signs, must be distinguished from the "sentences of syntactics," which are formed according to syntactical rules, and the relation of signs to objects is involved in the problem of the relation of the structure of language to the structure of nature.[183]

One of the oldest and most persistent theories is that languages mirror (correspond with, reflect, are isomorphic with) the realm of nonlinguistic objects. . . . It goes without saying that such a persistent tradition as lies behind the doctrine in question must have something to commend it; it is, nevertheless, significant that this tradition has progressively weakened and has even been repudiated by some of its most vigorous former champions. . . . But it is clear that, when a language as a whole is considered, its syntactical structure is a function of both pragmatic and empirical considerations and is not a bare mirroring of nature considered in abstraction from the users of the language.[184]

Among the historical antecedents of pragmatics are rhetoric and the interpretations put on the experimental sciences; and the social character of language as a system of signs mediating the responses of members of a community to one another and to their environment falls under the scope of pragmatics. As the rhetorical and social aspects of language are investigated, it might be anticipated that another aspect of "imitation"—that by which meanings acquire general acceptance and are manipulated in propaganda and persuasion—may be brought more fully to light. Such an inquiry, however, would have to be based on a study of actual languages, and it would tend further to weaken the distinction between implication, denotation, and meaning. The tendency in most semantic interpretations of poetry is in the opposite direction to establish a sharp line between denotary and connotatory, between cognitive and emotive uses of language, and to find the essence of poetry on one side of this line in the analysis of tropes, ambiguity, paradox, or irony.[185]

For Santayana, as for Democritus and Hume, beauty is identified with pleasure. It is constituted by "the objectification of pleasure"; it is "pleasure objectified."[186] All human functions, but particularly the senses, contribute to the materials of beauty, and the perception of form has a physiological and psychological basis. The beauty of material and of form is the objectification of certain pleasures connected with the process of direct perception; but beauty may result also from "expression," which is acquired by objects through association.

We not only construct visible unities and recognizable types, but remain aware of their affinities to what is not at the time perceived; that is, we find in them a certain tendency and quality, not original to them, a meaning and a tone, which upon investigation we shall see to have been the proper

[169]

characteristics of other objects and feelings, associated with them once in our experience. The hushed reverberations of these associated feelings continue in the brain, and by modifying our present reaction, colour the image upon which our attention is fixed. The quality thus acquired by objects through association is what we call their expression. Whereas in form or material there is one object with its emotional effect, in expression there are two, and the emotional effect belongs to the character of the second or suggested one. Expression may thus make beautiful by suggestion things in themselves indifferent, or it may come to heighten the beauty which they already possess.[187]

Two terms are distinguished in all expression: first, the object actually presented, the word, the image, the expressive thing; second, the object suggested, the further thought, emotion, or image, the thing expressed.

Imagination is the fundamental faculty, underlying all mental processes, in constructing these arbitrary expressions of sense and discourse.

The "sane" response to nature is by action only and by an economy which nature can accept and weave into her own material economy; but as to the terms of sense and discourse, they are all from the very beginning equally arbitrary, poetical, and (if you choose) mad; yet all equally symptomatic. They vary initially and intangibly from mind to mind, even in expressing the same routine of nature. The imagination which eventually runs to fine art or religion is the same faculty which, under a more direct control of external events, yields vulgar perception. The promptings and the control exercised by matter are continuous in both cases; the dream requires a material dreamer as much as the waking sensation, and the latter is a transcript of his bodily condition just as directly as the dream. Poetic, creative, original fancy is not a secondary form of sensibility, but its first and only form.[188]

Many species survive together, many rival endowments and customs and religions. If mythical systems decline at last, it is not so much by virtue of the maladjustments underlying their speculative errors—for their myths on the whole are wisely contrived—as because imagination in its freedom abandons these errors for others simply because the prevalent mood of mankind has changed, and it begins dreaming in a different key. "This world of free expression, this drift of sensations, passions, and ideas," is the "realm of Spirit." It is only for the sake of this free life that material competence and knowledge of fact are worth attaining. Facts for a living creature are only instruments; his play life is his true life.[189]

"Imitation" has a similarly fundamental and broad meaning extending the processes by which sensations are reflected on and understood (or in Hume's terminology the relation of ideas to the impressions of which they are copies) to the processes of art.

Imitation is a fertile principle in the Life of Reason. We have seen that it furnishes the only rational sanction for belief in any fellow mind; now we shall see how it creates the most glorious and interesting of plastic arts. The machinery of imitation is obscure but its prevalence is obvious, and even in the present rudimentary state of human biology we may perhaps divine some of its general features. In a motor image the mind represents prophetically what the body is about to execute: but all images are more or less motor, so that no idea, apparently, can occupy the mind unless the body has received some impulse to enact the same. The plastic instinct to reproduce what is seen is therefore simply an uninterrupted and adequate seeing; these two phenomena, separable logically and divided in Cartesian psychology by an artificial chasm, are inseparable in existence and are, for natural history, two parts of the same event. . . . In some such fashion we may come to conceive how imitative art is simply the perfection and fulfillment of sensation. The act of apperception in which a sensation is reflected upon and understood is already an internal reproduction. . . . Imitation cannot, of course, result in a literal repetition of the object that suggests it. The copy is secondary; it does not iterate the model by creating a second object on the same plane of reality, but reproduces the form in a new medium and gives it a different function. In these latter circumstances lies the imitative essence of the second image: for one leaf does not imitate another nor is each twin the other's copy. Like sensibility, imitation remodels a given being so that it becomes, in certain formal respects, like another being in its environment.[190]

To imitate mankind is merely to be assimilated to the million and improve nothing; but, if men are imitated under proper inhibitions and in the service of one's own ends, a double result is achieved— men are really understood and one's own being is preserved and enlarged and made ideally relevant to what it physically depends on. Assimilation is a way of drifting through the flux; representation, on the contrary, is a principle of progress.[191]

This logistic meaning of imitation is developed in many forms in contemporary theory. It underlies the use of *Einfühlung*, or empathy, in the analysis of art as well as the application of Freudian conceptions to aesthetic phenomena. Santayana has acknowledged his enthusiasm for the step Freud took in *Beyond the Pleasure Principle:* for Freud, as for Santayana, the dream becomes characteristic of the activities of conscious behavior, but, where Santayana traces imagination to its fulfilment in play, Freud analyzes the libido against a prior principle of Inertia or the tendency toward peace and death, by which the goal of all life becomes death.[192] The application of psychoanalytical principles to art does not consist simply in placing the work of art in the context of the psychological forces operative in the author and in those who appreciate his work; it consists rather in the exploration of forces that determine artist and audience as well as art. Thomas Mann saw Freud's significance for the future in the clarity which he brought to this interplay of life and art, by which life itself becomes imitation and myth.

But it is just this life as reanimation that is the life as myth. Alexander walked in the footsteps of Miltiades; the ancient biographers of Caesar were convinced, rightly or wrongly, that he took Alexander as his prototype. But such "imitation" meant far more than we mean by the word today. . . . Life, then—at any rate, significant life—was in ancient times the reconstitution of the myth in flesh and blood; it referred to and appealed to the myth; only through it, through reference to the past, could it approve itself as genuine and significant. The myth is the legitimization of life; only through and in it does life find self-awareness, sanction, consecration. . . . The artist in particular, a passionately childlike and play-possessed being, can tell us of the mysterious yet after all obvious effect of such infantile imitation upon his own life, his productive conduct of a career which after all is often nothing but a reanimation of the hero under very different temporal and personal conditions and with very different, shall we say childish means. The *imitatio* Goethe, with its Werther and Wilhelm Meister stages, its old-age period of *Faust* and *Divan*, can still shape and mythically mould the life of an artist—rising out of his unconscious, yet playing over—as is the artist way—into a smiling, childlike, and profound awareness.[193]

Imitation and Poetry

Expression is an imitation by which significance is acquired, and all psychic functions are basically imagination which in its free play constructs a world in which art supplies at once a rich realization of values and a key to the interpretation of significances and life.

V

The variety of meanings in which the term "imitation" has been used provides only a key or a schematism to the development of the problems of imitation in poetry. Acquaintance with the differences of meanings of the term is essential if either the discussion or the problems approached in the discussion are to be understood. The study of the meanings assumed by the term provides two important instruments for the study of criticism and of poetry: in the first place, the meanings assumed by "imitation" and by the related terms that are taken as basic in literary criticism and history are so interrelated that common problems recur in many forms of statement and in many approaches, and the range of problems treated, consequently, assumes some order and reason and ceases to seem to encompass an infinite diversity to be simplified only by assuming that a vast number of errors have been committed; in the second place, the different meanings of "imitation" are seen to focus attention on different aspects of poetry, and differences that seemed to result from irreconcilable clashes of doctrine are seen to be treatments of interrelated problems approached on assumptions which, in turn, make different, though commonly recognized aspects of poetry essential and central to its influence and nature.

The four aspects of poetry that have determined the broad meanings of "imitation," "imagination," and "expression," are (1) poetry considered as a mirror or embodiment of "values"; (2) poetry considered as an object constituted by the productive, imaginative, or linguistic art of the poet; (3) poetry considered as a means by which a state of mind or emotion is conveyed from poet to audience; and (4) poetry considered as a state of mind or emotional attitude and reaction. These different aspects of poetry in turn become central in theory and criticism. Any one of the four can be made the basis for the discussion of the remaining three, and the continuity of the discussion is secured by the fact that all four aspects must be treated in some form under each hypothesis. Consequently, it seems plausible at each turn of the discussion, since the discussion has become clear in each theory and since the nature of poetry marked off in all theories enters consideration in each, that philosophers and critics might come to agreement concerning whether poetry is an inspired expression of values which cannot be differentiated into kinds and which are not otherwise expressible; or an expressive object, unified, possessed of characteristic effects, and made by the art of the poet; or the expression of thoughts, either inspired thoughts in appropriate expression, or what has often been thought but never so well expressed, or common emotions in common or an unusual language; or, finally, the objectification of pleasure and the triumph of the pleasure principle. The outcome, however, is never the decision of this question about the nature of poetry, but instead there are erected irreducible oppositions of theories which are each made the basis for scholarly and painstaking explanations of apparent or real errors of earlier or contemporary critics. The development of these oppositions loses the advantages of both the diversity of aspects made prominent in the different theories and the continuity of discussion in which the same problems are treated under each of these aspects. The only means of continuing the discussion fruitfully seems to be to abandon, then, the set of terms basic to the oppositions and to discover a set which makes difficult or impossible some of the obvious errors that have been detected and anathematized. This is the force that leads to the sequence of theories based in turn on "imitation," "imagination," and "expression."

The return of "imitation" to basic importance in the discussion of poetry during the last fifteen or twenty years is an important sign both of the problems of contemporary aesthetics and criticism and of the availability of new devices for the treatment of recurrent and persistent dilemmas and oppositions. Croce's somewhat grudging defense of a proper meaning of imitation, Dewey's incisive analysis of its significance and of its limitations in the context of an analysis of expression, Santayana's wholehearted employment of the concept as central to reason in art, were earlier preparations for the recognition of problems which have led to the more recent insights into the implications and applications of imitation. The nature of these problems can be set forth briefly and clearly by tracing the history of their evolution in philosophy and criticism, and the history of criticism can be set forth briefly and clearly once the differences of meanings in which the words have been used have been explored in "historical semantics," which is an important preliminary to any form of disciplinary history—the history of philosophy, or art, or science, or criticism.

The Renaissance is a good starting point for the examination of the history of the use of "imitation" in modern discussions of poetry. It is a good starting point, not because medieval philosophers neglected the problems of aesthetics[194] or because devices of rhetoric, exegesis, hermeneutics, poetics, and the "fourfold" interpretation of literary texts have been without continuing influence and consequences, but rather because the attitude and atmosphere of literary criticism during the Renaissance have striking similarities to those recently prevalent. Literary criticism was strongly influenced during the Renaissance by the Platonic tradition, with its conception of the imitation of the ideal, and by the rhetorical tradition, with its conception of the imitation of the artist and of his writings, as developed by Cicero, Horace, Quintilian, and Longinus. Aristotle's *Poetics* also provided a technical vocabulary, a statement of problems, and an array of literary data.

The *Poetics* had been translated in the thirteenth century,[195] but it apparently had little influence in medieval philosophical or critical theory.[196] During the sixteenth century the *Poetics* was published in Greek as well as in Latin and vernacular translation and became the subject of lengthy commentary and criticism. Yet "imitation" was employed primarily in its Platonic or Horatian meanings, as imitation of the ideal or as imitation of literary models. These meanings were easily adjusted to the Aristotelian text, for Aristotle said that poetry is more philosophic and more serious than history, since it treats of the universal, and that tragedy imitates good men or men better than average; and these two tendencies of poetry, to the universal and to the better, to τὸ καθόλου and to τὸ βέλτιον, are taken to signify that the imitation of poetry is an idealization, while Horace was read as the handbook for which the *Poetics* might furnish the theory in which the imitation of models in order to please and instruct might serve as the practical elaboration of the proper pleasures of poetry. Renaissance critics combined these theories in varying proportions. Tasso, Robertelli, and Fracastoro stress the ideal element in imitation. Minturno treats imitation primarily in relation to the end of poetry to instruct and please, but in order to achieve that end poetry imitates the ideal. Julius Caesar Scaliger denies that imitation is the end of poetry—pleasure is the end—but there is imitation in all speech, since words are the images of things, and there are two means by which a poet may become perfect, imitation and judgment. The model should be selected carefully, and for Scaliger the model is Virgil. Finally, Castelvetro defines poetry as imitation and the imitation of action, but he differentiates between the imitation which is natural to all men and the imitation necessary to poetry, on the ground that poetry does not follow the example given by others or make the same thing that has already been made, but it makes something original and entirely different. Elements of all four conceptions of imitation enter into the discussion—the imitation of the ideal, of the literary model, of the actions of men, and verbal imitation productive of pleasure—but it is primarily the first two that set the interpretation of poetry. Aristotle's discussion of the unity of the plot undergoes a Horatian transformation into the rules of the three unities, and the Democritean conception of imitation by appearances or words accompanied by pleasure is transformed into a discussion of whether pleasure alone or pleasure and utility are the ends of poetry. This Platonic and Horatian interpretation of Aristotle was to persist for a long time,[197] but its characteristic form in the Renaissance is found in the relation philosophy itself assumed to art and to action. By the standards of philosophy in the seventeenth century, there was little philosophy during the

Renaissance, but it is more accurate to say that philosophy was not distinct from art and from action, that philosophy was stated in poetic form and poetry expressed philosophic truths, and that novelty was achieved by imitating models of antiquity in art, action, and thought, which were also instances and specifications of the ideal.[198]

For all the importance that "imitation" assumes in the philosophy and criticism of the Renaissance, the basic terms by which the uses of imitation are judged and regulated are found in "expression" and "action"—in what was said and done—to achieve the ends indicated by imitation and in the selection of ideals particularized in examples, models, and touchstones. The Renaissance man imitated antiquity to establish new art forms and new social structures, and his philosophy was an imitation intended to exhibit and employ instruments by which to facilitate achieving that end. Philosophers in the seventeenth century returned to speculation after the manner of the sciences, on the nature of things, including the nature of God and human nature and understanding. Philosophy is no longer identified with art, or criticism, or aesthetics (although the analogy of art is often applied to nature and used to provide principles of explanation or inquiry), but, instead, the determination of the principles of art is part of the task of philosophy. Consequently, although it is possible to find indications in each of the major philosophers of the period of how the problems of aesthetics would be treated according to his principles, none of them devotes much space in his major works to the analysis of art. The very considerable body of criticism and speculation on problems of aesthetics is found for the most part in the works of men who are concerned primarily with literature, art, or rhetoric and who apply the principles of the philosophers. Boileau's *Art poétique* has been compared to Descartes's *Discours de la méthode:* for Boileau, as for Descartes, *bon sens* is fundamental, and all precepts reduce to imitation of poets who have achieved clarity.[199] Joseph Addison employed principles he had learned from Locke to treat art and imagination logistically in his eleven papers on the "Pleasures of the Imagination."[200] Primary and secondary pleasures of the imagination are distinguished.

Primary pleasures of the imagination arise from actually seeing something, and sight is the most perfect and delightful of our senses. There are three sources of all the pleasures of the imagination in our survey of outward objects: the great (the sublime pleases us because it marks the end of our uneasiness at any restraint on our freedom), the new (the new or uncommon pleases us ultimately because it gratifies our curiosity), and the beautiful, first in our own species, and then in general (the sense of beauty is not a direct intuition of a lovely appearance but the sense of kind). The secondary pleasures of the imagination are from statuary, painting, description, and music. Our enjoyment is based on the comparison of ideas. We enjoy an example of art because of the resemblance it bears in our opinion to nature, and we enjoy nature for its resemblance to art. Portraits and statues are enjoyed as mimicry, even when the original is disagreeable or common or small, because of the comparison the mind makes. Edmund Burke, from like logistic beginnings, finds in imitation one of the sources of pleasure in the imagination, and imitation itself is one of the "passions of society."[201] Hobbes does not develop a special philosophy of art or aesthetics as part of the construction of the system of his philosophy, but the uses to which he puts the concept "imitation" in his *Answer to the Preface to Gondibert* establishes the kinds of poetry on differences of objects and manners of imitation. Sir Joshua Reynolds, finally, develops the series of meanings implicit in the basic dialectical distinction between the discovery of an ideal beauty and the imitation of artists which, when properly employed, prepares for it, although mere copying, whether of nature or of artists, is to be deprecated.[202] The imitation of models is a useful means of forming the taste, of discovering the central forms or types in nature, and of suggesting particular details which may be transplanted in your own work; but in its application to nature Reynolds uses "imitation" only in the sense of copying or reproducing nature, as distinguished from expressing or embodying Ideal beauty. There are therefore nonimitative arts (like music and architecture) as well as imitative arts, and even in painting and sculpture there are higher as well as lower species, and only the lower are, strictly speaking, imitative.

During the seventeenth century and the first half of the eighteenth, when philosophers for the most part sought the principles of their philosophy in the nature of things and critics and philosophers of art applied philosophic principles (after a time lag of about half a century) in the analysis of the arts, "imitation" was a basic term employed to distinguish art from nature and to mark the relations between the two. "Imitation" is a basic term precisely because it marks an ultimate difference among things, and to seek to explain it would be to seek principles that underlie or justify metaphysical princip es. The relations set up between art and philosophy are a mark and sign of this phase of philosophic discussion, whether art and philosophy be thought to be the same or distinct: in the seventeenth and eighteenth centuries "imitation" was a philosophic principle used to identify and analyze art, conceived as objects and actions of a particular kind, whereas in the Renaissance "imitation" was a means of acquiring a particular kind of expression or action, and philosophy itself was an art acquired by imitation. A corollary of this difference is the use to which the principle was put in the two periods. The recurrent problem in the seventeenth and eighteenth centuries was whether or not imitation is the principle of all the arts or only of some, and consequently whether imitation in poetry is different from imitation in sculpture or music. These are questions that have their occasion and inspiration in earlier statements and authorities, such as the comparison of painting and poetry by Simonides and Horace which had become a commonplace, or the distinction between poetry and history made by Aristotle, or the analogies between musical modes and moral characters stressed by Plato. But whereas writers in the Renaissance quoted these observations to make recommendations concerning imitations that tended to employ analogies among the arts, sciences, and practical techniques and that came to specificity in their applications, writers of the seventeenth and eighteenth centuries used the analogies and differences in the course of classifying the arts as modes of imitation or as variously imitative or nonimitative.

When the Abbé Charles Batteux sought the principle of all the arts in his *Beaux arts réduits à un même principe* in 1746, he found that principle in imitation. A genius, however, requires a support to raise and sustain him, and that support is Nature. "He cannot create it; he ought not destroy it; he can therefore only follow and imitate it, and consequently all that he produces can only be imitation."[203] To imitate is to copy a model, and the term "imitation," therefore, contains two ideas: the original or prototype which possesses the traits that are to be imitated and the copy which represents them. Nature is the prototype, but nature can be differentiated into four worlds: the existent world, the historical world, the fabulous world, and the ideal or possible world. From these beginnings Batteux enters into an encyclopedic and illuminating analysis of all the arts, including those which some of his contemporaries treated, following other conceptions of the principle of imitation, as nonimitative. The second of the *Three Treatises* of James Harris, published in 1744, was "A Discourse on Music, Painting, and Poetry." In it the three arts are distinguished primarily by their appropriate objects of imitation, the peculiarity of "poetic imitation" being that it "includes everything in it, which is performed either by Picture-Imitation or Musical; for its materials are words, and words are symbols by compact of all Ideas."[204] Music, moreover, may be considered, not as an imitation, but as deriving its efficacy from another source, the affections. Many writers had looked into the question of the relations of the arts when Lessing made his magisterial analysis of the relation of poetry to painting and sculpture, or the plastic arts, in the *Laokoon*, published in 1766. They included Dryden (*Parallel of Poetry and Painting*, published in 1695 as a preface to Du Fresnoy's Latin poem *De arte graphica*), Joseph Spence (*Polymetis, or an Inquiry concerning the Agreement between the Works of the Roman Poets and the Remains of the Ancient Artists, Being an Attempt To Illustrate Mutually from One Another*, published in 1747), Count

Imitation and Poetry

Caylus (Spence and Caylus are subjects of criticism by Lessing), the Abbé du Bos (*Réflexions critiques sur la poésie et la peinture*, published in 1719), Daniel Webb (*An Enquiry into the Beauty of Painting*, 1760, and *Observations on the Correspondences between Painting and Music*, 1760), Winckelmann (*Imitation of the Ancients in Painting and Statuary*, 1755), and Adam Smith ("Of the Nature of That Imitation Which Takes Place in What Are Called the Imitative Arts," published posthumously in *Essays on Philosophical Subjects*). According to Lessing, both poetry and the plastic arts are imitations, and he assumes that artists imitate other artists as well as nature. His profound and incisive analysis of the arts is to the end of differentiating them by their objects as well as their manner of imitation. Jean Jacques Rousseau, in preparation for his *Letter to M. d'Alembert on Spectacles*, in which he argues against D'Alembert's proposal that a theater for comedy be established in Geneva, composed his essay "On Theatrical Imitation" drawn from the dialogues of Plato.[205] Lord Kames, employing a similar conception of imitation to discover principles of criticism in human nature in his *Elements of Criticism*, published in 1762, was led instead to the conclusion that men naturally imitate virtuous actions,[206] but not those that are vicious, and that none of the arts imitates nature except painting and sculpture.[207] Edward Young, in his *Conjectures on Original Composition*, written in 1759, distinguishes between two kinds of imitation, one of nature, the other of authors; and, since we call the first "originals," we confine the term "imitation" to the second.[208] The ancients should be imitated but imitated aright: the man and not the composition should be imitated.[209] When Thomas Twining published his translation of Aristotle's *Poetics* in 1789, he prefaced it with two dissertations on poetical and on musical imitation. He distinguished four senses of imitation: by sound, by description, by fiction, and by personation.[210] Twining argues that Aristotle applies imitation to poetry in the sense of fiction and that he considered dramatic poetry peculiarly imitation, but he did not consider poetry as imitation in the other two senses, employed by modern writers, that is, as resemblance of sound and description.

Twining thinks it questionable whether poetry would have been placed in the class of imitative arts, if the drama had never been invented,[211] and music is imitative in so far as it has an effect on the passions and the imagination.[212]

The transition from philosophic examinations of the nature of things, including human nature and human understanding, to examinations of the forms of thought and the faculties of the mind, including those which treat of the nature of things, was sharply enough marked to constitute a revolutionary reorientation in the philosophy of Kant. For other philosophers, who preceded or followed him, it was a gradual and barely discernible shift of emphasis in the progressive development of a continuing philosophical analysis. For dialecticians, who were convinced before Hegel that the real is rational and the rational real, it made little fundamental difference whether the basic terms of the analysis were derived from things or from thoughts, while for operationalists, who looked for the definition of thought in their consequences, the separation of thought from its object was meaningless and a source of error. Philosophers who, like Hume, use a logistic method to derive ideas from impressions which they copy and to compound them in relations with other ideas, must suppose that there is some unexplorable relation between the course of nature and the succession of our ideas,[213] while philosophers who, like Kant, use a critical and problematic method to seek universality in the forms of thought must suppose a sharp difference between the phenomena for which our theoretic knowledge is true and the noumena among which we are guided in action by practical reason, with the result that practical action, by virtue of its contact with reality, assumes priority over theoretical science. Where philosophers of the seventeenth and early eighteenth centuries found a basic problem in the relation of mind, matter, and God, but were able to treat the relation of knowledge to its object without undue subtlety once the principles of these existences had been established, the philosophers of the nineteenth century faced fundamental problems concerning the relation of knowledge and its objects before they went on to treat of mind, matter, and God. The altered relation between philosophy and art is the least ambiguous sign of this change, and the treatment of the concept of "imitation" is one means by which to examine that altered relation. Philosophy no longer provides the principles which critics apply in the examination of the products of the arts; rather art and philosophy are both characterized by the faculties of the mind by which they are produced, perceived, and judged. Philosophy and art are themselves subjects of comparison, distinction, and competition, and philosophers find beauty and art, taste and genius, intruding into the center of their speculations rather than falling into place as side issues to be taken care of according to the principles they have set forth.

Art and criticism underwent changes which reflect these changes in the relation of art to philosophy. Relative to dialectical philosophy, with its two levels corresponding to Plato's two kinds of imitation, poetry sometimes assumes the position of the highest expression of reality to which philosophy at best approximates, but it also underwent a variety of inversions. In one, hidden and dark passions, dreams and fantasy might take precedence over rational or abstract thought—this is the Romantic inversion which had had its earlier expression in Manichaeism, Gnosticism, and the medieval romances. In another, since the dialectic of systematic thought is the same as the dialectic of historical development, matter may take the place of spirit, and the history of the science of society may take the place of the development of spirit, with the result that poetry becomes an ideology and an instrument in the class struggle rather than an expression of the Ideal—this is the inversion of dialectical materialism. In a third, the aesthetic is a stage which may prepare for or be guided by the fuller and more perfect expression of moral or religious stages—this is the moral and religious inversion which received varied expression in Kierkegaard and Tolstoi. Relative to an operational method, with its distinction of words and deeds, expression and content, and with its method of examining the works of the great which was refurbished in Matthew Arnold's use of touchstones, criticism can set forth the adventures of the soul among masterpieces, but the focus tends to fall on images or forms or symbols. The problematic method, directed to the investigation of the particular nature of the work of art, tended to philological and historical criticism and in general to the study of art in the context of society, while logistic criticism studied art in the reaction of the observer. Criticism turned to studies of the creative act, to adventures of appreciation, to cultural history and social analysis, and to the investigation of play, empathy, and dreams.

The concept of imitation appears in these transformations in two different ways. When the basic terms of analysis are taken from the processes and the faculties of the mind, "imitation" may either retain the rich diversity of meaning which was required when it served as a basic term relating objects made by artists to natural objects, or it may be simplified to a series of simple literal senses: some dialecticians of the nineteenth century call the creative process "imitation," some contrast it to "imitation"; some operational critics call the creative use of literary models "imitation," some contrast it to imitative processes bordering on plagiarism; some problematic philosophers call the construction of fiction or of poetic form "imitation," some restrict imitation to photographic reproduction; and the pleasure caused by an art object may be imitation or simple emotion. Imitative art in this simple literal sense is the antithesis of true art on a variety of grounds—because it is a lie, or a copy, or academic and traditional, or designed simply for amusement or to satisfy a degraded or decadent taste. Yet "imitation" also appears in these discussions in a second way in which it exercises its traditional function of relating what man does and makes to things as they exist and as they function apart from man. If the principles of knowledge, art, and social action are found in sensation, imagination, passions, will, and understanding, the results or products of these faculties or powers must be related to appropriate objects. Those relations were established by the formulation of new theories of "imitation." The relation may be directly between the thought and its object, as in the theory of "models" long employed to account for the relation between physical theory and the

[184]

aspects of phenomena to which they are applied.[214] The relation
may be in the institutions established among men in society or in the
processes of social action, and "laws of imitation" were sought as
the foundation of social groups[215] and as the basis of psychical distinctions of inner from outer.[216] The relation may finally be between
the observer and the object perceived as in the theory of *Einfühlung*,
or empathy. Yrjö Hirn summarizes the converging influence of the
theory of "imitation" on art toward the end of the nineteenth
century.

Contemporary science has at last learned to appreciate the fundamental
importance of imitation for the development of human culture [Hirn refers
particularly to the works of Tarde, Schmidkunz, and Baldwin]. And some
authors have even gone so far as to endeavour to deduce all sociological
laws from this one principle. At the same time natural history has begun to
pay more and more attention to the indispensability of imitation for the
full development of instincts, as well as for training in those activities
which are the most necessary in life.

It is fortunate for the theory of art that the importance of the imitative
functions has thus been simultaneously acknowledged in various depart-
ments of science. Whatever one may think of the somewhat audacious
generalisations which have been made in the recent application of this new
principle, it is incontestable that the aesthetic activities can be understood
and explained only by reference to universal tendency to imitate. It is
also significant that writers on aesthetic had felt themselves compelled to
set up a theory of imitation long before experimental psychologists had
begun to turn their attention in this direction. In Germany the enjoyment
of form and form-relations has since Vischer's time been interpreted as the
result of the movements by which not only our eye, but also our whole
body, follows the outlines of external things. In France Jouffroy stated the
condition for the receiving of aesthetic impressions to be a "power of
internally imitating the states which are externally manifested in living
nature." In England, finally, Vernon Lee and Anstruther Thompson have
founded a theory of beauty and ugliness upon this same psychical impulse
to copy in our own unconscious movements the forms of objects. And in
the writings of, for instance, Home, Hogarth, Dugald Stewart, and
Spencer, there can be found a multitude of isolated remarks on the influence
which is in a direct way exercised on our mental life by the perception of
lines and forms.[217]

"Imitation" is designed to serve the same function in this second group of meanings—in models of physical things, in laws of social relations, and in empathy of aesthetic forms—as in the first, but they are adapted to serve that function differently, for the "imitation" of the ideal, or of nature, or of artists, or of objects of perception depended on a relation between things, natural and artificial, and indicated a relation between psychological states and their objects, whereas "imitation" as models, repetitions, and empathy are efforts to explain psychological states that have or should contain their relations as operations similar to, expressions of, or reactions to, objects.

The reorientation of philosophy to principles derived from expression and communication, operation and action, instead of to principles derived from reason and understanding, will and the passions, was successful in removing both the dichotomy of knowledge and its object as well as the numerous families of dichotomies that cluster about these parents. The accomplishments of twentieth-century philosophy are usually stated in these terms: we have corrected the bifurcation of nature and we have abandoned the spectator theory of truth. To act and to express require both body and mind (whereas bodies moved and minds thought in the seventeenth century), and the tests for our knowledge are consensus and consequences, which make unnecessary the separation of knowledge and subject matter (whereas in the nineteenth century principles depended on the forms of thought or on the regularities of nature). We are only beginning to recognize that we have succeeded in avoiding these separations by accepting an equally troublesome distinction: if we are in direct contact only with what we do and say and make, with language and with operations, we come ultimately to the problem of the relation of what we say or make—artifacts, institutions, sciences—to what we do not say or make. This is the problem of the relation of art to nature. It is difficult to find characteristics by which to mark off the differences between the philosophy of the recent past and the philosophy of the nineteenth cen-

tury in spite of our sense of almost total difference—many of the
old problems are still discussed; many of the principles and terms
of the earlier discussion are still employed; and the names of nineteenth-century heroes are often invoked: Hegel, Mill, Marx,
Kierkegaard—but the difference in the relation of philosophy to
art is sharply marked, and the uses of "imitation" once again furnish a terminology in which it can be stated unambiguously. Philosophy no longer examines "things," and therefore it does not
uncover the principles by which art may be discussed as an object
and an objective function; philosophy no longer finds its subject
matter in the forms and processes of thought, and therefore it does
not enter into competition with art in related or identical psychological faculties; philosophy is a communication and an operation,
and, therefore, philosophy is itself an art.

Philosophy had the same relation to art in the Renaissance, but
the way in which philosophy is thought to be an art today is different in important respects from the Renaissance fashion. The
Renaissance philosopher thought of the fine arts, and, when his
speculations moved from poetry or painting to liberal arts, his attention centered on rhetoric, which could provide techniques for
either a theory of literature or a statesman's handbook. The modern
philosopher thinks of industrial arts or technology, and he concentrates, when he turns to the liberal arts, on logic, which may provide rules for constructing artificial languages from symbols or
theories of inquiry for the resolution of problems. The Renaissance
philosopher could therefore write poems with epic structures on
Infinity and Immensity, or histories in which past accomplishments
suggested precepts, or dialogues which mingled Pastoral, Courtly,
and Platonic elements. Modern deductive logical systems need no
translation into poetry, and modern speculations on the nature of
philosophy place it in a context in experience and civilization, and in
at least some of the forms of the modern art of philosophy, as in the
existentialist self-creation, formal philosophic analysis may have
alternative statement in drama, novel, and short story.

Bertrand Russell, in one of the phases of his formulation of this conception of philosophy, presented the discovery that logic is the essence of philosophy, if not as a Copernican, at least as a Galilean, revolution.

Modern logic, as I hope is now evident, has the effect of enlarging our abstract imagination, and providing an infinite number of possible hypotheses to be applied in the analysis of any complex fact. In this respect it is the exact opposite of the logic practised by the classical tradition. In that logic, hypotheses which seem *primâ facie* possible are professedly proved impossible, and it is decreed in advance that reality must have a certain special character. In modern logic, on the contrary, while the *primâ facie* hypotheses as a rule remain admissible, others, which only logic would have suggested, are added to our stock, and are very often found to be indispensable if a right analysis of the facts is to be obtained. The old logic put thought in fetters, while the new logic gives it wings. It has, in my opinion, introduced the same kind of advance into philosophy as Galileo introduced into physics, making it possible at last to see what kinds of problems may be capable of solution, and what kinds must be abandoned as beyond human powers. And where a solution appears possible, the new logic provides a method which enables us to obtain results that do not merely embody personal idiosyncrasies, but must command the assent of all who are competent to form an opinion.[218]

The interpretation of scientific theories or models, according to P. W. Bridgman, is an art similar to the art of constructing or inventing them.

The way in which conclusions about the properties of the mathematical model are to be translated into conclusions about the corresponding physical system is not capable of specification with logical precision, as we have already seen must always be the case when we apply probability theory to any concrete physical situation. We are really concerned more with an art than a science, an art which is to be learned only by observation of the way the inventers of the theory do it. The art is not difficult to learn, and the lack of logical precision is not disturbing in practice, because the expectation that observable results will ever arise from this lack of precision is of the same small order of magnitude as our expectation that we may some day see a pail of water freeze on the fire. What we have here is a special sort of intellectual tool, of great utility in meeting the situations of practice.[219]

Dewey views philosophy as an intellectual instrument or art by which a culture reconstructs itself in whole or in part.

Knowledge is still regarded by most thinkers as direct grasp of ultimate reality, although the practice of knowing has been assimilated to the procedure of the useful arts;—involving, that is to say, doing that manipulates and arranges natural energies. Again while science is said to lay hold of reality, yet "art" instead of being assigned a lower rank is equally esteemed and honored. And when within art a distinction is drawn between production and appreciation, the chief honor usually goes to the former on the ground that it is "creative," while taste is relatively possessive and passive, dependent for its material upon the activities of the creative artist. . . . But if modern tendencies are justified in putting art and creation first, then the implications of this position should be avowed and carried through. It would then be seen that science is an art, that art is practice, and that the only distinction worth drawing is not between practice and theory, but between those modes of practice that are not intelligent, not inherently and immediately enjoyable, and those which are full of enjoyed meanings. When this perception dawns, it will be a commonplace that art—the mode of activity that is charged with meanings capable of immediately enjoyed possession—is the complete culmination of nature, and that "science" is properly a handmaiden that conducts natural events to this happy issue. Thus would disappear the separations that trouble present thinking: division of everything into nature *and* experience, of experience into practice *and* theory, art *and* science, of art into useful *and* fine, menial *and* free. . . . Thought, intelligence, science is the intentional direction of natural events to meanings capable of immediate possession and enjoyment; this direction—which is operative art—is itself a natural event in which nature otherwise partial and incomplete comes fully to itself; so that objects of conscious experience when reflectively chosen, form the "end" of nature.[220]

Jean-Paul Sartre argues that existentialism is a humanism in which man *is* freedom and *invents* man, since existence precedes essence in the case of man unlike the case of a manufactured object—Sartre uses the example of a book or a paper-cutter—in which production precedes existence.

Atheistic existentialism, which I represent, is more coherent [*sc.* than the philosophies of the seventeenth and eighteenth centuries in which the essence man precedes the historical existence that we encounter in nature].

It declares that if God does not exist, there is at least a being in whom existence precedes essence, a being who can exist before being able to be defined by any concept, and that that being is man or, as Heidegger says, the human reality. What does it signify in this case that existence precedes essence? It signifies that man exists first, encounters himself, arises in the world, and that he defines himself later. If man is not definable as the existentialist conceives him, it is because he is nothing to begin with. He will be only afterwards, and he will be such as he will make himself. Thus there is no human nature, since there is no God to conceive it. Man only is, not only as he conceives himself, but such as he wishes himself, and since he conceives himself after existence, since he wishes himself after this burst to existence, man is nothing other than that which he makes himself. This is the first principle of existentialism. . . . But if existence truly precedes essence, man is responsible for that which he is. Thus the first step of existentialism is to place every man in possession of that which he is and to make the total responsibility of his existence rest on him. And when we say that man is responsible for himself, we do not mean that man is responsible for his strict individuality, but that he is responsible for all men.[221]

Philosophy is an art of forming hypotheses, or of interpreting theories, or of communicating, making, and possessing values, or of producing man himself and his significant world—and, in all these forms, philosophy is an existing activity or fact marching among and affecting the existence, significance, or value of other activities or facts.

Since philosophy is an art, it is difficult to raise questions concerning the nature of art, for it would be naïve and a sin against the logic of the art of philosophy to convert this proposition and suppose that art is therefore philosophy. If the art of philosophy is logic, all other arts—including poetry and literature—tend to become noncognitive; if the art of philosophy is an operation, all other arts have like operational definitions; if the art of philosophy is inquiry, art is not itself a process of problem-solving but a quality possessed by experience in the happy resolution of problems; if the art of philosophy is self-creation and self-definition, art has an "engagement," a commitment determined by the cultural ensemble in which it occurs. There is no easy way to relate these—and a vast

number of other basic hypotheses about the nature of art and poetry—directly to one another, yet they all follow as consequences
from the various ways in which art can be thought to be fundamentally and essentially "expression" and "communication," "operation" and "making."

One of the most definite and characteristic marks of modern
thought is found in the various elaborations of the basic conceptions
of "expression" and "operation," for they develop inversions—
based on the dichotomies of nineteenth-century idealisms and realisms, postivitisms and utilitarianisms—of the basic principles of
seventeenth-century philosophers. Philosophers of the seventeenth
century speculated on dreams, play, and games, but they supposed,
since man is a nature operating among other natures, that, in spite of
the fact that we may dream that we are awake when sleeping, we
can distinguish between dreaming and waking when we are awake,
that fantasy is a free association of ideas which is a poor guide and
an unreliable witness unless checked against the realities encountered in sensation or thought, that play is a relaxation from the business of life, and that games are governed by arbitrary rules that at
best imitate the conditions to which science and art must be adjusted. In modern speculation these relations have been inverted: we
discover the nature of waking by analyzing its hidden springs in
dreams; fantasy is the source not only of science and art but of
reality; life is fundamentally play, and we construct theories of
games to solve its problems. In the seventeenth century the nature
of man was often conceived to be a *conatus*, a continuing force or
action, impeded by the actions of external objects which cause passions; the ultimate resistance or weakening of that *conatus* was annihilation, at least of that part of man that is mortal, and death;
men sought principles and values in things, and, when values were
discovered, they had generality or universality, which men could
recognize because of "common notions," and which worked or
pleased because of a conformity or harmony in the nature of things
and the nature and habits of men. In modern speculation the reality
principle is inertia or death, and the pleasure principle is the result

of the impingement of external objects; "nothing" is the beginning, not the end, and one of the important metaphysical problems turns on whether existence emerges from the nothing as a result of the "Deed" or the "Word"; we do not agree because a proposition is true, but truth is recognized from the consensus of those competent to judge a proposition, and what pleases us is a psychological or a a cultural symptom, which may be taken as fact or as indication of a need for therapy or social action.

VI

At this level of generality, since it is a question of first principles—and in the present temper of philosophic thought, since we take our principles where we find them and as they are communicable—to ask whether the seventeenth-century or the twentieth-century philosophers are right about principles would be to raise a question of no significance. Even if there were some sense in which our principles could be shown to be less adequate than those sought when men speculated about things (and it is difficult even to imagine by what methods and on what principles the proof would proceed), the inversion has had profound effects in stimulating insight and inquiry and has led to bodies of knowledge of which there was little suspicion three hundred years ago. What is important is that a change of direction has been forced on speculation concerning literature and poetry during the last fifteen or twenty years within the context of contemporary principles, which can be traced to a growing recognition of problems that had previously been ignored. They are problems that focus on the nature of art and poetry, and their consideration gives promise of reducing the confusion and vast unordered proliferation of aesthetic and critical theories and, in doing so, of throwing light on the nature and problems of philosophy. Art as an expression creates and communicates *values:* those values have relations to other values, yet we have only the beginnings of theories by which to treat the homogeneities, the clashes, and the identities of values in their varieties of manifestation and expression. Art as an expression is a form given to a *content:* we have tended to concentrate on form and to find it primarily in the form of expression, dynamic, ambiguous, paradoxical, synecdochal, and we have only the beginnings of methods by which to treat content other than as a joining of the same and the different, the old and the new. Art as an expression is the objectification of *pleasure:* pleasure depends on taste, yet we have only a vague discomfort with the consequences of the generalization that art is what in fact pleases. Art as expression has an organic *unity* of its own, but we have made a mystery of what the art object is—the expression of an intuition, the expressive object, the objectification of pleasure, the process of communication. These are problems that affect the writing of poetry and the creation of art as well as appreciation and criticism They are exemplified in the cult of unintelligibility, the burying of recognizable meanings and sentiments in verbal structures and in the stream of consciousness, the searching for surrealistic values above cognitive recognition or for passionate or decadent values deep in hidden impulses, as well as for moral, religious, political, or social values; they are exemplified in the development of mass arts adapted to larger literate audiences and to new means of mass communication and in the leveling-out of what is published in books, produced in motion pictures, broadcast on radio and television; they are encountered in cultural regionalisms and the circumscribing of art in a culture; and they lead in the contacts of cultures to the effete cult of the exotic or the suspicion of treasonable cosmopolitanism.

These problems of the nature of art in orientation to and in distinction from other things are problems of "imitation" which reappear in new forms and sometimes under new names in theories of imagination and expression. The emergence of these problems concerning the nature of art has recently been accompanied by a renewed interest in themes of imitation in which they have been treated. W. J. Verdenius has raised the question of imitation in terms of the relation of art to the ideal.[222] Jean-Paul Sartre treats the aesthetic object as unreal. The painting or the poem is an "analogon" by which the artist constitutes an unreal object. Aesthetic enjoyment is only a manner of apprehending that unreal object, and, far from being directed to a real object, it serves to constitute the imaginary object by means of the real canvas.[223] Mikel Dufrenne distinguishes three aspects in the aesthetic object: the sensible, the object represented, and the world expressed. A work of art is characterized not only by its sensible qualities, which it owes to its matter, and its structure as a work of art, which constitutes its expression, but also by its subject, which it represents. Dufrenne elaborates, in explaining what is meant by representation, qualifications which recall the distinctions Aristotle makes in the aesthetic applications of his doctrine of imitation:

> The object represented is not necessarily a real object which would serve as a model for the creative enterprise: it can obviously be borrowed just as well from the universe of the fantastic, of the legendary, or be invented completely in all parts. And the representation is not necessarily an exact copy, reproduction, or statement of that object. If we wish to give representation its full extension, we shall say that there is a representation every time the aesthetic object invites us to leave the immediacy of the sensible, and proposes to us a sense with respect to which the sensible is only a means and fundamentally indifferent; that is to say, we have to explain this sense according to norms that do not belong to aesthetics, but to logic. That which characterizes representation and will oppose it later to sentiment is not so much the reality that is represented, it is this appeal to the concept: the represented object is an identifiable object which demands to be recognized and which awaits the reflection of an undetermined commentary; it invites me to turn from the appearance and to seek elsewhere its proper truth.[224]

Erich Auerbach has studied imitation in the sense of the relation of art to fact in the structure of the reality presented by poet and novelist in some of the characteristic relationships, actions, and situations represented in Western literature from Homer and the Old Testament to the present.[225] Kenneth Burke reverses this process by applying the five terms of his dramatistic analysis—Act, Scene, Agent, Agency, and Purpose—to set forth, not merely the ways in which the actions of men are presented in art, but "the basic forms of thought which, in accordance with the nature of the world as all men necessarily experience it, are exemplified in the attributing of motives,"[226] and proceeds thus from the analysis of drama to the classification of schools of philosophy and types of political constitutions. Francis Fergusson uses imitation to analyze the nature of drama as an imitation of action.[227]

One of the significant consequences of this direction of literary criticism is the emergence of a determined effort to isolate and analyze the characteristic structure of a poem or of a work of art. The history of literary criticism from the Renaissance to the present has shown this search for the unity of a work of art transformed recurrently into the discovery of the unity of something else: the dramatic unities based on characteristics of time, place, and action, unities of intuition, of adjustment of imagination to understanding, of the creative act, of association, of expression, of communication, of culture, and more vaguely of matter and form. These recent statements of the character of the poem or work of art derive their fundamental terms, as did Aristotle's statement, from the relation of the medium, its potentialities and exigencies, to the content imitated and expressed. Kenneth Burke, one of the most profound and perceptive of contemporary critics, expresses this relation in a series of striking examples.

Greek tragedy being much nearer to grand opera than to the style of modern naturalism, its "imitation" included many ritualistic elements (as with the masks of the actors and the traditional dance movements of the chorus) that could only be interpreted as *interferences* with imitation, if the term had merely some such meaning as the faithful depicting the "lifelike."

For a beginning, let us consider a scattering of terms that might help us loosen up our notion of "imitation." To an extent, we might substitute: "the *miming* of an action." (Recall where Chaplin, for instance, "imitates" a dancer by taking two forks, sticking a roll on the end of each, and acting "lifelike" *in terms of this* greatly disparate medium.) Or: "The ritual figuring of an action" (since Greek tragedy was built about "quantitative" parts that, whatever their origin in nature, were as ceremonious as the processional and recessional of the Episcopalian service). Or: "the stylizing of an action." (The characters in Greek tragedy stood for certain civic functions somewhat as with the heroic posturing of an equestrian statue in a public park.) Or: "the symbolizing of an action." (Hence, we would hold that our term, "symbolic action" aids greatly in the reclaiming of lost connotations here.)[228]

These and like conceptions and uses of "imitation" have made their appearance elsewhere in relations and circumstances that suggest, not mutual influence, but simultaneous common recognitions of problems. André Dhôtel, thus, finds "imitation" useful for the analysis of rhetoric in senses that recall Burke's.

In fact, imitation is realized beyond nature. It is natural to walk in order to go to the hunt or to the cinema. To imitate someone who walks is already to dance. However the dance (and *a fortiori* the word) marks an agreement which cannot be situated in the domain of normal necessities, but constitutes from the start *another* story which natural needs in no way imposed. Imagination no doubt, but also a measure for the imagination. Love (and love of the truth) is born of a word, the power of which, experienced diversely, doubles instinct or utility which unites creatures only for the time necessary to satisfy needs and without leading these creatures even to recognize themselves.[229]

Similar characteristics of poetry and art are indicated in Fergusson's distinction between plot and action, which is based on Aristotle's characterization of the plot as "the imitation of action" and the poet as "the maker of plots." Fergusson employs this distinction not only "to indicate a direction which an analysis of a play should take" but also to point to "the object which the dramatist is trying to show us and we must in some sense grasp if we are to understand his complex art: plotting, characterization, versification, thought and their coherence."[230] Dewey indicates these characteristics when he speaks of "the compelling force" of the artist's medium which leads him to modify the object he represents in order to represent it,[231] and Santayana emphasizes like aspects of art when he remarks that imitation does not result in a literal repetition of the object which suggests it but "reproduces the form in a new medium and gives it a different function."[232] "Imitation" in all these converging applications serves to "define" art, to indicate a direction and method of analysis, and to suggest criteria for evaluation by which it is possible to concentrate on qualities of the work of art without forgetting that it expresses values that go beyond it, or that it is conditioned by the circumstances in which it was produced, or that it is not effectively art, whatever qualities it possesses, if it communicates no significance and moves no feeling.

The concept of "imitation" may be used as a convenient index to relate the new problems of contemporary aesthetics and criticism to the methods and the principles by which they have been placed among other philosophic problems. We have revolted against the principles commonly employed during the nineteenth and early twentieth centuries, but we have not abandoned them, for we still employ the accustomed distinctions to explore the implications of our new principles. We base our philosophies on "experience," "existence," "action," "expression," "communication," and "language" rather than on the "association of ideas," "the forms of thought," "understanding," or "feeling." Yet we continue to seek the basic forms and operations of "experience" and "language" in epistemological terms: we identify experience with the "empirical" and then puzzle over the relation of "experience" not only to science, art, and society but also to sensations, passions, and unconscious impulses; we find the basic distinctions of language in their cognitive and emotive uses and then puzzle over the relations of science to values and of values to meanings and preferences. If "experience" is to be employed as a principle, science, art, morals, and religion must be included in experience, and as forms of experience they might be explored for data concerning the operations and mutual influences of reason, emotion, persuasion, and illusion, but it is improbable that the forms of experience will be characterized by the unique or preponderant importance of a single psychological process. The forms of expression, and their contents and uses, might throw light on the operations and mutual influences of reason, emotion, persuasion, and sensation, but it is improbable that linguistic categories based on psychological distinctions will provide workable basic principles in philosophy or any of its branches. This confusion of principles affects our efforts to justify new principles no less than our efforts to develop their consequences. Principles cannot be demonstrated, but they can be examined both in relation to the circumstances in which they arise and in relation to the subject matter to which they apply. We justify principles in the structure of science and proof historically (or sociologically or pragmatically) and semantically, but our justifications have been rendered easy and rhetorical by the superannuated and inapplicable forms of history and semantics which we have come in recent years to employ.

History is used, as it always has been in the treatment of philosophic principles, to advance our arguments and to simplify our problems. Our arguments are advanced by discovering their origin and historical development in the treatment of genuine problems, and our problems are simplified by discovering the causes of old errors in the historical circumstances in which they were committed (or in which they were not yet erroneous) and by assuming that changed circumstances make it unnecessary to examine the arguments by which they were supported in the past, much less those by which they might be supported in the present. The investigation of intellectual history proceeds therefore in two dimensions: one dimension extends through the spheres in which principles are sought in successive ages—such as substance and being, mind and understanding, or experience and language—the other dimension extends through the agents or forms, processes or relations employed in the determination of principles in these various spheres during any given period. By virtue of the temporal dimension, the principles of other ages seem strange, although particular periods or particular schools may anticipate the sphere of discussion favored by the historian, and it is likely that the historians who wrote during periods against which we have revolted—such as the age immediately preceding our own—have neglected or misunderstood the periods and schools rediscovered by our historians. By virtue of the dimension of contemporaneous discussion, earlier history becomes relevant to present-day problems because oppositions of basic principles tend to be repeated, though in different terms, from age to age. The two dimensions, although distinguishable in analysis, are inseparable in their historical operation. Existentialism and symbolic logic, thus, are recent developments in philosophy. They render the principles of our immediate predecessors, who did not find their principles in existence and experience or in the structure and verification of statements, not only false but conveniently unintelligible.[233] The history by which this becomes the case is dependent on the novel doctrine of the present no less truly than the novel doctrine is the outgrowth of the past history. History renders the positions of some previous philosophers absurd and makes their arguments easy to refute, while it removes the absurdity otherwise associated with the positions of other philosophers and makes their neglected arguments worthy of study.

The history of the concept of "imitation"—both in the version I have given of it and in the versions which I have sought to discredit—illustrates both of these processes. There are historians who have contended that the concept of "imitation" was never useful for the analysis of artistic or aesthetic facts as well as historians who have found that it was once adapted to the facts or to the knowledge of the time but that it has ceased to be useful, for a variety of reasons, at a period more or less distant from the present. I have used history to prove that the concept of "imitation" has resumed an important place in aesthetic and critical discussions during the past few years and that it has been used in a great variety of meanings which are not taken into account when the "doctrine of imitation" is refuted or the history of its decline is traced. The question of the fate of the concept of "imitation" is inseparable from questions of the uses of history and of the relation of history to philosophical principles and philosophical semantics. History may be used as a device by which to relate concepts and arguments to times and circumstances; if they are treated wholly in terms of characteristics accounted for by peculiarities of their historical contexts, it becomes unnecessary to examine what a concept means or what an argument assumes or proves before crediting or rejecting the argument and the concepts in which it is expressed. History may also be used to develop the richness of meanings that have been attached to words and justified by arguments; when meanings are reconstructed from the historical contexts of statements, they are seen to be relevant to problems which recur in altered forms and to their possible resolutions, whether a particular term and the arguments by which its meanings have been explored are adopted or abandoned. The philosophic uses of history are more extensive and more direct when history leads to an understanding of the philosophies developed in contemporaneous opposition to one another or in successive improvement, abandonment, refutation, and revival. Intelligent judgment of these uses of history depends, however, on clarification of the nature of intellectual history itself and of the historical "facts" which it sets forth, for divergent documented statements of what philosophers have said and of the evolution of their statements should have some discoverable relation to the common facts they treat, other than the negative relations which are explained by the errors and obtuseness of previous historians.

When a philosopher or an artist or a critic seeks information, thus, concerning the meaning of "imitation," he is apt to get the impression from those historical expositions of aesthetic and critical doctrines that are easily accessible that it is a simple doctrine, which has passed out of currency, abandoned because of its inadequacies. The same time lag appears in histories of aesthetics and criticism as in other forms of intellectual history: we have revolted against epistemological and idealistic principles, against forms of thought, faculties of the mind, and processes of emotion, will, and reason, yet we continue to use them as categories in our histories of aesthetic experience and artistic expression, and the implications of our revolts emerge with difficulty from the resuscitated forms of *Geistesgeschichte* that we build on Herder, Hegel, Dilthey, or Max Weber. If "imagination" and "creation" are the basic terms of aesthetic analysis, "imitation" becomes a derived term dependent for its meaning on those prior concepts. It may continue to be an important term, as it is in the analyses by which Tarde and other sociologists sought to examine the foundations of human associations and society or in the analyses by which Vischer, Hirn, and others sought to examine aesthetic experience and the origins of art. It may be abandoned as antithetical to the processes of imagination and creation. To understand the relation of history to philosophic argument, the allegations of historians who hold that "imitation" has ceased to be operative as a concept and the allegations of historians roughly contemporaneous who hold that it has been put to new uses and has found a new scientific foundation should be examined relative both to'the theories they employ and to the facts they report.

Wilhelm Dilthey states the reasons for the abandonment of the concept of imitation in terms of the new importance given to imagination. In *Die Einbildungskraft des Dichters: Bausteine für eine Poetik*, he seeks his building stones for a poetic, as his title indicates, in the imaginative power of the poet. The theory of imitation is then reoriented to imagination as a basic term. In that reorientation Dilthey finds that the "poetic created by Aristotle" (*die von Aristoteles geschaffene Poetik*), after a long history of dominance in poetry and criticism, has come finally to the end of its influence: it was an instrument employed by poets in their work in all ages of consciously artistic poetry up to the second half of the eighteenth century, and it was the standard of critics until Boileau, Gottsched, and Lessing; but anarchy reigns in the broader jurisdiction of poetry today (the nineteenth century), and the Aristotelian poetic is dead.[234] The Aristotelian poetic was a theory of forms (*Formenlehre*) and a technique based upon them. The rules of this poetic employed the principle of imitation (*Nachahmung*); it is an "objective" principle in much the same way as the logic and epistemology of Aristotle set perception and thought over against being, and then conceived being to be represented in thought. The Aristotelian poetic, based on this principle of imitation, was adapted and adjusted in a variety of ways in the techniques and in the interpretations of the early modern theater in Spain, England, and France. Even in Germany, Lessing based his dramaturgy on the poetic of Aristotle. Goethe and Schiller recognized their agreement with it in many respects,[235] but they also became aware of its inadequacy, and it was at this point in history, according to Dilthey, that the Aristotelian principle of imitation was rendered untenable by inquiry into the subjective powers of the human mind.[236] Imitation, then, is an "objectivist" principle which was useful in the development, and illuminating in the interpretation, of poetry, including the dramatic poetry of Lope de Vega, Shakespeare, Corneille, and Racine, but was found to be inadequate for Romantic poetry and was displaced by a "subjectivist" principle in Romantic philosophy and psychology.

The two dimensions which I have differentiated in treating the history of "imitation" reappear in Dilthey's history. The successive steps of the temporal sequence, moreover, are sketched in terms that correspond to my differentiation of principles derived from the examination of things (Dilthey's "objective principles") from principles derived from the examination of thoughts (Dilthey's "subjective principles"). But while our accounts agree in treating "imitation" as an objective principle, they do not agree in their statements of what happens to "imitation" when the relations it sets forth are referred to a subjective principle. Nor do they agree concerning the period in which the objective principle was abandoned or concerning the number of times this occurred. The accounts differ not only concerning the succession of ages but also concerning the character of contemporaneous philosophic speculation in particular ages. Both differences can be clarified by examining Dilthey's theory of poetry in relation to other theories, for on Dilthey's supposition such an examination would lead to the historical question: What does poetry become when it ceases to be the imitation of an already existent reality? According to the analysis of imitation which I have set forth, on the other hand, it would follow that a new theory based in imagination rather than imitation would take into account the same features of poetry that were the subject of inquiry in one of the theories of imitation and that, allowing for differences of emphasis, the structure of the theories would be comparable.

Dilthey remarks that the ground of the principle of imitation in human nature, according to Aristotle, is the pleasure men take in imitating (*Nachbilden*) and in the perception of imitations (*Nachbildung*). In his exposition of Aristotle's doctrine he translates μίμησις by *Nachahmung*, μιμεῖσθαι by *Nachbilden*, and μίμημα by *Nachbildung*. It would not be inaccurate to translate both *Nachahmung* and *Nachbildung* by "imitation," and many philosophers use the two words to cover a common range of meanings.[237] What is the "subjectivist" principle that Dilthey finds substituted for the untenable "objectivist" principle of imitation (*Nachahmung*)? It is imitation (*Nachbildung*). Or, to give the distinction he makes its utmost sharpness and to use two English words for the two German words, the poet does not *imitate* nature (in the sense of *Nachahmung*); he *reproduces* his experience (in the sense of *Nachbildung*) in imagination. "Here we enter into the most proper sphere of the poet: an experience that has been lived (*Erlebnis*) and its expression or its reproduction in imagination."[238] Poetic creation, according to the old poetic, Dilthey adds, is a kind of displacement, and Democritus, Plato, Aristotle, and Horace agree in treating it that way. The Romantics, on the other hand, emphasize the affinity of genius with madness, dream, and every variety of ecstatic condition.[239] The contemporaneous dimension is again prominent in this statement; it might be questioned whether Democritus, Plato, and Aristotle agreed on any fundamental point of their theories of art and its making, and also whether Horace followed any one of them. Whatever the resolution of those questions, one historical fact is difficult to gloss over—that the relation of artistic genius to madness, enthusiasm, and ecstasy was explored long before the Romantic philosophy of the nineteenth century, and Democritus and Plato both contributed profoundly to that inquiry.

Two senses of "imitation" are usually encountered in a dialectic, such as the Romantics and Dilthey employed—the inferior imitation is mere copying of phenomenal aspects of contingent things and should be avoided and discouraged, but the higher imitation does more than imitate either physical objects or subjective states of mind, for it attains values which are not encountered as such in contingent things and which cannot be explained by the subjective processes of the mind. It attains truth, and it is found to operate not only in poetry but also in philosophy and science. Dilthey's conception of "reproduction" has both of these characteristics. The function of the poet is to bring order and harmony into our emotional life, and the poet is therefore a man of vivid sensations, images, and lived experiences, who possesses also an unusual power both of expression and of understanding. He omits what is accidental or contingent in characters, events, or life in general and gives imaginative expression to what is essential. The essential thus selected from the actual is called the *typical*, and the image which embodies or expresses it is called a *type*. Thought produces concepts; artistic creation produces types.[240] When I observe a skater or a dancer, I can by effort and practice separate my ideas of fact from those of value. A type results, and in each department of human life types serve as norms. But the concept of the type may also emphasize a common trait shared by all members of the class. It is in this sense that Shakespeare presents types of all the passions.[241]

Reproduction (*Nachbildung*) or imaginative reconstruction is the only way in which we can understand another person: to reproduce is to relive—"*Nachbilden* ist eben ein *Nacherleben*."[242] The individual is also encountered in the interpretation of literature, in hermeneutics, and Dilthey finds the culmination in the development of hermeneutics in the analysis of Schleiermacher, who, beginning with the recognition that the interpretation of literature is one instance of the phenomenon of understanding, bases his system of interpretation and his theory of literature on the demonstration that understanding is inexplicable except as a reproduction or imitation (*Nachbildung*) of the creative process. The cycle of adjusting imitation to the critical theory is complete: the doctrine of the imitation of nature, according to which the artist expresses a natural form in an artificial medium, is untenable; its place is taken by the doctrine of reproduction or imitation (*Nachbildung*) of lived experiences, according to which the imaginative power of the poet adds to sensation (*Empfindung*) a formal construction (*Nachbildung*). Reproduction gives art an objective reference, not to particulars, but to types. The process of reproducing or reliving is "understanding," and the task of understanding is to discover a living system in the given.

Imitation and Poetry

Psychology and history take over much of the task of philosophy, which is, like art itself, defined as reproduction, and the beautiful is assimilated to the true, when Dilthey sets at the head of "Die drei Epochen der modernen Ästhetik und ihre heutige Aufgabe" in 1892 a quotation from Schiller: "Would that the demand for beauty might at last be given up and be replaced wholly and entirely by the demand for truth."[243]

This historical statement raises questions of fact as well as questions of theory. With respect to facts: Is it the case that the doctrine of imitation held undisputed sway until the eighteenth century and was then abandoned? Contrary facts might be alleged: that the doctrine of imitation was repeatedly refuted before the eighteenth century, that it was used in more than one meaning to express different and often incompatible doctrines, and that it continued to be used during the nineteenth and twentieth centuries—indeed, according to Yrjö Hirn, reviewing the history of the concept of imitation thirteen years after Dilthey pronounced it untenable, modern science has at last come to the support of critics who treated art as imitation by showing that aesthetic processes can be understood and explained only by reference to imitation. With respect to theory: Are "understanding" and "reliving" satisfactorily explained by imaginative "reproduction" (*Nachbildung*) of "types"? Karl Groos undertakes, in *The Play of Men* written more than a decade after Dilthey's statement, to explain inner "reliving" (*Nacherleben*) by outer "imitation" (*Nachahmung*).[244] Such questions of fact and of theory are inseparable: How are the facts determined in intellectual history? How are theories established or refuted in philosophical disputes? The very process which I have used to expound Dilthey's doctrine might seem to illustrate a like dilemma of facts selected by theories and theories established by facts: Dilthey demonstrates that the principle of imitation became untenable in the eighteenth century; my reply is to show that he continues to use one of the meanings of "imitation" in the nineteenth century. Do we use "history" in the same sense? Do we mean the same thing by "imitation"? The differences in our conceptions of history follow from different conceptions of historical semantics and result in different historical definitions of terms. In intellectual history semantics is in part a question of method, in part a question of fact: the history depends on the development of meanings assumed by terms, and the selection or statement of facts which results depends on the significations given to terms in use.

Semantics may serve to differentiate Dilthey's conception of history from the one I have tried to expound. Dilthey's purpose is to construct the living system within which philosophic discussion occurs, and he consequently sets philosophies forth in their psychological contexts and historical epochs. Philosophies are characterized by their epochs; concepts become untenable and are eliminated in the processes of historical evolution, while tenable concepts survive. My purpose is to advance philosophic discussion by clarifying problems, assumptions, inferential sequences, and errors based on paralogisms and fallacies, and I consequently seek the philosophic grounds and assumptions of proposed systems of explanation, including history and psychology. In any advanced cultural context or epoch many sets of philosophic assumptions are in operation and opposition; the philosophers of a period expose contemporary as well as past errors and find inspiration in ancient as well as recent truths. The difference between these purposes affects both dimensions of history, the contemporaneous cross-section and the temporal development. A period may be said to have a philosophy, and the philosophy of one period differs from those of others: Dilthey shows that the "philosophy" of the seventeenth century can be distinguished easily and interestingly from the philosophy of the Renaissance and from that of the eighteenth century. It is no less apparent, however, that the "philosophy" of the seventeenth century is the philosophy of Bacon, Hobbes, Locke, Descartes, Spinoza, and Leibniz, and that these great philosophers spent long efforts in developing the consequences of their basic differences. I find it more profitable for philosophic and scientific purposes to enter into the discussion with them and to try to follow through, say, Leibniz' refutations of Descartes, Spinoza, and Locke, on the supposition that we are engaged in like problems and employ like assumptions today, than to seek with Dilthey the living structure which explains by historical and psychological devices why they agree with each other and differ from us, on the supposition that we have passed beyond their concepts and problems.

If periods are distinguished from each other by their characteristic philosophies, the temporal dimension of history is a succession of philosophies. According to Dilthey, there are three large standpoints or classes of metaphysical systems: the naturalistic systems, which employ the principle of imitation in aesthetics; the transcendental systems, which, in aesthetics, seek a principle of creation in the creative powers of the subject; and the positivistic systems, which go their own way.[245] It seems a meager basis for philosophizing to suppose that history would justify the continued labors only of idealists, and such a supposition would provide only an equally unpromising basis for history, since the recounting of the past is reduced to the epitaphs of past philosophers written under three rubrics. Moreover, the prediction of the future has not been verified by the continued advance of idealistic and transcendental systems during the seventy-odd years since Dilthey wrote, unless history loads the dice with an idealistic account of the recent past. At best, an epochal account of the evolution of philosophies does not avoid the relativities of systems, for as many theories of the epochs or living contexts have been developed to explain why philosophers say what they say as there are philosophic systems. Dilthey himself does not always go back to the three basic metaphysics—thus, the three epochs which he distinguishes in "Die drei Epochen der modernen Ästhetik" are the seventeenth century with its natural or rational aesthetic, the eighteenth century with its empirical or aesthetic-sense aesthetics, and the nineteenth century with its historical method.

Meanings, like philosophies, are determined by periods. In Dilthey's semantics a term like "imitation" has a single meaning in the single philosophy of a period, and history traces the processes which lead to its abandonment or its continued use. The semantics I have practiced has two successive forms: "historical" semantics, in which terms are defined according to the assumptions, arguments, and conclusions of philosophical positions examined and differentiated historically, and "philosophical" semantics, in which terms are employed and related according to meanings adapted to a single set of assumptions and methods. The patterns of historical semantics provide useful preparation for philosophical semantics at least in so far as known errors and recognized achievements can be related to new terminologies and new methods. At least, it might forestall the facile mutual annihilation which philosophers practice ritualistically by fixing their own meanings on the terms which other philosophers employ, and it might shorten their puzzling over what other philosophers could possibly have been intended by statements they carefully elaborated and arguments they carefully constructed. Philosophical semantics consists, not in the determination of what the term *must* mean in the light of available knowledge and as a result of social conditions, but rather in the construction of a system of interrelated meanings in the light of other systems—their structures, their inferential consequences, their scope, deficiencies, and analogies.

History, however, is not an arbitrary exercise determined by philosophic purposes or by preferred semantics. It treats of facts and of interrelations found among facts. Facts should discriminate among the values of opposed theories and among the historical accounts in which theories are employed. Dilthey's method and the method I have used lead to sharply different statements of fact, and it would seem to be clearly the case that one of us, at least, must be in error in our apparently contradictory statements. Dilthey traces a history of the Aristotelian conception of imitation and discovers that it was employed by poets and critics until the middle of the eighteenth century, at which point it became untenable. I trace a history of what seems to be the same conception of imitation and discover that it was not used, or even stated, by any influential philosopher in the modern period, that is, since the Renaissance, until it reappeared in the doctrines of several twentieth-century philosophers. It might seem that a team of research workers with moderate experience, or even a single moderately assiduous and discerning scholar, should be able to determine which of these histories is more nearly correct. Yet a little thought and careful reading would show that any such expectation is thwarted by the fact that the two histories are histories of different phenomena. Dilthey is concerned with the "poetic created by Aristotle" (*die von Aristoteles geschaffene Poetik*), and he is quite content to pass over such fundamental differences, which indeed become trivial in this approach, as those that separated Democritus, Plato, Horace, and their numerous and variegated progeny from Aristotle. I am ready to give full importance to the fact that the *Poetics* (that is, the book) of Aristotle was far more frequently and persistently the subject of discussion, commentary, and application in the treatment of aesthetic problems prior to the middle of the eighteenth century than it has been since. The history I trace is the history of Aristotle's doctrine, not the history of the tradition and interpretation of his work. That history is based on the assumption that it is possible to determine what Aristotle meant (if it is not, we shall have like difficulties in understanding Dilthey or each other) and how it differed from the doctrines of his contemporaries and successors, whether or not they themselves or the historians who wrote about them thought the doctrine Aristotelian. Dilthey would have no hesitation in acknowledging the facts that underlie this assumption—he repeatedly points out that the men who comment on a doctrine, or adopt or use it, modify it in so doing, and I could ask for no better specification of doctrinal changes within a tradition than he gives, for example, when he points out that the poetic of Scaliger derives more from Hermogenes, Menander, and Diomedes than from Aristotle and Horace, and it makes Virgil rather than Homer the ideal poet.[246]

Both forms of history have, as is indeed true of all history and philosophy itself, a tinge of both arrogance and futility. How, it might be asked of me, can you pretend to state what Aristotle meant, and argue that he meant something that no one found in him for three hundred years during which his works were available and were to some extent read? And what is the use of tracing concepts and themes from period to period when it is obvious that a concept or an idea, even one that Aristotle happened to use, takes on a particular form in a particular period or culture, and that the differences are more important than the analogies it bears to the expressions of other times and places? My answer is that the history of the numerous and often contradictory interpretations that have been put upon the work of Aristotle as well as that of other philosophers is indication of the need for historical semantics, and, unless it is possible to differentiate meanings, there is no reason to suppose that any philosophic statement will convey a single sense or even a roughly coherent set of senses. The device by which I have suggested that Aristotle's (or any other philosopher's) meaning may be approximated is the methodical taking into account of the varieties of interpretations and the presentation of evidence for the accuracy and importance of one's own interpretations in the light of the alternative possibilities. The important characteristic of the method is that it is concerned with what the philosopher said, and it is based on the assumption that his reasons can be understood and might be valid and important in themselves for what they mean, and not merely as a sign of something else, like the philosopher's state of mind, or his times, or his class. It has contemporary as well as historical uses, yet it is not widely practiced today, because our methods discover many reasons which would make unnecessary the labor of reconstructing the meanings which Aristotle, say, gave to familiar terms and rediscovering the principles by which he came to conclusions which we judge, apart from those meanings and principles, to be banal or false. We might suppose that Aristotle did not mean what he said (as indeed no philosopher could), but psychological, social, or economic grounds must be found to give his statements significance; or we might suppose that isolated statements found in his works indicate an evolution from an early Platonic to a late scientific attitude through an intermediate period of transition, and therefore no effort should be wasted to seek a coherent doctrine even in a single work or a single book of a single work; or we might suppose that what he said is false today, although it may have been useful in the circumstances or adapted to the state of knowledge of his times, since he lived in a̓ pre-feudal, pre-industrial society based on slave labor, and the concepts which he developed and which had a long influence became untenable with the advent of Romantic poetry and the development of theories of madness.

How, it might, on the other hand, be asked of Dilthey, can you presume to reduce the philosophies of men who spent their lives differing one from another and giving their differences as precise statement and as solid grounds as ingenuity and trained subtlety could provide, to a single philosophy which can be identified by a date and a few concepts, and which must be separated from later philosophic speculation by a line which no living philosopher can cross on pain of dealing in untenable ideas? And what is the use of showing that ideas and attitudes, even those influenced by tradition, take on new forms in new cultural and ideological contexts, when it is obvious that the novelty occurs in ideas formed in a continuous dialogue in which the next step to novelty and to truths previously unstated is prepared by ideas developed in other times and other circumstances? His answer is that the unresolved differences of philosophers detract from the possible effectiveness of philosophy and indicate therefore the need to explain how these differences arise and how they are resolved. The device by which this may be accomplished is to set forth the structure of the intellectual character of an age in dynamic relations that permit the interplay of such differences. The important characteristic of the method is that it is concerned with the living forces that determine the meanings of statements, and its efficacy is not affected by the fact that philosophers quote dead philosophers and sometimes imagine that they are continuing their doctrines or systems, unaware of the modifications that are introduced into doctrines when they are fitted to the temper and problems of a later time.

Arguments which go back ultimately to basic assumptions and philosophic principles may ground those assumptions in history or in semantics, or arguments may be employed to establish or to question the principles assumed in history or semantics. The fate of reason, discussion, and argument is implicated in the uses of history and semantics, and the philosophic interest of history and semantics is in their effects on the use of reason. I have thus far tried to trace Dilthey's history and semantics and my own back to principles which are directly comparable. Dilthey's history is dialectical or epochal: as he traces the philosophies of successive periods, the concept of imitation held sway for a long time in poetry and criticism and then became untenable for the poetry and the philosophy of recent periods. My history is problematic and disciplinary: as I trace the problems that are discussed on varying assumptions within any given period through the succession of periods, I find that sometimes the concept of imitation is fundamental in the discussion of aesthetic problems and sometimes it is defined in terms of other concepts taken as fundamental, but the genuine problems discussed under the term "imitation" do not disappear; they return in many recognizable forms, often expressed in variants of, or substitutes for, the term "imitation." In Dilthey's semantics, terms like "imitation" are defined broadly and analogically in the context of a tradition, and they lose their meaning and importance when terms like "creation" and "imagination" make their appearance. In historical semantics, as I have tried to practice it, terms are defined narrowly and literally in the context of the basic assumptions and the related terms by which their meanings are set forth and developed in a particular philosophy, with the result that terms like "imitation" and "imagination" have many meanings, and either one may be used as fundamental in defining and applying the other.

I have no objection to dialectical history or analogical semantics, but I find grave dangers in the rigid and dogmatic form which Dilthey has given to them and which has been accentuated in statements that defer to Dilthey as an authority. Dialectical history in its various forms—Hegelian, Marxist, or Crocean, *Geistesgeschichte*, materialistic determinism, or historiography—has in recent years been made a substitute for philosophy and a substitute for rational analysis. If you can account for a doctrine by the circumstances in which it originated, there is no need to analyze it or to refute it; and, if you can present your own doctrine as the historical outcome of the progress of science or of altered economic, social, and ideological conditions, there is no need to examine the possibility that other doctrines may claim a like historical origin. The problem of semantics is then reduced to the problem of separating the right meaning of a term by means of other right terms from the wrong meanings based on wrong terms. Rational grounds of discussion disappear, and no other means of taking into account the claims of opposed theories of history and semantics remains than the facile and ineffective refutations provided in each theory for all others.[247]

This situation constitutes one of the basic intellectual problems of our times. The progress of science has at once exhibited new models for philosophy and provided new subject matter. The progress of communication has forced upon our attention the varieties of values esteemed in different cultures (and, by reflection, in our own) and has suggested that philosophy assumes a cultural form in the structures of values of a society. We can explain aspects of the development of science, knowledge, and institutions ideologically, psychologically, epistemologically, historically, and sociologically, but when we explain *why* men say what they do, we tend to discount *what* they mean when they say it. We profess an interest in other values than our own, and we do appreciate strange values, sometimes without the need of explanation, as in the plastic arts, sometimes after analysis and preparation, as in poetry, while other arts, like music, fall midway between—immediately effective on one level, dependent on another level, on training to be perceptible and on theory to be intelligible. But when we examine *what* men value apart from the values which we likewise feel, we seem to be forced to the disturbing conclusion that there is nothing too absurd, too useless, or too devoid of interest to be chosen as true, or good, or beautiful by some men, yet we cannot wholly abandon the question *why* what is preferred has, or should have, value. Two forces are at work which pull us paradoxically in opposite directions. When we try to explain our efforts to be objective in knowledge, we discover that knowledge is relative to impulses and preconceptions, times, languages, and cultures. When we try to discuss our efforts to express or achieve values felt or sought, we discover that communication and co-operation is possible only if we find common values underlying the diversity of expression and action. Philosophy has a double responsibility with respect to knowledge and with respect to values. Its task with respect to knowledge is not only to take account of science as a subject matter and to construct a science of sciences but also to contribute to the advance of knowledge by preserving the rational integrity of the dialogue and opposition of philosophies in their efforts to construct a science of sciences or a wisdom of action, and by continuing the labor of separating error, fiction, illusion, and lie from truth, in the confidence that they do approximate truth despite differences in assumption and environment and that they do open up some view of the good in attaining the better. Its task with respect to values is not only to set up criteria of action, judgment, and appreciation to govern the lives of men who accept the assumptions on which those criteria are based but also to contribute to the understanding of values that fall in the focus of other criteria and to the consequent enrichment of one's own values.

To accomplish these tasks, our concepts and methods must be flexible, and their use must be informed by insight into other possibilities. This flexibility and this insight can be advanced by the study of the recurrent themes of inquiry and the techniques by which they are developed. The alternative to such a view of multiple meanings and possibilities is to suppose that one concept has unique adequacy and one method unique validity. The study of "imitation" as a theme developed in the many meanings attached to the term can contribute to the appreciation of poetry and to its fuller operation in the community and the world, precisely because the richness of aesthetic and artistic phenomena cannot be exhausted by the analyses or the statements of any one philosophy or system of criticism. Our choice is either to make our concepts translucent enough to focus on identifiably different aspects of the same phenomena or to make them opaque by verbal disputes concerning whether art is in fact "imitation" or "imagination" or "expression." Is it true that a theory of imitation ignores the creative processes of artists and provides no place for that communication that makes art expressive, potentially to all men, of the values of a time? It would be difficult to find a theory of imitation of which such rigid limitations could be alleged plausibly. Aristotle, thus, says that the poet *imitates* actions and *makes* plots, and he describes the effect of dramatic poetry as a *catharsis*. He distinguishes carefully between the action imitated and the structure or synthesis of the plot as well as between the proper effects of proof, persuasion, and poetry. "Makes" in the Greek, is "creates" without benefit of the Book of Genesis, but with full awareness of the phenomena of enthusiasm and madness, and theories of imitation at various periods during the Middle Ages, and again during the seventeenth century, bridged any suspected gap between making and creating. The poet does not simply reproduce or represent what has happened: if that were the case, there would be no need for the elaborate analyses of plot, character, thought, language, melody, and spectacle which constitute the body of the poetic theory based by Aristotle on imitation, for it is these "parts" of the poem that the poet adds when he imitates action and realizes some of the potentialities of his poetic medium. At most, the theory of imitation commits Aristotle to trying to discover what the poet added, and what the audience appreciates, by examining the poem in which it is added and in which it is perceived rather than by digging into the soul of the artist or by exploring the structures of experience and cultures. His effort is to place the aesthetic object in a real world and to distinguish it from other objects in that world. The object imitated is not necessarily a real object—it may be legendary, ideal, or wholly imaginary. Imitation is not necessarily a copy of an object as it exists in fact or as it is described, recounted, or imagined elsewhere. A work of art is an imitation in so far as the subject to which it directs attention is rendered plausible and effective by devices proper to the art (it is great art when those devices are used well), and as imitation the work of art is distinct from natural objects, even though its matter is natural and its effect depends on a natural tendency to take pleasure in imitations. It is no less obviously the case that theories of creation based on "imagination," while emphasizing the vision of genius, take into account what is *represented*, if they consider what is said in a poem and how it is said; and they take into account what is *expressed*, if they consider the values which make the vision and the representation intelligible and effective. Nor, finally, do theories of "expression," which emphasize experience and communication, neglect the matter *reproduced* in content or employed as medium or the significant and dynamic form imaginatively *created* and *perceived*.

The study of the structure of problems, the recurrence of themes, and the diversity of techniques is a device by which to achieve flexibility and clarity in the use of concepts and methods. Poetry is not a recent invention of mankind, nor has the history of poetry been a cumulative sequence in which later poems are better because they built on and preserve earlier achievements, and since early poets were also critics and wrote about poetry in their poems, the history of theories of poetry is as long as that of poetry and reflects in the form of its doctrines the problems and fashions of its subject matter. Poets often write with a conception or even a theory of poetry in mind, yet it is not necessary to agree with the theory of a poet to appreciate his poetry, and a variety of theories should lead, sometimes at least, to an enriched reading of a poem rather than to a clash of opposed doctrines. Acquaintance with the changing themes and with the meanings assumed by concepts in criticism can contribute to understanding the phenomena of art and the accompanying discussion of critics. The study of concepts and of the structures in which they evolve their meanings will not establish agreement concerning terms or even a lexical prescription of the meanings in which terms can be used profitably or meaningfully. But the differences of philosophic systems might be stated in ways that contribute to the clarification of principles rather than the formation of schools, to the recollection of insights achieved, errors demonstrated, and problems delineated in other philosophies, and in general to understanding short of agreement. The concept of "imitation" is adapted to serve these purposes because it has had a long history during which it has been put to a large number of uses in many meanings, sometimes as a fundamental term in critical and aesthetic systems, sometimes as a term defined and used or criticized in a context determined by other more fundamental terms.

The treatment of problems of art and criticism may be advanced by insight into the meanings philosophers have explored and knowledge of the problems they have treated. The formation and efficacy of the philosophies which are reflected in criticism are not uniquely determined, however, by wisdom or learning. At best, insight and knowledge serve as propaedeutics and guides in the exploration and development of basic concepts and principles adapted to the peculiar problems and opportunities of a time. Philosophers, like everyone else, follow the intellectual fashions and the modes of speech in which they were formed—unconsciously, or consciously adapting philosophic criteria to current interests and assumptions—and they seldom merely repeat or borrow what they learn but rather adjust it to experience, knowledge, and problems that did not affect earlier or different formulations of those criteria. The history of philosophy has been a dialogue in so far as those exchanges have been possible, and the continuing themes and techniques have cut across differences of period and principle because philosophers have often found that many of their contemporaries, with whom they share forms of language and forms of thought, are far deader than a few chosen philosophers who are separated from them by varying distances of time and space.

At present, all our problems are affected, when they reach the level of philosophic generality, by changes that are interrelated and affect all human activities and values: the advances of knowledge that raise questions concerning its nature, structure, and methods, the contacts of cultures that raise questions of the relations of values, and the increased scope and efficacy of practical action that raise questions of co-operation and mutual understanding. These changes doubtless influence the present tendency to seek philosophic principles grounded in "experience" and "communication" which is reflected in the preoccupation of aesthetic theories with "expression." In this atmosphere it is as little likely, or indeed desirable, that aesthetics should return to "imitation" as a basic principle as that it should return to "imagination" or "creation." Both are dead and unpromising as basic themes, yet both serve as propaedeutic and guide in the formation of theories of "expression," and the problems of "imitation" and "imagination" have their place in those theories. Thus, when Matisse explains what he means by "expression," the facts which are treated in theories of "imitation" and "imagination" are not slighted, and acquaintance with those theories might serve to enrich the significance of what Matisse means by "expression" rather than merely to arouse impulses to refute him in the name of "imitation" or "imagination."

Expression for me is not to be found in the passion which blazes from a face or which is made evident by some violent gesture. It is in the whole disposition of my picture—the place occupied by the figures, the empty space around them, the proportions—everything plays its part. Composition is the art of arranging in a decorative manner the various elements which the painter uses to express his sentiments. In a picture every separate part will be visible and will take up that position, principal or secondary, which suits it best. Everything which has no utility in the picture is for that reason harmful. A work of art implies a harmony of everything together (*une harmonie d'ensemble*): every superfluous detail will occupy in the mind of the spectator, the place of some other detail which is essential.[248]

The emphasis on the arrangement of "parts" in the work of art and the distinction between natural and artistic expression bring the statement into direct relation with theories of imitation. "Composition," "the art of arranging" the various elements, "sentiments," and the "mind of the spectator" provide place for the data of theories of "imagination" and "creation." The greater affinity of the statement to theories of imitation than to theories of imagination, to the "objective" rather than the "subjective" principle, is seen in the fact that the results of the creative process are found by seeking what is "essential" in the arrangement of the parts of the picture rather than by plunging into the subconscious of the artist.

The concept of imitation has, moreover, a second use which is more directly philosophic in character than its propaedeutic use in clarifying the structure of theories, and the recent increase in explicit discussions of imitation is indication of the nature of the problems to which it applies. The concepts of "experience" and "communication" are adapted to treat the emergence of values and their common effectiveness, but values, if they are genuine, must have objective contacts. Theories of imitation, when they are formed in a context of metaphysical principles of being and substance, explore the relation of aesthetic objects to other entities; they may also be adapted, in a context of principles found in action and statement, to explore the objective references and grounds of experience and communication. The concept of imitation brings prominently to attention four distinct ways in which a poem, or any other work of art, reaches and depends upon objectivity: in the values expressed and perceived, in the poem or other object made and recognized, in the form of expression employed, and in the sensibilities affected. These are at once the areas of problems which extend from aesthetics to the whole scope of our speculation and action and the grounds of differences which are now separating philosophies of experience and expression into schools and factions. We shall need all the insight that can be derived from earlier disputes of schools to prevent doctrinal differences from obscuring the converging meanings and from obstructing the practical consequences of philosophical analysis. But the problems are clear, and the concept of imitation can serve to sketch their interrelations and their implications.

The diversity of values and of value systems, in the first place, has been forced on our attention by experience of different cultures, traditions, classes, philosophies, religions, and arts; we must find the means of treating the values that underlie the different forms in which they are expressed if we are to understand them in theory or

advance them in action. These are problems that were treated in
dialectical theories of imitation, in which not only arts but actions
and things were analyzed as imitations of eternal ideas or values.
Viewed from the standpoint of experience, the problem is best
stated in inverted form—not how art and speculation imitate eternal
values but how common values which are unchanged by differences
of expression may be discerned in what we esteem as good and
what we accept as true. Theories of values have all but lost contact
not only with morals and preferences but even with ethics and aesthetics, and our judgment of what is good or beautiful has little
bearing on our analysis of action or taste. The contacts of cultures
may, however, lead to the recognition of contacts of philosophic
systems that mediate between the two extremes at which it is assumed either that a philosophy has no relation to morality or art or
that a philosophy must be used to impose courses of action or
modes of expression derived by deductive inference and reinforced
by political power or social constraint.

The dependence of art on its social and cultural context, in the
second place, has been made increasingly apparent by the history of
art, by sociological and anthropological studies, and by the predicament of art in an age of political dictatorships, mass communication, and cultural barriers and restrictions; we must find the means
of distinguishing aesthetic values from the social conditions in
which they originate if they are to be cultivated as values in themselves and therefore to influence our cultures as values and not as
devices of propaganda or escape. These are problems that were
treated in problematic theories of imitation, in which poetry was
considered an imitation of the actions of men. We have learned that
poems and other objects of art are formed in cultural contexts; if
we understood the structures and values of art objects, we would
have an insight into cultures which is lacking when we have no
independent means of understanding the values by which a culture
is characterized.

Language and communication, in the third place, is one of the
centers of our attention, and our "practical" criticism of poetry has

tended to emphasize linguistic devices, but at the expense of separating language from what language expresses and of making criticism and history irrelevant or hostile to each other. These are
problems that were treated in operational theories of imitation, in
which men imitate the achievements and devices of other men, and
the recrudescence of interest in rhetoric and in rhetorical tropes,
commonplaces, and inventions marks the continuity of the analysis.

The study of human aptitudes, sensibilities, and passions, finally,
has intensified our propensity to define art relative to the person
who takes pleasure in it. The resulting problems are those treated
in logistic theories of imitation, which base imitation on laws of
nature, but we have now reached a point at which we might
profitably pause in discriminating pleasures by physical symptom or
introspective report for the purpose of constructing a vocabulary
for the discussion of art, and instead analyze the object of art,
which is the objectification of pleasure, for the purpose of discovering means by which to discriminate subjective states. These are
four different ways in which art is related to nature and to natural
processes. They present serious problems not only for art and criticism but for practical action and philosophy. The term "imitation"
may or may not be used in treating them, but the doctrines of imitation which were developed to treat like problems in the past can be
put to use as analytical instruments both to prepare the way for new
theories and to explore the objective grounds on which they can be
based.

APPENDIX

Remarks on the Occasion of the Seventieth Birthday of Thomas Mann (June 6, 1945) Made at a Dinner Given to Him in Chicago, June 29, 1945

Thomas Mann began his speech at the celebration of Freud's eightieth birthday, nine years ago in Vienna, by speculating concerning the propriety of selecting a poet and man of letters to do honor to a man of science. Those reflections may well return to his mind tonight and lead him again, as have the characters in his novels, to philosophic speculations concerning the relations of art and science, for his friends—with irony or with insight—have chosen a philosopher to do him honor on his seventieth birthday. There is irony in the selection, since the deep-seated antipathy which separates philosophy from poetry finds expression both in the philosopher's conviction that poetic feeling and diction weaken and obscure the truths vindicated by logical rules and the goods defined by moral prescriptions and also in the poet's knowledge that formal rules and traditional prescriptions yield truths that achieve neither progress nor conviction and goods that achieve neither justice nor utility. But the irony has its basis in an insight that philosophy and poetry merge in their higher reaches where truth encompasses mysteries and beauty expresses truths.

This same irony and its accompanying insight provide the themes and the forms of Thomas Mann's novels and short stories. It is the irony and the insight which have through the ages constituted the genius of Platonism and which, with a further turn of irony, have found expression for the forces that move in our times, not in the dialectic of a philosopher who writes with the sensitivity of a poet, but in the tales of a novelist who writes with the profundity of a philosopher. Plato gave dramatic and poetic expression at once to the demonstration that the poet, inspired by divinity or madness, perceives truths and achieves values not otherwise accessible to man, and also to the conviction of the philosopher and the lawgiver that the teller of tales, whose morals and meanings are contrary to law and to truth, cannot be tolerated in either the perfect state of the *Republic* or the second-best state of the *Laws*. The novels of Thomas Mann mark him a philosopher who brings to life intellectuals, wordy and ineffectual, like Settembrini, or sinister, like Naptha, in the company of poets, like Tonio Kröger, who possess—and are sick with—knowledge, and men of feeling, like Pieperkorn. Plato took an art form, the mime, a conversation-dialogue employed by Sophron, Xenarchus, and others to exhibit characters opposed to each other in the discussion of themes, and transformed it to the uses of philosophy in the dialogue which provides, in the oppositions of characters and principles, an instrument for the discovery of truth. Mann took the novel, a narrative of characters and actions, which contemporary novelists were employing to set forth the relations of men to each other and the flow of their thoughts, and transformed it, using philosophy to explore the foundations of those relations and the significance of those compelling and questioning sequences. When Mann wrote *Buddenbrooks*, the novel was passing, as an art form, from a structure adapted primarily to plot and narration to a structure in which the development of the character of men, of families, and of times assumed primacy. He completed and published the *Magic Mountain* at a time when novelists built their narratives about the internal dialogue and the stream of thought that constituted the life of their characters. He almost alone among novelists built a new structure for the novel on the intellectual content which animates the associations of men and the flow of their thoughts and feelings, and he revolutionized the novel by using philosophy to give it form, as Plato had revolutionized the mime by putting it to a philosophic use. The change in the form of the novel no less than the change of

its content removed the antithesis between art and phil
cording to Thomas Mann, "the supremacy of the novel in ...
writing" is a consequence "of the crisis in which the novel finds
itself and of the fact that it must issue forth from this crisis as something new, hitherto unknown and more intellectual."

Poetry merges with philosophy in the philosophy of Plato, and
arguments depend in Plato's philosophy on poetic insight into character, situation, and feeling and on poetic use of language; yet at
the height of his poetic artistry Plato was suspicious of poets. The
novel becomes intellectual in the art of Thomas Mann, and plots
develop an argument which sets forth the confrontation of full and
varied philosophies; yet at the height of his speculations Mann retained his fears of the literal-minded limitations of purely intellectual analyses. He reproached Freud, properly, for esteeming
philosophy too little, and he expressed his conviction that "in
actual fact philosophy ranks before and above the natural sciences
and that all method and exactness serve its intuitions and its intellectual and historical will." Yet he came to philosophy and to his
intellectual preoccupations by way of Schopenhauer and Nietzsche,
Novalis and Kierkegaard, by speculating on will rather than by
celebrating reason, and he found himself in the realm of the psychology of the unconscious even before he read Freud. Plato is a poet,
but he argues that the true poet is one who knows and is therefore a
philosopher. Thomas Mann is a philosopher, but he sees the true
philosopher as one who transcends the limits of rationality in his
understanding and who is therefore a poet. Profound differences
separate a philosophy which finds the criteria of poetry in truth
from an art which finds the criteria of philosophy in poetic insight,
yet the two philosophies find similar preoccupations when they
treat of love. In the *Symposium* Plato has Socrates repeat the tale of
Diotima which culminates in the ladder of loves that men mount
from physical to spiritual and finally to transcendent beauty.
Thomas Mann has Hans Castorp recognize the attractive force of
love: "It is love, not reason, that is stronger than death," and although the magnificent tale of Castorp's effort to mount the ladder

of loves ends with the recognition that his "prospects are poor," his recognition of love in the adventures of the flesh and in the spirit of a dream removes all bitterness from the contemplation of his undetermined fate. In both versions of the movement of love the direct influence of music on the spirit of man gives ground and form to the more indirect influences of the refinements of argument.

The art of Thomas Mann is a structure of dialectic in which the normal unreflective life of the bourgeois is set over against the thoughtful creative life of the artist; in which knowledge is set once more against art; analysis against form; disease, physical or mental, against health; tradition against change. It is a dialectic, however, not a static or literal opposition, for art, as a departure from the normal, is grounded in and strengthened by its roots in the normal, and as antithesis to knowledge it is insight and consciousness of knowledge; form is the consequence and resolution of analysis; health is based on experience of the unhealthy; and innovation is dependent on tradition. The oppositions of our times merge and are reconciled in the evolution of the tales which Thomas Mann spins out of them. He realizes in his storytelling the functions of wisdom and philosophy for our times. When Aristotle sought to define the nature of wisdom, he found it equally exemplified in the philosopher—the lover of wisdom, *Philosophos*—and in the lover of myths—*Philomythos*. The modern world might well learn this wisdom from Thomas Mann, for we have lost our sense of the profundities of truth because we have confused truths with facts that we can see and feel and test by their utility, and we have come to suspect the myth, because we suppose literal-mindedly that, unlike history, the myth did not happen and therefore is not true. Thomas Mann has employed the monumental cycle of the Joseph novels to teach us that the myth is true precisely because it has happened so many times that it must be retold again and again to explore the dimensions and varieties of its truth. There is no first time in human history, but every beginning turns out to be the twilight of another beginning. "What concerns us," he concludes, "is time's abrogation and dissolution in the alternation of tradition and prophecy."

Appendix

The lover of myth, the *philomythos*, does not need explanation—except on festive occasions such as these—by those who aspire to the love of wisdom, to *philosophia*, for his art is explained in his works. The problems of the artist are the subject of his novels and short stories—the artist's struggles with the man of action (which was once even carried to the extreme of supposing that the artist could be a nonpolitical man) and the man of science. But ultimately all three—doer, knower, and maker—are transformed into one: the maker. Even in the face of this resolution we easily forget that the poet is, as his name implies, the maker. Yet the recognition of the poet as maker is essential to appreciate what Thomas Mann says of his collected short stories—that they are "an autobiography in the guise of a fable." They are the autobiography of a poet—of a maker—who could say with Tonio Kröger, "I am looking into a world unborn and formless, that needs to be ordered and shaped." His works have been the creation of an artistic order so conceived that it is also the discovery of an intelligible order in the materials from which the art has been constructed and the projection of a practical order in the ends accessible in future action and life illuminated by artistic vision.

Notes

NOTES TO CHAPTER I

1. Karl Menninger, *Love against Hate* (New York: Harcourt, Brace, 1942), pp. viii–ix.
2. Hermogenes Περὶ μεθόδου δεινότητος 36 (*Hermogenis opera*, ed. H. Rabe [Leipzig: Teubner, 1913], pp. 453–55).
3. Athenaeus *Deipnosophistae* v. 182: "But in the symposium of Epicurus there is an assemblage of flatterers praising one another, while the symposium of Plato is full of men who turn their noses up in jeers at one another; for I pass over in silence what is said about Alcibiades. In Homer, on the other hand, only sober symposia are organized." Cf. *ibid*. 187–88: "Again, Epicurus in his symposium puts questions about indigestion in order to get omens from it; following that he speaks about fevers. What need is there even to speak of the lack of proportion which pervades his style? As for Plato—I pass over the man who was bothered by the hiccups and cured by gargles of water and still more by the insertion of a straw to tickle his nose and make him sneeze; for he wanted to introduce fun and mockery—Plato, I say, ridicules Agathon's balanced clauses and antitheses, and also brings on the scene Alcibiades, who avows that he is consumed with lust. Nevertheless, while writing that kind of stuff, they banish Homer from their state. . . . Nevertheless, even the symposium described by Xenophon, although it is praised, admits occasions for censure not fewer than these. Callias, for example, gets the symposium together when his favorite Autolycus had been crowned victor in the pancratium at the Panathenaea. And immediately the guests on the couches give their attention to the lad, even though his father is seated beside him. . . . Homer, on the other hand, has not undertaken to tell us anything of the sort even though he has Helen before him."
4. Plutarch *Quaestiones conviviales* vi. prooemium 686B–C.
5. Cicero *De senectute* xiii. 45.
6. Plato *Phaedrus* 265A–B.
7. Plato *Symposium* 206E.
8. *Ibid*. 211B; cf. *Phaedrus* 249D–250C.
9. Plato *Laws* iii. 653B–C.
10. *Ibid*. 666A–667A; cf. 672D.
11. *Ibid*. 670A–671E.

12. Plato *Gorgias* 492C. Cf. *Republic* i. 332D ff., where Polemarchus defines justice as "benefiting friends and harming enemies," and *ibid.* ii. 362C, where Glaucon makes the same action the prerogative and property of the unjust man.

13. Plato *Gorgias*, 507E–508A.

14. Plato *Republic* v. 457D–458D; cf. *ibid.* 461E–464A.

15. *Ibid.* 475C–477E.

16. Plato *Laws* iii. 693B–C.

17. Plato *Republic* ix. 580D–581C.

18. *Ibid.* viii. 558D.

19. *Ibid.* 568A–C.

20. *Ibid.* ix. 572D–573C.

21. Plutarch *Quaestiones conviviales* i. prooemium 612D–E.

22. Methodii *Convivium decem virginum sive de castimonia*, Oratio I. 1. 4 (*Patrologia Graeca*, XVIII, 36B–37A, 44C–45A).

23. John 13:34.

24. John 15:9–10.

25. The history begins properly in the time of the Apostles: cf. I Cor. 11:20–29; II Pet. 2:13; Jude, chap. 12. For the apologetic defense of Christian ἀγάπαι, cf. Tertullian *Apologeticus adversus gentes pro Christianis* 39 (*Patrologia Latina*, I, 531–41); Minucius Felix *Octavius* viii–ix, xxxi (*PL*, III, 266–73, 349–53); Cyprian *Ad Quirinum testimonia contra Judaeos* iii. 3 (*PL*, IV, 733–34). Clement of Alexandria distinguishes between the love of God and of neighbor, which is the celestial banquet in heaven, and the terrestrial banquet: the latter dinner (δεῖπνον) is a consequence of charity (ἀγάπη), but it is not itself charity (*Paedagogus* ii. 1 [*PG*, VIII, 388A]), and Clement sets forth the rules that should govern the conduct of Christians in symposia (*ibid.* 4 [*PG*, VIII, 440–45]). After the establishment of the church the excesses are again subject of criticism; cf. Gregory Nazianzen *Praecepta ad virgines* 117–24 (*PG*, XXXVII, 587–88); Augustine *Epistola* 22. i. 1–6 (*PL*, XXXIII, 90–92). The anonymous *Commentary on Job*, attributed to Origen, urges the importance of fasting and abstinence from excessive food and drink (Book iii [*PG*, XVIII, 506]): "Nisi enim tua misericordia conservaverit, quomodo possumus effugere tanta pericula ciborum sane ac potuum, quae frequenter plus repunt ac serpunt, quam malignae ac venenosae bestiae?"

26. I John 2:15–17: "Love not the world, neither the things that are in the world. If any man love the world, the love (ἀγάπη, *caritas*) of the Father is not in him. For all that is in the world, the lust (ἐπιθυμία, *concupiscentia*) of the flesh, and the lust of the eyes, and the pride of life, is

not of the Father, but of the world. And the world passeth away, and the
lust thereof: but he that doeth the will of God abideth for ever."
    27. Augustine *Confessions* xiii. 9. 10. Cf. *Epistola* 55. x. 18 (*PL*, XXXIII,
212–13); *ibid*. 157. ii. 9 (*PL*, XXXIII, 677).
    28. Augustine *Epistola* 167. iv. 15 (*PL*, XXXIII, 739).
    29. Acts 8:9–13, 18–24; Irenaeus *Contra haereses* i. 23. 1–3 (*PG*, VII,
670–72); *Philosophumena* vi. 1. 7–20, ed. Cruice (Paris, 1860), pp. 243–66.
    30. Augustine *Contra epistolam Manichaei* xiii. 16 (*PL*, XLII, 182–83);
Contra Faustum ii. 4 (*PL*, XLII, 211); *De moribus Manichaeorum* xviii.
65–66 (*PL*, XXXII, 1372–73).
    31. *Marsilio Ficino's Commentary on Plato's "Symposium": The Text and a
Translation*, with an Introduction by S. R. Jayne (Columbia, Mo.: University
of Missouri, 1944). A triple love is distinguished according to their
respective objects and the natural inclinations of men; cf. *Commentary*
vi. 9 (p. 193): "Hence, as we said, a triple Love arises, for we are born or
reared with an inclination to the contemplative, the practical, or the
voluptuous life. If to the contemplative, we are lifted immediately from the
sight of bodily form to the contemplation of the spiritual and divine. If to
the voluptuous, we descend immediately from the sight to the desire to
touch. If to the practical and moral, we remain in the pleasures only of
seeing and the social relations. People of the first type are of such strength
of character that they are exalted most highly; those of the last type are so
weak that they are pressed to the depths; but those of the middle type remain
in the middle region. And so all love begins with sight. But the love of
the contemplative man ascends from sight into the mind; that of the
voluptuous man descends from sight into touch; and that of the practical
man remains in the form of sight. Love of the first is attracted to the highest
daemon rather than to the lowest, that of the second is drawn to the lowest
rather than to the highest, and that of the last remains an equal distance
from both. These three loves have three names: love of the contemplative
man is called divine; that of the practical man, human; and that of the
voluptuous man, animal." The ladder of love takes on both Neoplatonic
and Christian characteristics; cf. *ibid*. v. 6 (p. 175): "Beauty is a certain
vital and spiritual charm (*gratia*) first infused in the Angelic Mind by the
illuminating light of God, thence in the souls of men, the shapes of bodies,
and sounds; through reason, sight, and hearing, it moves our souls and delights
them; in delighting them, it carries them away, and in so doing, inflames
them with burning love." The ascent from body, to soul, to Angelic
Mind, to God, is a progressive emancipation from limitations; cf. *ibid*. vi. 17
(p. 211): "The same comparison which exists among these four exists
among their respective beauties. Certainly, the beauty of the Body consists

in the composition of its many parts; it is bound by space and moves along in time. The beauty of the Soul suffers the changes of time, of course, and contains a multitude of parts, but is free from the limits of space. The beauty of the Angelic Mind, on the other hand, has number alone; it is immune to the other two [space and time]. But the beauty of God suffers none of these limitations. You see the beauty of the Body. Do you wish to see also the beauty of the Soul? Subtract the weight of the matter itself from the bodily form and the limits of space; leave the rest; now you have the beauty of the Soul. Do you wish to see the beauty of the Angelic Mind? Take away now, please, not only the spacial limit of place, but also the sequence of time; keep the multiple composition, and you will find there the beauty of the Angelic Mind. Do you wish still to see the beauty of God? Take away, in addition to those above, that multiple composition of forms, leave the simple form, and there you will have found the beauty of God."

32. The translation of *A Platonick Discourse upon Love by Pico della Mirandola* by Thomas Stanley, author of one of the first histories of philosophy in English (1656), has been edited by E. G. Gardner (Boston: Merrymount Press, 1914). In his Introduction (pp. ix–x) the editor translates the opening section of the fourteenth-century commentary on the canzone of Guido Cavalcanti attributed to Egidius Colonna. "Being in a dark wood, and travelling along a hard and rough path, I rested from my labour, and slept. In my slumber I had this vision. Methought that I ascended a very high mountain, from which was seen almost all the world, and above this mountain there was another even higher, from which things yet more distant were beheld. On the first mountain stood a most beauteous Lady, and before her there was a fire so great that it gave warmth to all the world; on the other mountain, which was higher, stood two Ladies, and between them there was a most fair fountain, to which I was wont to go oftentimes to drink. Wherefore, wishing to go thither to drink, as was my usage, it behoved me to pass in front of the first Lady, and, as I passed, I saw a Squire kneeling before her, to whom the Lady was saying these words: 'Thou knowest me by my face and by my bearing right well, that I am Love.' And he answered her: 'My Lady, it is very sooth.' And the Lady said to him: 'Now hearken to me, and listen well to what I would tell thee. I have sent to the world two messengers of mine, to wit, Solomon and Ovidius Naso; the one led me into the world with music and song, and the other wrought the art wherewith I should be brought. From then until now I have sent no messenger, but those that have spoken of me have done so either for their own desire of knowledge or because they were heated by this fire. I have chosen thee for my third messenger, and this has been done

with reason; for as the first was divine in his sweetness, and the second was a most perfect poet, so art thou a philosopher full of wisdom; and because thou art not a slave of Love, but a friend, I command thee not, but I pray thee to renew my memory in the world, and to tell of my nature and secret conditions, upon which the other speakers have not touched.' Having heard this, that noble Squire answered the Lady, and said: 'My Lady, what you pray of me shall be done, but, because the world is full of divers fashions, tell me the fashion that you would have me adopt in my speech.' And the Lady made reply: 'I will tell thee one condition of mine, which is that I can verily give the desire of speaking, but cannot give the wisdom and the fashion; but hie thee to those Ladies on the mountain, who are the two Philosophies, Moral and Natural, and they will teach thee the fashion of speaking.' " Pico continues the Neoplatonic Christian transformation of the ladder of love to cosmological and theological terms; cf. *A Platonick Discourse* ii. 20 (pp. 43–44): "As when the Ideas descend into the Minde, there ariseth a desire of enjoying that from whence this Ideal Beauty comes; so when the species of sensible Beauty flow into the Eye, there springs a twofold Appetite of Union with that whence this Beauty is deriv'd, one sensuall, the other rational; the Principles of Bestial and Humane Love. If we follow the Sense, we judge the Body, wherein we behold this Beauty, to be its Fountain; whence proceeds a desire of Coition, the most intimate union with it. This is the Love of irrational Creatures. But Reason knows that the Body is so far from being its Original, that it is destructive to it, and the more it is sever'd from the Body, the more it enjoyes its own Nature and Dignity: we must not fix with the species of Sense, in the Body; but refine that species from all reliques of corporeal infection. And because Man may be understood by the Rational Soul, either considered apart, or in its union to the Body; in the first sense, Humane Love is the Image of the Celestial; in the second, Desire of sensible Beauty; this being by the Soul abstracted from matter, and (as much as its nature will allow) made intellectual. The greater part of Men reach no higher than this; others more perfect, remembering that more perfect Beauty which the Soul (before immerst in the Body) beheld, are inflam'd with an incredible desire of reviewing it, in pursuit whereof they separate themselves as much as possible from the Body, of which the Soul (returning to its first Dignity) becomes absolute Mistress. This is the Image of Celestial Love, by which Man ariseth from one perfection to another, till his Soul (wholly united to the Intellect) is made an Angel. Purged from Material dross and transformed into spiritual flame by this Divine Power, he mounts up to the Intelligible Heaven, and happily rests in his Father's bosome." The discourse placed in the mouth of Pietro Bembo in the *Cortegiano* of Baldassare Castiglione ends with a prayer (Count Baldesar Castiglione, *The Book of the Courtier*, trans. L. E. Opdycke [New York: Liveright, 1929], iv. 70 [pp. 302–3]): "What mortal tongue, then, O most holy Love, can praise thee worthily? Most fair, most good, most wise, thou springest from the union of beauty and goodness and divine wisdom, and abidest in that union, and by that union returnest to that union as in a circle. Sweetest bond of the universe, joining things celestial to things terrestrial, thou with benignant sway inclinest the supernal powers to rule the lower powers, and turning the minds of mortals to their origin, joinest them thereto. Thou unitest the elements in concord, movest nature to produce—and that which is born, to the perpetuation of life. Thou unitest things that are separate, givest perfection to the imperfect, likeness to the unlike, friendship to the unfriendly, fruit to the earth, tranquility to the sea, vital light to the heavens. . . . Deign, then, O Lord, to hear our prayers, pour thyself upon our hearts, and with the splendour of thy most holy fire illumine our darkness and, like a trusted guide, in this blind labyrinth show us the true path. . . . Accept our souls, which are offered thee in sacrifice; burn them in that living flame which consumes all mortal dross, to the end that, being wholly separated from the body, they may unite with divine beauty by a perpetual and very sweet bond, and that we, being severed from ourselves, may, like true lovers, be able to transform ourselves into the beloved, and rising above the earth may be admitted to the angels' feast, where, fed on ambrosia and immortal nectar, we may at last die a most happy and living death, as died of old those ancient fathers whose souls thou, by the most glowing power of contemplation, didst ravish from the body and unite with God." In the *Dialoghi d'amore* of Leone Abarbanel or Leone Ebreo, the Platonizing Renaissance conception of Love is harmonized with Judaism; cf. Leone Ebreo, *Dialoghi d'amore: Hebraeische Gedichte*, ed. C. Gebhardt (Heidelberg: Carl Winter, 1929); *The Philosophy of Love (Dialoghi d'amore)* by Leone Ebreo, trans. F. Friedeberg-Seeley and J. H. Barnes (London: Soncino, 1937).

33. *The Table Talk of Martin Luther*, trans. William Hazlitt (London: Bell, 1895), pp. xcviii–c, 7, 14, 19, 20, 22, 23, and *passim*, esp. *Of Discord*, pp. 314–15.

34. S. Freud, *Civilization and Its Discontents*, trans. J. Rivière (New York: Cape & Smith, 1930), pp. 143–44.

35. A. Nygren, *Agape and Eros* (London: Society for Promoting Christian Knowledge, 1939), II, Part II, 466.

36. M. C. D'Arcy, S.J., *The Mind and Heart of Love* (New York: Holt, 1947), pp. 314–22.

NOTES TO CHAPTER II

1. Cf. John Burnet, *Early Greek Philosophy* (3d ed.; London: Black, 1920), p. 31: "It is not very often that Plato allows himself to dwell on the history of philosophy as it was before the rise of ethical and epistemological inquiry; but when he does, he is always illuminating. His artistic gift and his power of entering into the thoughts of other men enabled him to describe the views of early philosophers in a sympathetic manner, and he never, except in a playful and ironical way, sought to read unthought-of meanings into the words of his predecessors. He has, in fact, a historical sense, which was a rare thing in antiquity."

2. Cf. Burnet (*ibid.*, pp. 31–32): "As a rule, Aristotle's statements about early philosophers are far less historical than Plato's. He nearly always discusses the facts from the point of view of his own system, and that system, resting as it does on the deification of the apparent diurnal revolution of the heavens, made it very hard for him to appreciate more scientific views. He is convinced that his own philosophy accomplishes what all previous philosophers had aimed at, and their systems are therefore regarded as 'lisping' attempts to formulate it (*Met.* A. 10. 993ª15). It is also to be noted that Aristotle regards some systems in a much more sympathetic way than others. He is distinctly unfair to the Eleatics, for instance, and in general, wherever mathematical considerations come into play, he is an untrustworthy guide. It is often forgotten that Aristotle derived much of his information from Plato, and we must specially observe that he more than once takes Plato's humorous remarks too literally."

3. For a more extreme disapproval of dialectic and the Platonic philosophy, however, see W. Fite, *The Platonic Legend* (New York: Scribner's, 1934). During the Middle Ages this criticism took the form of disapprobation of Plato's analogical method and metaphorical language; cf. R. McKeon, "Aristotelianism in Western Christianity," in *Environmental Factors in Christian History*, ed. J. T. McNeill, Matthew Spinka, and H. R. Willoughby (Chicago: University of Chicago Press, 1939), pp. 224 ff.

4. F. C. S. Schiller, "From Plato to Protagoras," in *Studies in Humanism* (London: Macmillan, 1907), pp. 22–70; George Grote, *Plato and the Other Companions of Socrates* (London: Murray, 1885), II, 210 ff. and *passim*; *A History of Greece* (London: Murray, 1888), VII, 29 ff.; E. Dupréel, *Les Sophistes: Protagoras, Gorgias, Prodicus, Hippias* (Neuchâtel: Griffon, 1948), pp. 19–25, 37–38, 54–55, 99–101, 125, 189, 263–65, 281–82.

5. *De anima* i. 2. 403ᵇ20 ff.

6. *De caelo* i. 10. 279ᵇ5 ff.

7. *Metaphysica* ii. 1. 993^{b}11 ff.

8. *Ibid.* iii. 1. 995^{a}24 ff.

9. *Ibid.* iv. 4. 1006^{a}5 ff.; *Analytica posteriora* i. 3. 72^{b}5 ff.; *Topica* i. 1. 100^{a}25 ff. and 2. 101^{a}37.

10. *Rhetorica* i. 1. 1355^{a}18 ff.

11. *Physica* viii. 1. 251^{a}8.

12. *Ibid.* ii. 4–6. 195^{b}31 ff.

13. *Ibid.* viii. 9. 265^{b}17 ff.; 7. 260^{a}20 ff.

14. *De caelo* ii. 13. 294^{a}12 ff.

15. *De generatione et corruptione* i. 8. 324^{b}25.

16. *Meteorologica* ii. 1. 353^{b}5 ff.

17. *Ibid.* 7. 365^{a}12 ff.

18. For an exhaustive enumeration and painstaking illustration of such "faults" cf. H. Cherniss, *Aristotle's Criticism of Presocratic Philosophy* (Baltimore: Johns Hopkins Press, 1935). Although the book may be consulted at random with the confidence that one or more errors in Aristotle's citation of his predecessors will be found on almost any page, the reader may be particularly interested in the statement of the method of criticism (Foreword, pp. ix–xiv) and in the enumeration of "common errors which recur in all or many of Aristotle's discussions of the Presocratics" (pp. 359 ff.). Cf. also Cherniss, *Aristotle's Criticism of Plato and the Academy* (Baltimore: Johns Hopkins Press, 1944), Vol. I.

19. *Politica* ii. 1–6. 1261^{a}4–1266^{a}30. In judging Aristotle's selection of points from the *Republic*, it is well to bear in mind that he is quoting from that work primarily in the interests of political doctrine as he understands it and that to his mind a great portion of the *Republic* consists of digressions foreign to the main subject (*ibid.* 6. 1264^{b}39 ff.). The principle of selection is, as usual, determined by Aristotle's philosophy, and the restatement is determined by his terminology and problems, but until an explanation of Socrates' own restatement and selection at the beginning of the *Timaeus* of the arguments he himself presented in the *Republic* makes them square with modern conceptions of historical accuracy, the suspicion of a possible justification should be left to Aristotle's treatment of the same dialogue. There is no Gordian knot in either problem, nor are such drastic devices needed as Cornford's supposition (*Plato's Cosmology* [New York: Harcourt, Brace, 1937], pp. 3–6, 11) that Socrates does not in the *Timaeus* refer to the argument of the *Republic*.

20. *Lives of the Philosophers* i. 1.

21. *Republic* iv. 435E. Plato sometimes seems to attribute this judgment of national characters to education rather than to climate. Since science and therefore education are functions of climate and, conversely, the no-

tion of the influence of climates is a scientific theory, the two explanations are not necessarily contradictory in his dialectic. In the *Laws* (747B), after showing arithmetical studies to be valuable for banishing meanness and covetousness from the souls of pupils, Plato adds that if the legislator does not make use of such instruction "he will unintentionally create in them, instead of wisdom, the habit of craft, which evil tendency may be observed in Egyptians and Phoenicians and many other races." Cf., on the other hand, the praise of progressive methods used by the Egyptians for teaching mathematics to the young (819B).

22. *Epinomis* 987D.

23. *Timaeus* 22B.

24. Cf., for example, *Politica* iii. 14. 1285ª19: "For barbarians being more servile than Hellenes, and Asiatics than Europeans, do not rebel against a despotic government. Such royalties have the nature of tyrannies because the people are by nature slaves; but there is no danger of their being overthrown, for they are hereditary and legal."

25. *Op. cit.*, p. 313, n. 5.

26. The four arguments or "paradoxes" of Zeno concerning motion are stated in Aristotle's *Physica* (vi. 9. 239ᵇ5 ff.; cf. *ibid*. 2. 233ª21 ff.; viii. 8. 263ª4 ff.; and *Topica* viii. 8. 160ᵇ8 ff.). Our information concerning the "paradoxes" of the one and the many are preserved from the report of Eudemus in his *Physics* and Alexander's commentary on it as quoted by Simplicius.

27. *Physica* i. 3. 186ᵇ1 ff.

28. *Metaphysica* iii. 4. 1001ᵇ6 ff.; *Physica* iv. 2. 209ª23 ff. and 3. 210ᵇ23 ff.

29. *De generatione et corruptione* ii. 9. 335ª24 ff.; *Metaphysica* i. 3. 984ª17 and 4. 985ª11.

30. *De generatione et corruptione* i. 2. 315ª34 ff.

31. Cf. *Sophistes* 246A; *Timaeus* 46D, etc. Diogenes Laertius (ix. 40) supplies a reason for Plato's failure to take note of Democritus: "Plato, who mentions almost all the early philosophers, never once alludes to Democritus, not even where it would be necessary to controvert him, obviously because he knew that he would have to match himself against the prince of philosophers." It is indicative of the influence of Aristotle on the interpretation of the history of philosophy that scholars have more recently treated the philosophy of Plato, notwithstanding that silence, as the perfect opposite to that of Democritus, much as Aristotle treats it. According to Erich Frank (*Plato und die sogenannten Pythagoreer* [Halle, 1923], pp. 119 ff.), Plato's thought is, notwithstanding his failure to mention Democritus, a "mighty dialogue with materialism"; and Paul Shorey (*What Plato Said* [Chicago: University of Chicago Press, 1933], p. 345) finds the influence

of Democritus throughout Plato. What Aristotle presented as a dialectical opposition of ideas is made in the interpretation of passages in the dialogues into a historical influence.

32. *Meno* 76C; *Laws* x. 889B; cf. *Sophistes* 243E; *Theaetetus* 152E; *Politicus* 272D; *Timaeus* 45C.

33. *Phaedrus* 270A; *Phaedo* 96A ff.; *Apology* 26D; cf. *Hippias Major* 283A and *Timaeus* 46C.

34. There are several references to the Sophists in the *Ethica Nicomachea* (ix. 1. 1164ᵃ22, 31; x. 9. 1180ᵇ35, 1181ᵃ12), but they have to do with their actions and professions as teachers rather than with their doctrines. There are similarly two references to Gorgias in the *Politica*, one contrasting his method of defining the virtues (ironically) with that of Socrates (i. 13. 1260ᵃ27 ff.), the other citing his (ironical) definition of citizens (*ibid.* iii. 2. 1275ᵇ27).

35. *Timaeus* 29B ff. and *Politicus* 269D, 272B–273E.

36. *Timaeus* 46D. Cf. *ibid.* 47E: "The foregoing part of our discourse, save for a small portion, has been an exposition of the operations of Reason; but we must also furnish an account of what comes into existence through Necessity. For, in truth, this Cosmos in its origin was generated as a compound, from the combination of Necessity and Reason. And inasmuch as Reason was controlling Necessity by persuading her to conduct to the best end the most part of the things coming into existence, thus and thereby it came about, through Necessity yielding to intelligent persuasion, that this Universe of ours was being in this wise constructed at the beginning." Cf. *ibid.* 68E.

37. Cf. the myth of the *Politicus* 269C; *Laws* iii, iv, and x (892B and 903B ff.); the myth of the *Republic* x. 616C; *Timaeus* 20E–25C; *Critias* 108E ff.; the myth of the *Protagoras* 320D ff. for some of the numerous forms which the dialectical oppositions narrated in such conflicts can take.

38. *Physica* ii. 7–9. 198ᵃ35 ff.; cf. *Analytica posteriora* ii. 11. 94ᵇ27; *De partibus animalium* i. 1. 639ᵇ12 ff.

39. *Timaeus* 26C, 29D, 30B, 48D. Cf. *Laws* iii. 683E: "For we have come to the same view now, as it appears, in dealing with facts of history; so that we shall be examining it with reference not to a mere abstraction, but to real events."

40. *Republic* ii. 369B ff.

41. Questions of value, even in the age of Cronus, are referred to dialectic as a criterion (*Politicus* 272B–D) and in other ages to imitate the age of Cronus is to "order both our homes and our States in obedience to the immortal element within us, giving to reason's ordering the name of 'law' " (*Laws* iv. 714A).

42. *Meteorologica* i. 3. 339^{b}28; cf. *Politica* ii. 5. 1264^{a}1; vii. 10. 1329^{b}24 and, for the cosmological and biological basis of the theory, *De generatione et corruptione* ii. 10. 336^{b}1 ff.

43. *Metaphysica* xii. 8. 1074^{b}1.

44. *Ibid.* i. 1. 980^{a}26; cf. 981^{b}13.

45. *Ibid.* ii. 1. 993^{a}30.

NOTES TO CHAPTER III

1. *Poetica* 13. 1453^{a}12–23.

2. Thucydides *History of the Peloponnesian War* i. 126–27. The identity of the matricide Alcmaeon with the ancestor of the Athenian family of the Alcmaeonidae is doubtful; cf. Bethe in Pauly-Wissowa-Kroll, *Real-Encyclopaedie*, Vol. I, col. 1554, ll. 48–64, *s.v.* "Alkmaion." Uncertainties in historical evidence, however, serve as frequently to advance as to impede the fortunes of political debate and the victories of international rhetoric.

3. *History of the Peloponnesian War* i. 22.

4. *Ibid.* 23.

5. Herodotus *Histories* vii. 104.

6. *Ibid.* viii. 144.

7. Thucydides *History of the Peloponnesian War* i. 68–70.

8. *Ibid.* 120–21.

9. Cf. R. McKeon, "The Problems of Education in a Democracy," in *The Bertrand Russell Case*, eds. J. Dewey and H. M. Kallen (New York: Viking Press, 1941), pp. 101–9.

10. *History of the Peloponnesian War* ii. 65.

11. *Gorgias* 515C–E.

12. *Politica* ii. 12. 1274^{a}5–11; *Constitution of Athens* 27.

13. *Meno* 94A–B; *Protagoras* 319E–320B.

NOTES TO CHAPTER IV

1. *Republic* x. 607B–C.

2. For a more detailed statement of meanings of "imitation" and of related terms in Plato's philosophy cf. R. McKeon, "Literary Criticism and the Concept of Imitation in Antiquity," in *Critics and Criticism: Ancient and Modern*, ed. R. S. Crane (Chicago: University of Chicago Press, 1952), pp. 149–59.

3. Plato *Timaeus* 28A–29A.

4. *Ibid.* 48E–49A, 50C–51B.

5. *Ibid.* 29B–D.

6. Plato *Phaedrus* 265A–B.

7. *Ibid.* 245A.

8. *Ibid.* 248D–E.

9. Plato *Ion* 533D–534E.

10. Plato *Meno* 99A–D.

11. Plato *Sophist* 236C–E.

12. Isocrates *Against the Sophists* 15–18. For a fuller statement of the rhetorical analysis of "imitation" in antiquity cf. McKeon, *op. cit.*, pp. 168–72.

13. For a more detailed statement of the meaning of "imitation" and of related terms in Aristotle, cf. McKeon, *op. cit.*, pp. 160–68.

14. Aristotle *De generatione et corruptione* ii. 10. 336ª31–337ª7.

15. Aristotle *Metaphysica* xii. 10. 1075ª11–1076ª4. Cf. also *Politica* ii. 2. 1261ª37–ᵇ4.

16. Diogenes Laertius *Lives of Eminent Philosophers* iii. 25: "And, as he [Plato] was the first to attack the views of almost all his predecessors, the question was raised why he makes no mention of Democritus." Cf. *ibid.* ix. 40: "Aristoxenus in his *Historical Notes* affirms that Plato wished to burn all the writings of Democritus that he could collect, but that Amyclas and Clinias the Pythagoreans prevented him, saying that there was no advantage in doing so, for already the books were widely circulated. And there is clear evidence for this in the fact that Plato, who mentions almost all the early philosophers, never once alludes to Democritus, not even where it would be necessary to controvert him, obviously because he knew that he would have to match himself against the prince of philosophers, for whom, to be sure, Timon has this meed of praise; 'Such is the wise Democritus, the guardian of discourse, keen-witted disputant, among the best I ever read.' "

17. Sextus Empiricus *Adversus mathematicos* viii. 6: "Plato and Democritus supposed that only intelligibles are true; but whereas Democritus did so because nothing sensible exists by nature—since the atoms which compose all things possess a nature which is void of every sensible quality—Plato did so because sensibles are always becoming and never being, as their substance keeps flowing like a river, so that it does not remain the same for two moments together, and (as Asclepiades said) does not admit of being pointed out twice owing to the speed with which it flows."

18. Plutarch *Adversus Colotem* 8. 1110; cf. H. Diels, *Die Fragmente der Vorsokratiker* (5th ed.; Berlin: Weidmann, 1935), Demokritos, A 57, B 141, 167, Vol. II, pp. 98–99, 170, 178.

19. Diels, Demokritos, B 33, p. 153. Cf. *ibid.*, B 39, p. 155: "One must either be good or imitate a good man," and B 154, p. 173: "We have become

pupils of the animals in the most important things: of the spiders in weaving and darning, of the swallow in housebuilding, and of the songsters such as swan and nightingale in singing, through imitation (κατὰ μίμησιν)."

20. Diels, Leukippos, A 29, 30, 31, pp. 78, 79; Demokritos, A 1, 51, 121, 135 (51), pp. 84, 98, 112, 115.

21. Diels, Demokritos, A 49, B 9, 117, 125, pp. 97, 139, 166, 168.

22. *Ibid.*, B 26, 142, pp. 148, 170.

23. *Ibid.*, B 145, 82, 302, pp. 171, 160, 222.

24. *Ibid.*, B 59, p. 157.

25. *Ibid.*, B 17, 18, 21, pp. 146, 147. Cf. also *ibid.*, B 112, p. 164: "It is the mark of the divine understanding to be always considering something beautiful."

26. *Ibid.*, B 194, 207, 105, pp. 185, 187, 163.

27. Plato *Protagoras* 325E–326D.

28. Isocrates *Antidosis* 246–48.

29. Nature or natural ability is developed by three means in the training of an orator: "art," which consists of precepts; "imitation," which consists of use of a model; and "exercise," which consists of practice in speaking. Cf. Cicero *De oratore* ii. 21. 89: "Assuredly Nature herself was leading him into the grand and glorious style of Crassus but could never have made him proficient enough, had he not pressed forward on the same way by careful imitation, and formed the habit of speaking with every thought and all his soul fixed in contemplation of Crassus." Cf. *ibid.* 22. 90: "Let this then be my first precept, that we show the student whom to imitate, and to imitate in such a way as to strive with all possible care to attain the most excellent qualities of his model. Next let practice be added, whereby in imitating he may reproduce the pattern of his choice and not express him as time and again I have known many imitators do, who in imitating hunt after such characteristics as are easily imitated or even abnormal and possibly faulty." Cf. *ibid.* 23. 98: "And indeed we see that there are many who imitate no man, but gain their object by nature, without following the likeness of any model." Cf. *ibid.* 8. 34: "Can any music be composed that is any sweeter than a well-balanced speech? Is any poem better rounded than an artistic period in prose? What actor gives keener pleasure by his imitation of real life than your orator affords in his conduct of some real case?"

30. Cicero *Orator* 2. 8–9.

31. Cicero *De natura deorum* i. 32. 90; 37. 103.

32. *Ibid.* ii. 32. 81–82. Cf. *ibid.* 22. 57–58: "For he [*sc.* Zeno] holds that the special function of art is to create and generate, and that what in the processes of our arts is done by the hand is done with far more skillful craftsmanship by nature, that is, as I have said, by that 'craftsmanlike'

(*artificiosus*) fire which is the teacher of the other arts. And on this theory, while each department of nature is 'craftsmanlike,' in the sense of having a method or path marked out for it to follow, the nature of the world itself, which encloses and contains all things in its embrace, is called by Zeno not merely 'craftsmanlike' (*artificiosus*) but actually a 'craftsman,' whose foresight plans out the work to serve its use and purpose in every detail."

33. Plotinus *Enneads* v. 8. 1. Plotinus and Epictetus both liked to refer to the universe as a poem or a drama. Cf. *Enneads* iii. 2. 17: "In the true poem, which men endowed with poetic nature imitate in part, the soul is the actor; it receives its role from the poet of the universe. . . ." Cf. also Epictetus *Encheiridion* 17: "Remember that you are an actor in a play, the character of which is determined by the Playwright. . . ." Cf. *Discourse* i. 29. 41; iv. 7. 13; Frag. 11.

34. Seneca *Ad Lucilium epistula* 65. 3.

35. Marcus Aurelius *To Himself* xi. 10.

36. Augustine *De vera religione* 31. 57 (*Patrologia Latina*, XXXIV, 147).

37. Augustine *Contra Faustum Manichaeum* xxxii. 20 (*PL*, XLII, 509).

38. Augustine *De Trinitate* iii. 4. 9 (*PL*, XLII, 873).

39. Augustine returns repeatedly to the distinction between image and likeness in the course of his explications of Scripture. Cf. Gen. 1:26–27: "And God said, Let us make man in our image and likeness: and let them have dominion over all the earth, and over every creeping thing that creepeth on the earth. And God created man in his own image." Cf. Gen. 5:1 and 9:6; Wisd. of Sol. 2:23; Eccles. 17:1. Cf., also, I Cor. 11:7. There is, moreover, a Platonic turn in the biblical use of "image" and "likeness." In the Platonic dialectic all things, including man, are imitations, and virtue and knowledge consist in imitation, reminiscence, and participation, but art which is an imitation of an imitation has consequences inconsistent with knowledge, virtue, and beauty. In the Old Testament man is made in the image and likeness of God, but he is prohibited from making images and likenesses. Cf. Exod. 20:4: "Thou shalt not make unto thee a graven image (*sculptile*) nor any likeness (*similitudo*) of anything that is in heaven above, or that is in the earth beneath, or that is in the water under the earth." Deut. 5:8 repeats the injunction in the same terms, *sculptile* and *similitudo*, but in Deut. 4:15–18 the terms employed are *sculpta similitudo* and *imago*; in Ps. 97:7 they are *sculptile* and *simulacrum*.

40. Augustine *De Genesi ad litteram liber imperfectus* 16. 57 (*PL*, XXXIV, 242). Cf. *De diversis quaestionibus 83*, Quaest. 74 (*PL*, XL, 85–86): "Image and equality and likeness must be distinguished. For where there is an image, there is necessarily a likeness but not necessarily an equality; where there is an equality, there is necessarily a likeness,

but not necessarily an image; where there is a likeness there is not necessarily either an image or an equality. Where there is an image there is necessarily a likeness but not necessarily an equality, as there is an image of man in a mirror because it is expressed of him; there is also a likeness, but not an equality, because many things are lacking in the image which are present in the thing of which it is expressed. Where there is an equality, there is necessarily a likeness, but not necessarily an image, as when there is an equality in two comparable eggs there is also a likeness, for whatever is present in one is present also in the other, but there is no image because neither is expressed of the other. Where there is a likeness there is not necessarily either an image or an equality, for every egg in so far as it is an egg is like every other egg, but a partridge egg, although in so far as it is an egg it is like a hen's egg, is nonetheless neither an image of it, since it is not expressed of it, nor equal, since it is smaller and of another species of animal. But when it is said, 'not necessarily,' it should also be understood that it can sometimes be the case. Therefore, there can be an image in which there is also an equality, as image, equality, and likeness would be found in parents and children if the interval of time were lacking, for the likeness of the son is expressed of the father so that it is rightly called an image, and it can be of the same dimensions, so that it is also rightly called an equality, except in so far as the parent preceded in time."

41. Augustine *De musica* i. 4. 6 (*PL*, XXXII, 1086–87).

42. The term "imitation" is prominent in Augustine's controversies against the Pelagians, for the problem of original sin turned on the question whether sin is transmitted by generation or by imitation. When Augustine taunted Julian to carry out his promise to explain the homonyms and equivocal terms that enter into the discussion of "imitation" (*Opus imperfectum contra Julianum* ii. 51 [*PL*, XLV, 1163]), Julian distinguishes between *generation*, which is properly imputed to the sexes, and *imitation*, which is always of souls. Good imitation is distinguished from bad by citing exhortations and prohibitions from Scripture. Imitation is good when it is of God, the angels, and the apostles: of God (Matt. 5:48)—"Ye therefore shall be perfect, as your heavenly Father is perfect"; of the angels (Matt. 6:10)—"Thy will be done, as in Heaven, so on earth"; of the apostles (I Cor. 11:1)—"Be ye imitators of me, even as I also am of Christ." Imitation is bad when it is of the devil, men, and animals: of the devil (Wisd. of Sol. 2:25)—"They imitate him who are of his heart"; of men (Matt. 6:16)—"Be not, as the hypocrites, of sad countenance: for they disfigure their face, that they may be seen of men to fast"; of animals (Ps. 31:9)—"Be ye not as a horse, or as the mule, which have no understandings." The error of the Pelagians concerning imitation, according to

Augustine, arises from their supposition that imitator and what is imitated must have the same nature. Cf. *Opus imperfectum contra Julianum* vi. 34. (*PL*, XLV, 1588–89): "For imitation is in the will; but when it is good, 'the will,' as it is written (Prov. 8:35), 'is prepared by the Lord.' Therefore no one imitates unless he has willed, but man dies and rises again, willy nilly. Moreover, imitation itself does not always require that that which is to be imitated and that which imitates be of the same nature: otherwise we would not be able to imitate the justice and piety of Angels whose nature is diverse from ours, which nonetheless we request of the Lord in prayer when we say, 'Thy will Be done, as in heaven, so on earth' (Matt. 6:10), as you have yourself confessed. Nor would we imitate God the Father, whose nature is far different from ours, yet the Lord says, 'Be as your Father who is in heaven' (Matt. 5:48); and it is said by the prophet (Lev. 11:44): 'Sanctify yourselves therefore and be ye holy; for I am holy.' It does not follow therefore that we are not able to imitate Christ because he was in the world in the likeness of sinful flesh, whereas we are in sinful flesh." Among other texts frequently cited are I Cor. 4:16: "I beseech you therefore, be ye imitators of me," and Eph. 5:1: "Be ye therefore imitators of God, as beloved children"; cf., also, Matt. 11:29 and 16:24.

43. Bonaventura *Collationes in Hexaëmeron* xii. 2–3 (*Opera omnia S. Bonaventurae* [Quaracchi: Typographia Collegii S. Bonaventurae, 1891], V, 385a). Alexander of Hales entitles one of the questions treated in his *Summa theologica* "On the Creation according to quality or on created Beauty" (*Summa theologica* Lib. I, Pars I, Inquis. I, Tract. 2, Quaest. 3: "De creatura secundum qualitatem seu de pulcritudine creati" ([Quaracchi: Typographia Collegii S. Bonaventurae, 1928], II, 99–108). The editors of this edition devote a special section of their Introduction to the aesthetics of Alexander (Sec. 4: "De aesthetica Alexandri Halensis," pp. xl–xlii). Alexander's argument is that the universe is beautiful because it exhibits the traces of divine beauty (*ibid.*, Inquis. I, Tract. II, Quaest. 3, cap. 5, n. 81 [II, 301a]: "Pulcritudo ergo creaturae est vestigium quoddam perveniendi per cognitionem ad pulcritudinem increatam"; cf. *ibid.*, n. 40, p. 55). Alexander and Bonaventura distinguish two aspects of artistic creation—what is made within and what is depicted or sculpted without. These may lead to the distinction of two kinds of work, that of pure imagination, such as the plastic representation of the devil whom one has never seen, and works of imitation, such as portraits, or it may be used to distinguish two aspects of any work of art, for even the portrait is a representation of the artist's conception of the model. The "image" is thus at once expressive of the genius of the artist and imitative of an existent or imag-

ined reality (cf. Bonaventura *Commentaria in sententiarum Librum I*, Dist. XXXI, Pars II, Art. 1, Quaest. 1 [*Opera omnia*, I, 540]).

44. Bonaventura *Commentaria in sententiarum Librum II*, Dist. XVI, Dubium 4 (*Opera omnia*, II, 407b–408a).

45. Bonaventura *In Hexaëmeron* xii. 14–17 (*Opera omnia*, V, 386b–387b).

46. *Ibid.* xiii. 12 (*Opera omnia*, V, 390a).

47. Bonaventura *Commentaria in sententiarum Librum I*, Dist. I, Pars I, Art. unicus, Quaest. 2, ad 4 (*Opera omnia*, I, 73). Cf. É. Gilson, *La Philosophie de Saint Bonaventure* (Paris: Vrin, 1924), chap. vii, "L'Analogie Universelle." Cf. also Thomas Aquinas *Summa theologica*, Ia, Quaest. 45, Art. 7, and *Contra Gentiles*, Pars I, cap. 13, for his treatment of the distinction between *vestigium* and *imago*. Duns Scotus draws up a systematic scheme in which he locates *vestige* and *image* in a context of related terms. Cf. *Collationes* xxxv (Joannis Duns Scoti, *Opera omnia* [Paris: Vives, 1891], V, 288–89): "The difference between an image (*imago*), a shadow (*umbra*), and a vestige or footprint (*vestigium*) and a likeness (*similitudo*) must be stated.—To understand this difference it must be known that all of them involve relation and respect; but a *likeness* does not involve causality, while a *vestige* does involve causality, according to Augustine in question 64 of the *Book of 83 Questions.*—A *shadow* has a confused conformity to an interposed body. I say *confused* because seeing a shadow, we know the interposed body, but we do not know *what figure* it has, since a rotund body sometimes forms a different figure in shadow.—An *image* represents the thing, not as genus or species alone, but as individual and as lineaments, that is, as it is long, broad, etc.—A *vestige* represents the thing in a medium manner: more perfectly than a *shadow* and less perfectly than an *image.* . . . A *vestige* differs from an *image*, because it represents a quantitative *part*, while an *image* represents a *whole*, not however because the *vestige* represents a *universal*, while the *image* represents a *particular*. Therefore, since it is left by the passage of a part, like to the part, it is an *image* of the *part* and a *vestige* of the *whole*, because it represents the *whole* animal by reason of the *part*." The specific difference between *vestige* and *image* can be stated in terms of imitation; cf. *Opus Oxoniense*, Book I, Dist. III, Quest. ll, n. 517 (*B. Ioannis Duns Scoti Commentaria Oxoniensia*, ed. M. F. Garcia [Quaracchi: Collegium S. Bonaventurae, 1912], I, 472): "As was said in the question on the *vestige*, I say that the *image* is representative of the whole, and in this it differs from the *vestige* which is representative of the *part*; for if the whole body were impressed in dust, as the foot is impressed, what is left behind in the former case would be the *image* of the *whole*, just as what is left behind in the latter case is an *image* of the *part*

and a *vestige* of the *whole*.—However, this expressive conformity of the whole does not suffice, but *imitation* is required, for according to Augustine in question 74 of the *Book of 83 Questions*, in so far as two eggs are like, one is not the image of the other, because it is not formed to imitate it; and therefore it is required that the image be formed to *imitate* that of which it is the image and to *express* it."

48. Bonaventura *Commentaria in sententiarum Librum I*, Dist. XXI, Pars II, Art. 1, Quaest. 3, ad 5 (*Opera omnia*, I, 544).

49. Aristotle *Topics* vi. 2. 140ª14–15.

50. Bonaventura *Commentaria in sententiarum Librum I*, Dist. XXXI, Pars II, Art. 1, Quaest. 1, Contra 4 (*Opera omnia*, I, 540a).

51. Bacon, *Novum organum*, Book I, Aphorism 11.

52. Bacon, *The Dignity and Advancement of Learning*, Book V, chap. ii.

53. Bacon, *Novum organum*, Book I, Aphorism 129.

54. Bacon, *The Dignity and Advancement of Learning*, Book II, chap. xiii.

55. *Ibid.*

56. Bacon, *Novum organum*, Book I, Aphorism 23.

57. Bacon, *The Dignity and Advancement of Learning*, Book VII, chaps. i–iii.

58. Descartes, *Discours de la méthode*, Première partie (*Œuvres de Descartes*, ed. C. Adam and P. Tannery [Paris: Cerf, 1902], VI, 4).

59. *Ibid.* (*Œuvres*, VI, 10).

60. *Ibid.*, Quatrième partie (*Œuvres*, VI, 28). Descartes returns to the analogy of the theater and the world in another context in the *Cogitationes privatae* (*Œuvres*, X, 213): "Ut comoedi, moniti ne in fronte appareat pudor, personam induunt: sic ego, hoc mundi theatrum conscensurus, in quo hactenus spectator existiti, larvatus prodeo."

61. *Ibid.*, Sixième partie, (*Œuvres*, VI, 68).

62. *Ibid.* (*Œuvres*, VI, 71).

63. *Regulae ad directionem ingenii*, Regula 1 (*Œuvres*, X, 359–60).

64. *Olympica* (*Œuvres*, X, 179).

65. *Ibid.* (*Œuvres*, X, 184; cf. p. 217).

66. *Regulae ad directionem ingenii*, Regula 8 (*Œuvres*, X, 395): ". . . atque si statim in secundo gradu illuminationis naturam non possit agnoscere, enumerabit, per regulam septimam, alias omnes potentias naturales, ut ex alicujus alterius cognitione saltem per *imitationem*, de qua postea, hanc etiam intelligat. . . ." (Italics mine.)

67. *Ibid.* (*Œuvres*, X, 397): "Haec methodus siquidem illas ex mechanicis artibus *imitatur*, quae non aliarum ope indigent, sed tradunt ipsaemet quomodo sua instrumenta facienda sint." (Italics mine.)

68. *Ibid.*, Regula 14 (*Œuvres*, X, 438–39). Systematic doubt is explained similarly by an analogy to painting in the *Recherche de la vérité par la lumière naturelle* (*Œuvres*, X, 507–8): the imagination of children is compared to a blank tablet on which ideas are set forth like portraits drawn of things from nature. The senses, inclination, instructors, and the understanding are the painters. The understanding, which is the best, comes last and spends many years of apprenticeship, following the example of its masters without daring to correct their faults. The best device, under the circumstances, is to erase all images and to start the picture anew rather than waste time correcting them.

69. *Discours de la méthode*, Cinquième partie (*Œuvres*, VI, 43–44).

70. *Ibid.* (*Œuvres*, VI, 56).

71. *Ibid.*, Première partie (*Œuvres*, VI, 7).

72. Descartes, *Epistola VI*, "Censura quarumdam Epistolarum Domini Balzacii" (*Œuvres*, I, 7).

73. *Epistola DXLIX à Chanut* (*Œuvres*, V, 327). Cf. E. Krantz, *Essai sur l'esthétique de Descartes: Étudiée dans les rapports de la doctrine cartésienne avec la littérature classique française au XVIIᵉ siècle* (Paris: Germer Baillière, 1882), p. 78.

74. *Epistola VI* (*Œuvres*, I, 7).

75. *Ibid.* (*Œuvres*, I, 7–8). Descartes develops this analysis of literary qualities in defense of M. de Balzac. According to F. Ogier, the fault of which De Balzac was accused was imitation. His accusers could not deny that what he said was excellent, but they held that he did nothing but resay them and that he was praised for the virtues of others rather than for his own. "They add that sometimes he writes in another fashion than artisans speak, that his style is not popular enough, that he has a good opinion of himself, that he is sad when he is ill and that he finds a worse taste in pain than did the Stoic philosophers" (*Apologie pour Monsieur de Balzac* [Paris: Jolly, 1673], pp. 5–6). He defends De Balzac by criticizing a blind deference to the authority of the ancients, since they themselves made progress by improving on the models they used, by distinguishing between imitating and robbing the ancients, and, finally, by setting in opposition to the theft and imitation of mediocre spirits the emulation by which heroic spirits advance beyond their models.

76. Cf. Krantz, *op. cit.*, p. 93, where the argument is advanced that the *Art poétique* plays the same role in the history of literary criticism that the *Discours de la méthode* plays in the history of philosophy: the foundations of both are laid in self-knowledge, in the *cogito* of the thinker and in the self-examination of the poet; and since the essence of the beautiful is the true, according to the *Art poétique*, the criterion of beauty, like that of truth, is

found in clarity, and the chief problems of poetry are the rules for the expression of beauty. Cf., also, Lanson, "L'Influence de la philosophie cartésienne sur la littérature française," *Revue de la métaphysique et de morale*, IV (1896), 517.

77. Thomas Hobbes, *Leviathan*, Introduction (*The English Works of Thomas Hobbes*, ed. W. Molesworth [London: Bohn, 1839], III, ix).

78. *Ibid.*, Part I, chap. i (*Works*, III, 1–3).

79. *Ibid.*, Part IV, chap. xlv (*Works*, III, 648–49).

80. *The Answer of Mr. Hobbes to Sir William Davenant's Preface before Gondibert* (*Works*, IV, 443–44). (Italics Hobbes's.)

81. *Ibid.* (*Works*, IV, 445).

82. *Ibid.* (*Works*, IV, 449–50).

83. *Ibid.* (*Works*, IV, 453).

84. Hobbes, *The Iliads and Odysses of Homer*, "To the Reader, concerning the Virtues of an Heroic Poem" (*Works*, X, iii–iv).

85. N. Malebranche, *Méditations chrétiennes*, ed. H. Gouhier, *IV. Méditation* (Paris: Aubier, 1928), pp. 65–69.

86. Malebranche, *De la recherche de la vérité*, ed. F. Bouillier, II, 1, chap. 7, ii (Paris: Garnier, 1879), I, 166.

87. Malebranche, *Entretiens sur la métaphysique et sur la religion*, ed. P. Fontana, Cinquième entretien (Paris: Colin, 1922), I, 122.

88. *De la recherche de la vérité*, II, 3, chap. 1, iii, p. 235.

89. *Ibid.*, chaps. 3, 4, and 5.

90. *Ibid.*, IX⁰ *Éclaircissement*, Sur II, 3, chap. 3 (II, 367–68). Malebranche quotes Quintilian (*Institutio oratoria* viii. 2. 12) for evidence that obscurity is employed deliberately to gain a reputation for erudition. His analysis of imitation, likewise, shows points of similarity to Quintilian's (*ibid.* x. 2. 2–3): "And it is a universal rule of life that we should wish to copy what we approve in others. It is for this reason that boys copy the shapes of letters that they may learn to write, and that musicians take the voices of their teachers, painters the works of their predecessors, and peasants the principles of agriculture which have been proved in practice, as models for their imitation. In fact, we may note that the elementary study of every branch of learning is directed by reference to some definite standard that is placed before the learner. We must, in fact, either be like or unlike those who have proved their excellence. It is rare for nature to produce such resemblance, which is more often the result of imitation."

91. Kant, *Critique of Pure Reason*, "Preface to the Second Edition" (1787), B xvi–xvii.

92. Boethius *Consolation of Philosophy* v. prosa iv. 75–77: "Omne enim quod cognoscitur non secundum sui uim sed secundum cognoscentium

potius comprehenditur facultatem." Cf., also, *ibid.* 92–94: "nam superior comprehendendi uis amplectitur inferiorem, inferior uero ad superiorem nullo modo consurgit," and 115–20: "Uidesne igitur ut in cognoscendo cuncta sua potius facultate quam eorum quae cognoscuntur utantur? Neque id iniuria; nam cum omne iudicium iudicantis actus existat, necesse est ut suam quisque operam non ex aliena sed ex propria potestate perficiat." Poema iv, which immediately follows, treats satirically the Stoic analysis of the impressions of sense in terms of marks on a blank tablet and images in a mirror. It should be noted that the Latin word *iudicium* as used in the above passage is Cicero's translation for both κριτήριον and κρίσις; cf. Cicero *Academica* ii. 142: "One view of criterion (*iudicium*) is that of Protagoras, who holds that what seems true to each person is true for each person, another is that of the Cyrenaics, who hold that there is no criterion whatever except the inward emotions (*permotio intima*), another that of Epicurus, who places the whole criterion (*omne iudicium*) in the senses and in notions of things and in pleasure; Plato however held that the whole criterion of truth and truth itself is detached from opinions and from the senses and belongs to the mere activity of thought and to the mind." Cf. also Augustine *De civitate Dei* viii. 7, where he contrasts the Platonic logic to that of the Epicureans, who placed the criterion of truth (*iudicium veritatis*) in the bodily senses and that of the Stoics, who loved the art of disputation called dialectic and thought it to be derived from the senses from which the mind receives notions of those things which it explicates in definition. Augustine speculates on how the Stoics, when they affirmed only a wise man to be beautiful, had any notion of such beauty from their senses.

93. Diogenes Laertius *Lives of Eminent Philosophers* vii. 45–46: "An imagination is an imprint on the soul: the name having been appropriately borrowed from the imprint made by the seal upon the wax. There are two species of imagination, the one apprehensive, the other non-apprehensive. The apprehensive imagination, which they take to be the criterion of reality, is defined as that which proceeds from a real object, agrees with that object itself, and has been imprinted seal-fashion and stamped upon the mind; the non-apprehensive imagination is defined as that which does not proceed from any real object, or, if it does, fails to agree with the reality itself, not being clear and distinct." Cf. *ibid.* 49–51: "The Stoics agree to put in the forefront the doctrine of imagination and sensation, inasmuch as the criterion by which the truth of things is tested is generically an imagination, and again the theory of assent and that of apprehension and thought, which precedes all the rest, cannot be stated apart from imagination. For imagination comes first; then thought, which is capable of expressing itself,

puts into the form of a proposition that which the subject receives from an imagination. . . . According to them, some imaginations are aesthetic [i.e., sensuous] and others are not: the aesthetic imaginations are the impressions conveyed through one or more sense-organs, while the non-aesthetic imaginations are those received through the mind itself, as is the case with incorporeal things and all the other imaginations which are received by reason. Of aesthetic imaginations some come from real objects and are accompanied by yielding and assent on our part. But there also are imaginations that are only appearances (ἔμφασις), purporting, as it were, to come from real objects." Cf. Galen, *Historia philosopha* (H. Diels, *Doxographi Graeci* 91 [Berlin: De Gruyter, 1929], p. 635): "The Stoics held the senses always to be true but imaginations to be, some true, some false, and they held that sensations can fall into error in only one way and things known intellectually in two, for imagination is both of sensibles and intelligibles." Diogenes Laertius adds that the Stoics also divided imaginations into rational (λογική) and irrational, artistic (τεχνική) and nonartistic. Cf. Sextus Empiricus *Adversus mathematicos* vii. 227–60. According to Sextus, the Stoics also made a fourfold division of imaginations according to probability: some being probable, some improbable, some both probable and improbable, and some neither probable nor improbable.

94. Diogenes Laertius vii. 100–101.

95. Cicero *De officiis* i. 4. 14: "And it is no mean manifestation of Nature and Reason that man is the only animal that has a feeling for order, for propriety, for moderation in word and deed. And so no other animal has a sense of beauty, loveliness, harmony in the visible world; and Nature and Reason, extending the analogy of this from the world of sense to the world of spirit, find that beauty, consistency, order are far more to be maintained in thought and deed, and the same Nature and Reason are careful to do nothing in an improper or unmanly fashion, and in every thought and deed to do or think nothing capriciously." Cf., also, *ibid*. i. 36. 130.

96. Cicero *Tusculan Disputations* iv. 13. 31.

97. Sextus Empiricus *Adversus mathematicos* vii. 203–4: "Epicurus asserts that there are two things which are correlative—namely, imagination and opinion,—of which imagination, which he also terms 'evidence' [i.e., 'clearness'], is constantly true. For just as the primary passions—that is to say pleasure and pain—come about owing to certain agents and in accord with those agents (pleasure, for instance, from things pleasant and pain from things painful), and it is impossible for the agent productive of pleasure ever to be not pleasant, or that which is creative of pain to be not painful, but of necessity that which gives pleasure must in its real nature be pleasant and that which gives pain painful,—so also in the case of the im-

aginations, which are passions of ours, the agent which is productive of each of them is always and wholly imagined, and as being imagined, it is incapable of being productive of the imagination without being in very truth such as it appears. In the case, also, of the particular sensations one must argue in like manner. Thus the visible object not only appears visible, but actually is such as it appears; and the audible object not only appears audible but also really is so in truth; and so on with the rest." Opinions, on the other hand, may be either true or false. Cf., also, Diogenes Laertius x. 31: "Now in *The Canon* Epicurus affirms that our sensations and preconceptions and our passions are the criteria of truth; the Epicureans generally make imaginative presentations of the understanding also to be criteria." Even the phantasms of madmen and those perceived in dreams are true, for they produce effects, i.e., motions in the mind, whereas that which is unreal never produces motions.

98. This passage from his treatise "On Ends" was repeatedly quoted in antiquity; cf. Athenaeus, *Deipnosophistae* xii. 546e; Cicero *Tusculan Disputations* iii. 18. 41; *De finibus* ii. 3. 7; Diogenes Laertius x. 6; cf. C. Bailey, *Epicurus: The Extant Remains*, Frag. 10 (Oxford: Clarendon Press, 1926), p. 122. Athenaeus goes on to several related quotations from Epicurus, including, "The beginning and root of all good is the pleasure of the belly, and all wise and exquisite things have in this their standard of reference," and "We should prize the Good and the virtues and such things as that, provided they give us pleasure; but if they do not give pleasure, we should renounce them." Diogenes Laertius adds a quotation from Epicurus' Letter to Pythocles: "Hoist all sail, my dear boy, and steer clear of all culture (παιδεία)."

99. Athenaeus xii. 547a; Bailey, *op. cit.*, Frag. 79, p. 138.

100. Sextus Empiricus *Adversus mathematicos* vii. 169.

101. *Ibid.* 160–62.

102. *Ibid.* 217–21.

103. Simplicius *In Aristotelis categoriarum c. 9* (ed. C. Kalbfleisch [Berlin: Reimer, 1907]), p. 333, ll. 32–33.

104. Philostratus *The Life of Apollonius of Tyana* vi. 19.

105. Longinus *On the Sublime* ix. 1: "Now, since the first, I mean natural genius (μεγαλοφυές), plays a greater part than all the others [*sc.* the other four sources of the sublime in literature], here too, although it is rather a gift than an acquired quality, we should still do our utmost to train our minds into sympathy with what is noble, and as it were, impregnate them with lofty inspiration." Cf. *ibid.* xiii. 2: "Here [*sc.* Plato, in the *Republic*] is an author who shows us, if we will condescend to see, that there is another road besides those we have mentioned, which leads to sublimity. What and

what manner of road is this? Zealous imitation of the great historians and poets of the past." Finally, cf. *ibid.* xv. 1: "Weight, grandeur, and energy in writing are very largely produced, dear pupil, by the use of imaginations. (That at least is what some people call the actual images formed in the mind.) For the term 'imagination' is applied in general to an idea which enters the mind from any source and engenders speech, but the word has now come to be used of passages where, inspired by strong emotion, you seem to see what you describe and bring it vividly before the eyes of your audience." Longinus sums up his treatment of this first source of sublimity (*ibid.* 12): "This must suffice for our treatment of sublimity in ideas, as produced by greatness of mind (μεγαλοφροσύνη) or imitation or imagination."

106. Baumgarten, *Aesthetica, Prolegomena* 1, p. 1.

107. *Ibid.*, 4, p. 2.

108. *Ibid.*, 5–12, pp. 3–5.

109. *Ibid.*, 31, pp. 12–13.

110. *Ibid.*, 54 and 56, pp. 22–24.

111. *Ibid.*, 104, pp. 47–48.

112. Cf. *ibid.*, 285, pp. 170–71, where imitation is presented as Cicero's first precept, and 410, pp. 259–60, where specification is given to the advice of "Horace, Cicero, and Longinus" to imitate the great, not only by practicing in imitation of *exemplaria* of sublime writers, but also by perceiving, as in a mirror, the deeds and words of the illustrious men of all ages.

113. Sectio XVIIII, pp. 131–56, treats "Tenue cogitandi genus"; Sectio XX, pp. 156–67, "Medium cogitandi genus"; and Sectio XXI, pp. 167–87, "Sublime cogitandi genus," while Sectio XXII proceeds to the "Vices Opposite to the Sublime" and Sectio XXIII to "Amplifying Arguments." Cf. C. Julius Victor, *Ars rhetorica Hermagorae, Ciceronis, Quintiliani, Aquili, Marconanni, Tatiani*, Cap. XXII (C. Halm, *Rhetores Latini minores* [Leipzig: Teubner, 1863], p. 438): "Elocutionis" genera sunt tria, vehemens, quod Graeci βαρύ, tenue quod Graeci ἰσχνόν, medium, quod Graeci μέσον dicunt." Cf. also Fortunatianus *Ars rhetorica* iii. 9 (*ibid.*, p. 126).

114. Hume, *A Treatise of Human Nature*, Book II, Part I, Sec. 8, "Of Beauty and Deformity," ed. L. A. Selby-Bigge (Oxford: Clarendon, 1896), p. 299. (Italics Hume's.)

115. Hume, *An Enquiry concerning Human Understanding*, Sec. XII, Part 3, ed. L. A. Selby-Bigge (2d ed.; Oxford: Clarendon, 1902), p. 165: "Morals and criticism are not so properly objects of the understanding as of taste and sentiment. Beauty, whether moral or natural, is felt, more properly than perceived. Or if we reason concerning it, and endeavor to fix its standard, we regard a new fact, to wit, the general tastes of mankind, or

some such fact, that may be the object of reasoning and enquiry." Cf. *An Enquiry concerning the Principles of Morals*, Sec. I, p. 173: "Some species of beauty, especially the natural kinds, on their first appearance, command our affection and approbation; and where they fail of this effect, it is impossible for any reasoning to redress their influence, or adapt them better to our taste and sentiment. But in many orders of beauty, particularly those of the finer arts, it is requisite to employ much reasoning, in order to feel the proper sentiment; and a false relish may frequently be corrected by argument and reflection."

116. Hume, *Essays Moral, Political, and Literary*, Part I, 18, "The Sceptic" (ed. T. H. Green and T. H. Grose [London: Longmans, Green, 1912], I, 217).

117. Cf. *ibid.*, Part I, 14, "Of the Rise and Progress of the Arts and Sciences," p. 187: "A strong genius succeeds best in republics: A refined taste in monarchies. And consequently the sciences are the more natural growth of the one, and the polite arts of the other."

118. *Treatise*, Book 1, Part IV, Sec. 7, p. 265.

119. *Ibid.*, p. 267.

120. *An Enquiry concerning Human Understanding*, Sec. II, pp. 17 and 19; cf. *Treatise*, Book I, Part I, Sec. I, pp. 3–4. Cf. also *ibid.*, Sec. VII, Part I, p. 62: "It seems a proposition, which will not admit of much dispute that all our ideas are nothing but copies of our impressions, or, in other words, that it is impossible for us to *think* of anything, which we have not antecedently *felt*, either by our external or internal senses," and *ibid.*, Part II, p. 78: "Every idea is copied from some preceding impression or sentiment; and where we cannot find any impression, we may be certain that there is no idea."

121. *Treatise*, Book II, Part III, Sec. 3, p. 415; cf., also, *ibid.*, Sec. 10, p. 448, and Book III, Part I, Sec. 1, p. 458.

122. Kant, *Critique of Pure Reason*, A 124: "We have therefore a pure imagination as one of the fundamental faculties of the human soul, on which all knowledge *a priori* depends. Through it we bring the manifold of intuition on one side in connection with the condition of the necessary unity of pure apperception on the other. These two extreme ends, sense and understanding, must be brought into contact with each other by means of the transcendental function of imagination, because, without it, the senses might give us phenomena, but no objects of empirical knowledge, therefore no experience." Cf., also, *ibid.*, A 94: "There are three original sources, or call them faculties or powers of the soul, which contain the conditions of the possibility of all experience, and which themselves cannot be derived from any other faculty, namely, sense, imagination, and apperception."

123. *Ibid.*, A 22, n. 1: "The Germans are the only people who at present [1781] use the word *aesthetic* for what others call criticism of taste. There is implied in that name a false hope, first conceived by the excellent analytical philosopher, Baumgarten, of bringing the critical judgment of the beautiful under rational principles, and to raise its rules to the rank of a science. But such endeavors are vain. For such rules or criteria are, according to their principal sources, empirical only, and can never serve as definite *a priori* rules for our judgment in matters of taste; on the contrary, our judgment is the real test of the truth of such rules." Cf. *Critique of Judgment*, Part I Division I, Book I, 15 (trans. J. H. Bernard [2d ed.; London: Macmillan, 1914], p. 77): "But objective internal purposiveness, i.e. perfection, comes nearer to the predicate of beauty [*sc.* than objective external purposiveness, i.e., the utility of the object]; and it has been regarded by celebrated philosophers as the same as beauty, with the proviso, *if it is thought in a confused way.* It is of the greatest importance in a Critique of Taste to decide whether beauty can thus actually be resolved into the concept of perfection." Baumgarten presents the ends of aesthetics as the "perfection of sensitive knowledge as such" and identifies it with beauty (cf. *Aesthetica*, 14, p. 6).

124. *Critique of Judgment* 34, pp. 159–60: "By a principle of taste I mean a principle under the condition of which we could subsume the concept of an object and thus infer by means of a syllogism that the object is beautiful. But that is absolutely impossible. For I must feel the pleasure immediately in the representation of the object, and of that I can be persuaded by no grounds of proof whatever. Although, as Hume says, all critics can reason more plausibly than cooks, yet the same fate awaits them. . . . [Transcendental Criticism] should develop and justify the subjective principle of taste, as an *a priori* principle of the Judgment. This Critique, as an art, merely seeks to apply, in the judging of objects, the physiological (here psychological), and therefore empirical, rules, according to which taste actually proceeds (without taking any account of their possibility); and it criticises the products of beautiful art just as, regarded as a science, it criticises the faculty by which they are judged." Cf. *ibid.*, 6–8, pp. 55–63, where the beautiful is contrasted to the pleasant and the good as that which is represented as the object of universal satisfaction: judgments of taste differ from judgments about the pleasant which are not universal and from judgments about the good which have logical and not merely aesthetical universality. Or, to put it another way, the satisfaction of the pleasant depends on sensation, that of the good on a definite concept, whereas the satisfaction of the beautiful and the sublime is referred to concepts but indeterminate concepts. The satisfaction of the beautiful and the

sublime is connected with the mere presentation of the object or with the faculty of presentation; consequently, in the case of a given intuition, this faculty of presentation or the Imagination is considered as in agreement with the faculty of concepts of the Understanding or Reason (cf. *ibid.*, Part I, Div. I, Book II, 23, p. 101).

125. *Critique of Judgment*, Introduction, iii, pp. 14–17.

126. *Ibid.*, Part I, Div. I, Book I, 22, pp. 96–97. (Italics Kant's.)

127. *Ibid.*, 17, pp. 84–85. Cf. *ibid.*, 32, pp. 155–56: The works of the ancients may be used as models to indicate *a posteriori sources of taste.* "Not that these [*sc.* prior authors] make mere imitators of those who come after them, but rather by their procedure they put others on the track of seeking in themselves principles and so of pursuing their own course, often a better one. . . . *Following*, involving something precedent, not 'imitation,' is the right expression for all influence that the products of an exemplary author may have upon others."

128. *Ibid.*, 42, pp. 181–82.

129. *Ibid.*, 46, p. 188. (Italics Kant's.)

130. *Ibid.*, 49, pp. 197–98. (Italics Kant's.)

131. *Ibid.*, pp. 203–4.

132. *Ibid.*, 51, p. 210.

133. Novalis, *Fragmente der Letzten Jahre* (*Gesammelte Werke*, ed. C. Seelig [Herrhberg-Zürich: Bühl, 1946], IV, Frag. 3053, 301).

134. Novalis, *Das Allgemeine Brouillon* (*Gesammelte Werke*, III, Frag. 1701, 264).

135. F. Schlegel, "Gespräch über die Poesie," *Friedrich Schlegel, 1794–1802: Seine prosaischen Jugendschriften*, ed. J. Minor (Vienna: Konegen, 1882), II, 361–62.

136. F. W. J. Schelling, *Philosophie der Kunst*, Abschnitt I, 16 (*Schellings Werke*, ed. M. Schröter [Munich: Beck und Oldenbourg, 1927], III, 402–3).

137. S. T. Coleridge, *Biographia literaria*, chap. xii (*The Complete Works of Samuel Taylor Coleridge*, ed. Professor Shedd [New York: Harper & Bros., 1853], III, 342).

138. *Ibid.*, chap. xiv (*Complete Works*, III, 363–64).

139. *Ibid.*, chap. xviii (*Complete Works*, III, 421). Cf., also, *Table Talk* (*Complete Works*, VI, 468): "Imitation is the mesothesis of Likeness and Difference. The difference is as essential as the likeness; for without the difference, it would be a Copy or Fac-simile. But, to borrow a term from astronomy, it is a librating mesothesis: for it may verge more to likeness, as in painting, or more to difference, as in sculpture." This dialectical differentiation of two levels or kinds of imitation, the higher of which is identical with invention or creation, received many forms of expression during

the nineteenth century, some untouched by the movements of German idealism. Quatremère de Quincy, thus, in his *De l'imitation dans les beaux-arts* (Paris: Treuttel et Würtz, 1823), refers glancingly (Préambule, p. vi) to metaphysicians, like Kant, and to theoreticians, like Sülzer, before engaging in his effort to search out the elementary principles of imitation and of imitative resemblance, from which to deduce (*faire sortir*) the doctrines and the rules of taste, which will provide the foundations of a general theory of the fine arts (p. 15). "Imitation" has a very broad application for Quatremère de Quincy. "One should be able to explain almost the whole of man, natural and social, by imitation. What is there, in fact, in his habits, or in his tastes, or in his works, that cannot be traced back to the imitative instinct? To embrace the theory of imitation in its universality, therefore, would be to submit to an infinite analysis all the acts of human life, all the objects which enter into the relations of social existence" (p. v). The basic distinction is of faculties of the mind and of kinds of models corresponding to the faculties—those of a moral order and those of a physical order. Quatremère de Quincy distinguishes kinds of imitation, therefore, according to faculties, objects, and means; and these principles provide sharp differentiations among the arts. "In whatever manner one analyzes that which constitutes the general model of moral imitation or the imitation of the arts of poetry, one will find there, as in the model of physical imitation, the same diversity of points of view; one will see that no art can embrace more than one of them, because each is limited to a single aspect by the laws of its nature; one will be convinced that these laws are founded on the elementary separations of the faculties of the soul, to which each art is forced to address itself separately, and on the qualities of the objects of imitation that can be reunited in a single and identical image. In fact, as will be seen, the unity of the soul itself stands in the way of its being able to receive two simultaneous impressions from two imitations at a time, that is to say, in a single and identical moment and from a single and identical art in a single and identical work" (p. 37). In the case of nature and the mechanical arts, we do not perceive two distinct objects, a model and an image, but a single object is seen twice; but in the fine arts, we contemplate them as distinct objects and derive pleasure (which is the end of imitation) from the exercise of judgment in comparing model and image. Physical imitation is addressed directly to the organs of the body, moral imitation to the faculties of the mind. Imitation in the fine arts can further be divided according to the faculty to which it appeals, sense or understanding, and ideal imitation is creation or invention. "And as *idea*, according to the metaphysical definition of the word, is the notion engraved in spirit, *ideal* applied to works of imitation, designates the quality characteristic of the work in so far as it is produced by the principle of the notions which belong to the work of spirit and understanding. . . . Consequently, leaving aside all question of the origin of ideas, our theory, in agreement with language which is a kind of universal reason, recognizes in the works of imitation, as in the double faculty whose concourse is necessary to them, two kinds of qualities which divide them into two classes. The works of the first class, produced particularly by the action of the senses, have for positive and exclusive model the individual work of nature, and it is the essence of this manner of imitating to conform to that which it takes for its model without pretending to add anything, to remove anything, or to change anything, in it. This is imitation in the world of realities. The works of the second class are especially the product of that faculty of understanding, which gives them as model, not only that which the exterior sense sees in reality, but that which can only be discovered by this organ which scrutinizes the causes and the reasons of nature in the formation of things and beings. Since a like model does not exist anywhere materially, and since the spirit which copies it is also that which discovers it, the works which are the result of it are given the names of creation and of invention. This is *ideal imitation*" (pp. 189–90).

140. Dewey stated the problem of contemporary philosophy in these terms; cf. *The Quest for Certainty: A Study of the Relation of Knowledge and Action* (New York: Minton, Balch, 1929), p. 291: "Neither self nor world, neither soul nor nature (in the sense of something isolated and finished in its isolation) is the center, any more than either earth or sun is the absolute center of a single universe and necessary frame of reference. There is a moving whole of interacting parts; a center emerges wherever there is effort to change them in a particular direction."

141. Cf. *ibid.*, pp. 298–99.

142. Dewey is explicit in his purpose to analyze art and beauty in their reference to experience; cf. *Art as Experience* (New York: Minton, Balch, 1934), p. 326: "Art is a quality that permeates an experience; it is not, save by a figure of speech, the experience itself. Esthetic experience is always more than esthetic. It is a body of matters and meanings, not in themselves esthetic, *become* esthetic as they enter into an ordered rhythmic movement toward consummation. . . . The material of esthetic experience in being human—human in connection with the nature of which it is a part— is social. Esthetic experience is a manifestation, a record and celebration of the life of a civilization, a means of promoting its development, and it is also the ultimate judgment upon the quality of a civilization." Cf., also,

ibid., pp. 129–30: "Beauty, conventionally assumed to be the especial theme of esthetics, has hardly been mentioned in what precedes. It is properly an emotional term, though one denoting a characteristic emotion. . . . In case the term is used in theory to designate the total esthetic quality of an experience, it is surely better to deal with the experience itself and show whence and how the quality proceeds."

143. John of Salisbury, who acknowledged his great admiration for Cicero, devoted his two chief works, the *Metalogicon* and the *Polycraticus*, to the related problems of language and action.

144. *Biographia literaria*, chap. xiv (*Complete Works*, III, 374).

145. *Ibid.*, chap. xv (*Complete Works*, III, 381).

146. *Ibid.*, chap. xvii (*Complete Works*, III, 395–96).

147. *Ibid.* (*Complete Works*, III, 405).

148. *Ibid.* (*Complete Works*, III, 394).

149. Aristotle *De interpretatione* 1. 16^{a}3–9.

150. Kant, *Critique of Judgment*, Part I, Div. I, Book I, 49, p. 198.

151. *Ibid.*, p. 202. (Italics Kant's.)

152. *Ibid.*, 51, pp. 206–7. (Italics Kant's.)

153. Incerti Auctoris *Ad Herennium* i. 2. 3; cf. Cicero *De inventione* i. 7. 9.

154. Baumgarten, *Aesthetica*, Pars I, Cap. i, Sec. 1, 18–20, pp. 7–8.

155. *Ibid.*, Vol. II, *Praefatio* 3r.

156. Hume, *Treatise*, Book III, Part II, Sec. 2, p. 490.

157. Hume, *Enquiry concerning the Principles of Morals*, Sec. 9, Part I, pp. 273–74: "But the sentiments, which arise from humanity, are not only the same in all human creatures, and produce the same approbation and censure; but they also comprehend all human creatures; nor is there any one whose conduct or character is not, by their means, an object to every one of censure or approbation. On the contrary, those other passions, commonly denominated selfish, both produce different sentiments in each individual, according to his particular situation; and also contemplate the greater part of mankind with the utmost indifference and unconcern. . . . The distinction, therefore, between these species of sentiment being so great and evident, language must soon be moulded upon it, and must invent a peculiar set of terms, in order to express those universal sentiments of censure or approbation, which arise from humanity, or from views of general usefulness and its contrary. Virtue and Vice become then known, which arise from humanity; morals are recognized; certain general ideas are framed of human conduct and behaviour; such measures are expected from men in such situations." Cf. *ibid.*, Sec. 1, p. 174: "The very nature of

language guides us almost infallibly in forming a judgment of this nature; and as every tongue possesses one set of words which are taken in a good sense, and another in the opposite, the least acquaintance with the idiom suffices, without any reasoning, to direct us in collecting and arranging the estimable or blameable qualities of men."

158. B. Croce, *Aesthetic, as Science of Expression and General Linguistic*, trans. D. Ainslie (2d rev. ed.; New York: Noonday, 1953), p. 8. (Italics Croce's.)

159. *Ibid.*, pp. 12–13: "We have frankly identified intuitive or expressive knowledge with the aesthetic or artistic fact, taking works of art as examples of intuitive knowledge and attributing to them the characteristics of intuition, and *vice versa*. . . . What is generally called *par excellence* art, collects intuitions that are wider and more complex than those which we generally experience, but these intuitions are always of sensations and impressions. Art is expression of impressions, not expression of expression."

160. *Ibid.*, pp. 14–15. Cf., also, *ibid.*, p. 120: "It is clear from the preceding theorem that the activity of judgment which criticizes and recognizes the beautiful is identical with what produces it. The only difference lies in the diversity of the circumstances, since in the one case it is a question of aesthetic production, in the other of reproduction. The activity which judges is called *taste;* the productive activity is called *genius;* genius and taste are therefore substantially *identical*." (Italics Croce's.)

161. *Ibid.*, pp. 67–68: ". . . a classification of intuition-expressions is certainly permissible, but is not philosophical: individual expressive facts are so many individuals, no one of which is interchangeable with another, save in its common quality of expression." Cf. *ibid.*, p. 72: "But in the aesthetic fact there are none but proper words: the same intuition can be expressed in one way only, precisely because it is intuition and not concept."

162. *Ibid.*, p. 99.

163. *Ibid.*, pp. 140 ff.

164. *Ibid.*, pp. 16–17. (Italics Croce's.) Cf., also, *ibid.*, pp. 107–8: "From this comes the illusion that the artist *imitates nature*, when it would perhaps be more exact to say that nature imitates the artist, and obeys him. The illusion that *art imitates nature* has sometimes found ground and support in this illusion, as also in its variant, more easily maintained, which makes of art the *idealizer of nature*. This last theory presents the process out of its true order, which indeed is not merely upset but actually inverted; for the artist does not proceed from external reality, in order to modify it by approximating it to the ideal; he goes from the impression of external nature

to expression, that is to say, his ideal, and from this passes to the natural fact, which he employs, as instrument of reproduction of the ideal fact." (Italics Croce's.)

165. Dewey, *Art as Experience*, p. 3.

166. *Ibid.*, pp. 18 and 24.

167. *Ibid.*, p. 26.

168. *Ibid.*, pp. 52–54.

169. *Ibid.*, pp. 60–61.

170. *Ibid.*, p. 66: "The act of expression is not something which supervenes upon an inspiration already complete. It is the carrying forward to completion of an inspiration by means of the objective material of perception and imagery." Cf. *ibid.*, p. 75: "Nor are there in fact two operations, one performed upon the outer material and the other upon the inner and mental stuff. The work is artistic in the degree in which the two functions of transformation are effected by a single operation."

171. *Ibid.*, p. 73: "Only the psychology that has separated things which in reality belong together holds that scientists and philosophers think while poets and painters follow their feelings. In both, and to the same extent in the degree in which they are of comparable rank, there is emotionalized thinking, and there are feelings whose substance consists of appreciated meanings or ideas. As I have already said, the only significant distinction concerns the kind of material to which emotionalized imagination adheres. Those who are called artists have for their subject-matter the qualities of things of direct experience; 'intellectual' inquirers deal with these qualities at one remove, through the medium of symbols that stand for qualities but are not significant in their immediate presence."

172. *Ibid.*, pp. 76–77: ". . . emotion is esthetic when it adheres to an object formed by an expressive act. . . . Expression is the clarification of turbid emotion; our appetites know themselves when they are reflected in the mirror of art, and as they know themselves they are transfigured. Emotion that is distinctively esthetic then occurs. It is not a form of sentiment that exists independently from the outset. It is an emotion induced by material that is expressive, and because it is evoked by and attached to this material it consists of natural emotions that have been transformed." This is an excellent reformulation of the essential point of Aristotle's doctrine of catharsis. Cf., also, *ibid.*, p. 78: "Esthetic emotion is thus something distinctive and yet not cut off by a chasm from other and natural emotional experiences, as some theorists in contending for its existence have made it to be."

173. *Ibid.*, p. 79.

174. *Ibid.*, p. 103.

175. *Ibid.*, pp. 83, 85, 97–98.

176. *Ibid.*, p. 81. Cf., also, *ibid.*, p. 105: "In the end, works of art are the only media of complete and unhindered communication between man and man that can occur in a world full of gulfs and walls that limit community of experience."

177. *Ibid.*, p. 326. Cf., also, *ibid.*, pp. 270–71.

178. *Ibid.*, pp. 129–30: "Beauty, conventionally assumed to be the especial theme of esthetics, has hardly been mentioned in what precedes. It is properly an emotional term, though one denoting a characteristic emotion. . . . In case the term is used in theory to designate the total esthetic quality of an experience, it is surely better to deal with the experience itself and show whence and how the quality proceeds. In that case, beauty is the response to that which to reflection is the consummated movement of matter integrated through its inner relations into a single qualitative whole."

179. *Ibid.*, p. 267: "In what precedes, I have said nothing about imagination. 'Imagination' shares with 'beauty' the doubtful honor of being the chief theme in esthetic writings of enthusiastic ignorance. More perhaps than any other phase of the human contribution, it has been treated as a special and self-contained faculty, differing from others in possession of mysterious potencies. Yet if we judge its nature from the creation of works of art, it designates a quality that animates and pervades all processes of making and observation. It is a *way* of seeing and feeling things as they compose an integral whole. It is the large and generous blending of interests at the point where the mind comes in contact with the world. When old and familiar things are made new in experience, there is imagination." Cf., also, *ibid.*, p. 268: "Possibilities are embodied in works of art that are not elsewhere actualized; this *embodiment* is the best evidence that can be found of the true nature of imagination," and pp. 272–73: "Esthetic experience is imaginative. This fact, in connection with a false idea of the nature of imagination, has obscured the larger fact that all *conscious* experience has of necessity some degree of imaginative quality. . . . The work of art, however, unlike the machine, is not only the outcome of imagination, but operates imaginatively rather than in the realm of physical existences." (Italics Dewey's.)

180. *Ibid.*, p. 221. Cf. *ibid.*, p. 7: "Under such conditions, it is not surprising that the Athenian Greeks, when they came to reflect upon art, formed the idea that it was an act of reproduction, or imitation. There are many objections to this conception. But the vogue of the theory is testimony to the close connection of the fine arts with daily life; the idea would not have occurred to any one had art been remote from the interests of life.

For the doctrine did not signify that art was a literal copying of objects, but that it reflected the emotions and ideas that are associated with the chief institutions of social life." This Aristotelian conception of imitation shines through even later Platonizing interpretations, such as that of Sir Joshua Reynolds; cf. *ibid.*, pp. 284–86. The chief defect of the theory of representation or imitation is in the character attributed to the art object and the supposition that its medium is something objective; Dewey's remedy for this defect is to treat form and matter as two experiences integrated in the experience of a new expressive object. The difference between these positions is precisely the difference between a theory of imitation developed according to the problematic method employing metaphysical principles derived from nature and existence, and one developed according to a like method employing pragmatic principles derived from experience and expression. Cf. *ibid.*, pp. 287–88: "The fatal defect of the representative theory is that it exclusively identifies the matter of a work of art with what is objective. . . . Since the physical material used in production of a work of art is not of itself a medium, no rules can be laid *a priori* down for its proper use. The limits of its esthetic potentialities can be determined only experimentally and by what artists make out of its practice; another evidence that the *medium* of expression is neither subjective nor objective, but is an experience in which they are integrated in a *new* object."

181. *Ibid.*, p. 90. Dewey extends his theory of representation to "abstract" art, which might seem an exception to his statements about expressiveness and meaning, by quoting from Dr. Albert Barnes; cf. *ibid.*, pp. 93–94: "Reference to the real world does not disappear from art as forms cease to be those of actually existing things, any more than objectivity disappears from science when it ceases to talk in terms of earth, fire, air and water, and substitutes for these things the less easily recognizable 'hydrogen,' 'oxygen,' 'nitrogen,' and 'carbon.' . . . When we cannot find in a picture representation of any particular object, what it represents may be the qualities which *all* particular objects share, such as color, extensity, solidity, movement, rhythm, etc. All particular things have these qualities; hence what serves, so to speak, as a paradigm of the visible essence of all things may hold in solution the emotions which individualized things provoke in a more specialized way."

182. C. W. Morris, *Foundations of the Theory of Signs* ("International Encyclopedia of Unified Science," Vol. I, No. 2 [Chicago: University of Chicago Press, 1938]), p. 7.

183. *Ibid.*, p. 22: "To speak of the relation of signs to the objects they designate presupposes, in order to refer both to signs and to objects, the language of syntactics and the thing-language. This reliance upon syn-

tactics is particularly evident in discussing languages, for here a theory of formal linguistic structure is indispensable. For example, the constantly recurring question as to whether the structure of language is the structure of nature cannot properly be discussed until the terms 'structure' and 'structure of a language' are clear; the unsatisfactoriness of historical discussions of this question are certainly in part due to the lack of such preliminary clarification as syntactics has today supplied."

184. *Ibid.*, pp. 26–28.

185. W. Empson is aware of this tendency and its implications; cf. *Seven Types of Ambiguity* (2d ed.; London: Chatto & Windus, 1947), p. 234: "I must devote a final chapter to some remarks about what I have been doing; about the conditions under which ambiguity is proper, about the degree to which the understanding of it is of immediate importance, and about the way in which it is apprehended. For the first of these the preface to *Oxford Poetry*, 1927, stated an opposition very clearly; that there is a 'logical conflict, between the denotary and the connotatory sense of words; between, that is to say, an asceticism tending to kill language by stripping words of all association and a hedonism tending to kill language by dissipating their sense under a multiplicity of associations.' The methods I have been using seem to assume that all poetical language is debauched into associations to any required degree; I ought at this point to pay decent homage to the opposing power."

186. G. Santayana, *The Sense of Beauty, Being the Outlines of Aesthetic Theory* (New York: Scribner's, 1896), pp. 52–53. Like Hume, Santayana denies the universality of aesthetic principles because of the differences of the circumstances and experiences of men; cf. *ibid.*, pp. 41–42: "That the claim of universality is such a natural inaccuracy will not be hard to show. There is notoriously no great agreement upon aesthetic matters; and such agreement as there is, is based upon similarity of origin, nature, and circumstance among men, a similarity which, where it exists, tends to bring about identity in all judgments and feelings. It is unmeaning to say that what is beautiful to one man *ought* to be beautiful to another. If their senses are the same, their associations and dispositions similar, then the same thing will certainly be beautiful to both. . . . Evidently this obligation of recognizing the same qualities is conditioned by the possession of the same faculties. But no two men have exactly the same faculties, nor can things have for any two exactly the same values."

187. *Ibid.*, p. 193.

188. Santayana, *Realms of Being* (New York: Scribner's, 1942), Preface, pp. ix–x.

189. *Ibid.*, pp. x–xi. It is in respect to this treatment of Spirit that

Santayana aligns his speculations with those of Democritus; cf. *ibid.*, p. 845: "In placing it [*sc.* Spirit] here, in the animal psyche, my system takes its place in the train of Democritus and Epicurus who, although they did not deny the existence of gods, assigned to them no dominion over nature, and in that sense may be called atheists."

190. Santayana, *Reason in Art* (New York: Scribner's, 1917), pp. 144–47.

191. *Ibid.*, pp. 147–48.

192. Santayana, "A Long Way Round to Nirvana," *Some Turns of Thought in Modern Philosophy* (Cambridge: Cambridge University Press, 1933), pp. 87–91. Cf., also, Freud, "Humour," *Collected Papers* (London: Hogarth Press, 1950), V, 215–21, in which the characteristics of humor are found in the denial of the claim of reality and the triumph of the pleasure principle, which is strong enough to assert itself in the face of adverse real circumstances.

193. T. Mann, "Freud and the Future," *Freud, Goethe, Wagner* (New York: Knopf, 1937), pp. 35–40.

194. Edgar de Bruyne's *Études d'esthétique médiévale* (3 vols.; Bruges: "De Tempel," 1946) is indication of the extreme richness of materials that have been subject to relatively little scholarly study.

195. Cf. G. Lacombe, *Aristoteles Latinus* (Rome: Libraria dello Stato, 1939), p. 18; A. Gudeman, *Aristotles Poetik* (Berlin: De Gruyter, 1934), pp. 29, 457–58; E. Franceschini, "La Poetica di Aristotele ne secolo XIII," *Atti del R. Instituto di Scienze, Lettere ed Arti* (Venice), XCIV (1935), 523–48.

196. Roger Bacon is one of the few medieval philosophers who seems to quote from the *Poetics*, but his sources were Arabic, and there is no indication that he had the text of Aristotle or that his references are to that text. Cf. R. Bacon, *Opus tertium*, ed. J. S. Brewer, Cap. 64 (London: Longman, Green, Longman & Roberts, 1859), p. 266: "For as I proved in the *Opus Majus*, particularly in two places, and as I expounded in the fifth part of the *Moral Philosophy*, the poetic argument, which is moral and theological, ought to be constructed with metrical and rhythmic beauty, as Aristotle teaches in his book on this argument, and Avicenna and all the others teach this. For Alfarabi says this in his book *On the Sciences*, in the chapter on logic, that this argument ought to be sublime and beautiful by the beauty of meter and rhythm, in order that the mind may be borne suddenly and forcefully to a love of the thing if it is good or to its detestation if it is bad." Poetic is treated as a form of argument, since in the organization of the sciences elaborated by Alfarabi poetic is a part of logic. Cf., also, *ibid.*, Cap. 75, p. 306.

197. Dryden also combines the Horatian and the Democritean concep-

tions of imitation and attributes the result to Aristotle; cf. "An Essay of Dramatic Poesy," *Dramatic Essays* ("Everyman's Library" [London: Dent, 1912]), where Lisideius gives a definition of a play (which neither Aristotle, nor Horace, nor any other had ever done) as "a just and lively image of human nature, representing its passions and humours, and the changes of fortune to which it is subject, for the delight and instruction of mankind" (p. 10); Crites advocates imitation of the ancients who were faithful imitators and wise observers of nature, and he refers to Horace as "an excellent comment" on Aristotle (pp. 11–12); while Eugenius, without departing from the basic assumptions concerning imitation, argues that our greater knowledge of human nature makes it possible for us to make more perfect images than the ancients and to achieve the pleasure which comes from resemblance of truth and nature. Coleridge laid greater stress on the Platonic side of the interpretation with equal confidence that it was Aristotle's; cf. *Biographia literaria*, chap. xvii (*Complete Works*, III, 399): "I adopt with full faith, the principle of Aristotle, that poetry, as poetry, is essentially ideal, that it avoids and excludes all accident; that its apparent individualities of rank, character, or occupation must be representation of a class; and that the persons of poetry must be clothed with generic attributes, with the common attributes of the class; not with such as one gifted individual might possibly possess, but such as from his situation it is most probable beforehand that he would possess."

198. Machiavelli professed to open a new way for practical action to the common benefit of all; he states this way in the Introduction to the first book of the *Discourses on Livy*: "When we consider the general respect for antiquity, and how often—to say nothing of other examples—a great price is paid for some fragments of an antique statue, which we are anxious to possess to ornament our houses with, or to give them to artists to imitate them in their own works; and when we see, on the other hand, the wonderful examples which the history of ancient kingdoms and republics presents to us, the prodigies of virtue and of wisdom displayed by the kings, captains, citizens, and legislators who have sacrificed themselves for their country—when we see these, I say, more admired than imitated, or so much neglected that not the least trace of this ancient virtue remains, we cannot but be at the same time as much surprised and afflicted." Cf. *ibid.*, chaps. v and vi (where the constitution of Rome is taken as a model for imitation); cf., also, *The Prince*, chap. vi: "Let no one marvel if in speaking of new dominions both as to prince and state, I bring forward very exalted instances, for men walk almost always in the paths trodden by others, proceeding in their actions by imitation," and chap. xiv: "But as to exercise for the mind, the prince ought to read history and study the actions of

eminent men, see how they acted in warfare, examine the causes of their victories and defeats in order to imitate the former and avoid the latter, and above all, do as some eminent men have done in the past, who have imitated some one, who has been much praised and glorified, and have always kept his deeds and actions before them as they say Alexander the Great imitated Achilles, Caesar Alexander, and Scipio Cyrus."

199. Boileau, *Art poétique*, Canto I, ll. 45–48:

> "Tout doit tendre au bon sens; mais, pour y parvenir,
> Le chemin est glissant et pénible à tenir;
> Pour peu qu'on s'en écarte, aussitôt l'on se noie;
> La raison pour marcher n'a souvent qu'une voie."

Cf. ll. 28 and 40. Cf., also, ll. 139–42, where the model of Malherbe is proposed for imitation:

> "Tout reconnut ses lois; et ce guide fidèle
> Aux auteurs de ce temps sert encore de modèle;
> Marchez donc sur ses pas; aimez sa pureté.
> Et de son tour heureux imitez la clarté."

Or, again, Canto II, ll. 25–28:

> "Entre ces deux excès la route est difficile;
> Suivez, pour la trouver, Théocrite et Virgile;
> Que leurs tendres écrits, par les Grâces dictés,
> Ne quittent point vos mains, jours et nuit feuilletés."

200. *Spectator*, Nos. 411–22.

201. E. Burke, *A Philosophical Enquiry into the Origin of Our Ideas of the Sublime and Beautiful* (London: Robertson, 1824), "Introduction, On Taste," pp. 14–15: "But in the imagination, besides the pain or pleasure arising from the properties of the natural object, a pleasure is perceived from the resemblance which the imitation has to the original: the imagination, I conceive, can have no pleasure but what results from one or other of these causes. And these causes operate pretty uniformly upon all men, because they operate by principles in nature, and which are not derived from any particular habits or advantages. Mr. Locke very justly and finely observes of wit, that it is chiefly conversant in tracing resemblances: he remarks at the same time, that the business of judgment is rather in finding differences." Cf. *ibid.*, Part I, Sec. 12, p. 60: "Sympathy, Imitation, and Ambition": "Under this denomination of society, the passions are of a complicated kind, and branch out into a variety of forms agreeable to that variety of ends they are to serve in the great chain of society. The three

principle links in this chain are *sympathy, imitation,* and *ambition.*" Cf., also, *ibid.,* Sec. 16, pp. 84–86, "Imitation."

202. Sir Joshua Reynolds, *Discourses Delivered to the Students of the Royal Academy,* ed. R. Fry (New York: Dutton, n.d.), "Third Discourse": x, pp. 53–55: "But though there neither are, nor can be, any precise invariable rules for the exercise or the acquisition of these great qualities [*sc.* taste and genius], yet we may truly say, that they always operate in proportion to our attention in observing the works of Nature, to our skill in selecting, and to our care in digesting, methodising, and comparing our observations. . . . This long laborious comparison should be the first study of the Painter who aims at the greatest style. By this means, he acquires a just idea of beautiful forms; he corrects nature by herself, her imperfect state by her more perfect. His eye being enabled to distinguish the accidental deficiencies, excrescences, and deformities of things, from their general figures, he makes out an abstract idea of their forms more perfect than any one original; and what may seem a paradox, he learns to design naturally by drawing his figures unlike to any one object. This idea of the perfect state of Nature, which the Artist calls the Ideal beauty, is the great leading principle by which works of genius are conducted. By this Phidias acquired his fame. He wrought upon a sober principle which has so much excited the enthusiasm of the world; and by this method you, who have courage to tread the same path, may acquire equal reputation. This is the idea which has acquired, and which seems to have a right to the epithet of *divine;* as it may be said to preside, like a supreme judge, over all the productions of Nature, appearing to be possessed of the will and intention of the Creator. . . . But the investigation of this form, I grant is painful, and I know but of one method of shortening the road; this is, by a careful study of the works of the ancient sculptors; who, being indefatigable in the School of Nature, have left models of that perfect form behind them, which an artist would prefer as supremely beautiful, who had spent his whole life in that single contemplation."

203. M. l'Abbé Batteux, *Principes de la littérature* (rev. ed.; Lyon: Leroy, 1802), I, 17–18.

204. James Harris, *Three Treatises,* in *The Works of James Harris,* ed. by his son the Earl of Malmsbury (London: Wingrace, 1801), I, 42.

205. J. J. Rousseau, *De l'imitation théâtrale: Essai tiré des dialogues de Platon (Œuvres complètes de J. J. Rousseau,* ed. V. D. Musset-Pathay [Paris: Dupont, 1824], II, 385–411). Rousseau does not use the materials of this essay in his letter to D'Alembert but instead employs a logistic conception of imitation: the question of good and bad spectacles is determined by their effects on man, and, although man is one, he is modified by religions,

governments, laws, customs, prejudices, and climates; the theater pictures human passions, the original of which is in the hearts of men, and there are as many species as there are audiences to take pleasure in varieties of passions (*Lettre à M. d'Alembert* [*Œuvres complètes*, II, pp. 20–22]).

206. Henry Home Lord Kames, *Elements of Criticism* (7th ed.; Edinburgh: Bell & Creech, 1788), I, 180: "In short, with respect to all virtuous actions, it will be found by induction, that they lead us to imitation by inspiring emotions resembling the passions that produceth these actions. And hence the advantage of choice books and choice company."

207. *Ibid.*, II, 2–4: "Of all the fine arts, painting only and sculpture are in their nature imitative. An ornamented field is not a copy or imitation of nature, but nature itself embellished. Architecture is productive of originals, and copies not from nature. Sound and motion may in some measure be imitated by music; but for the most part music, like architecture, is productive of originals. Language copies not from nature, more than music or architecture; unless, where, like music, it is imitative of sound or motion. . . . Words have a separate effect on the mind, abstracting from their signification and from their imitative power: they are more or less agreeable to the ear, by the fulness, sweetness, faintness, or roughness of their tones. These are but faint beauties, being known to those only who have more than ordinary acuteness of perception. Language possesseth a beauty superior greatly in degree, of which we are eminently sensible when a thought is communicated with perspicuity and sprightliness. This beauty of language, arising from its power of expressing thought, is apt to be confounded with the beauty of the thought itself: the beauty of thought, transferred to the expression, makes it appear more beautiful."

208. *The Works of the Author of the Night Thoughts* (London: Owen, 1783), V, 89.

209. *Ibid.*, pp. 95–96: "Must we then, you say, not imitate ancient authors? Imitate them, by all means; but imitate aright. He that imitates the divine Iliad, does not imitate Homer; but he who takes the same method, which Homer took, for arriving at a capacity of accomplishing a work so great. Tread in his steps to the sole fountain of immortality; drink where he drank, at the true Helicon, that is, at the breast of nature. Imitate; but imitate not the composition, but the man. For may not this paradox pass into a maxim? viz. 'The less we copy the renowned ancients, we shall resemble them the more.' . . . Let us build our compositions with the spirit, and in the taste, of the ancients; but not with their materials: thus will they resemble the structures of Pericles at Athens, which Plutarch commends for having had an air of antiquity, as soon as they were built."

210. Thomas Twining, *Aristotle's Treatise on Poetry Translated: With*

Notes on the Translation, and on the Original; and Two Dissertations, on Poetical, and Musical, Imitation (2d ed.; London: Hansard, 1812), I, 4–34.

211. *Ibid.*, p. 58.

212. *Ibid.*, p. 66: "The whole power of Music may be reduced, I think, to *three* distinct effects;—upon the *ear*, the *passions*, and the *imagination*: in other words, it may be considered as simply delighting the *sense*, as raising *emotions*, or, as raising *ideas*. The last two constitute the whole of what is called the *moral*, or *expressive* power of Music; and in these only we are to look for anything that can be called *imitation*. Music can be said to imitate, no farther than as it *expresses* something." (Italics Twining's.)

213. Hume, *An Enquiry concerning Human Understanding*, Sec. V, Part II, pp. 54–55: "Here, then, is a kind of pre-established harmony between the course of nature and the succession of our ideas; and though the powers and forces, by which the former is governed, be wholly unknown to us; yet our thoughts and conceptions have still, we find, gone on in the same train with the works of nature. Custom is that principle, by which this correspondence has been effected; so necessary to the subsistence of our species, and the regulation of our conduct, in every circumstance and occurrence of human life."

214. The use of "models" came into particular prominence in the development of theories of the structure of the atom, but it has had broader applications. Cf. Ernst Mach, *The Science of Mechanics*, trans. T. J. McCormack (3d ed.; Chicago: Open Court, 1907), pp. 492–94: "The atomic theory plays a part in physics similar to that of certain auxiliary concepts in mathematics; it is a mathematical *model* for facilitating mental reproductions of facts. . . . Natural phenomena whose relations are not similar to those of functions with which we are familiar, are at present very difficult to reconstruct. But the progress of mathematics may facilitate the matter. As mathematical helps of this kind, spaces of more than three dimensions may be used, as I have elsewhere shown. But it is not necessary to regard these, on this account, as anything more than mental artifices. This is the case, too, with *all* hypotheses formed for the explanation of new phenomena. Our conceptions of electricity fit in at once with the electrical phenomena, and take almost spontaneously the familiar course, the moment we note that things take place as if attracting and repelling fluids moved on the surface of the conductors. But these mental expedients have nothing whatever to do with the phenomenon *itself*." (Italics Mach's.) It is customary to contrast twentieth-century "mathematical models" with classical "physical models." Cf. P. W. Bridgman, *The Nature of Physical Theory* (Princeton: Princeton University Press, 1936), chap. viii, "Mathematical Models and Probability," and esp. *ibid.*, p. 93: "We have seen that recent theoreti-

cal physics makes use of mathematical models instead of the physical models of classical theory. The fundamental requirement in a mathematical model is that it shall serve as a calculating device, from which we may compute the answer to any question regarding the physical behavior of the corresponding physical system. Since the experimental accuracy with which any measurement can be made is limited, we cannot expect to check with complete precision the demands of any mathematical model. It is conceivable that two formally quite different models might give numerical results which were the same within the errors of experiment, but which differed in higher order terms. Under these conditions either model would serve equally well as a calculating device, and we would have to choose between them on other grounds, usually on the ground of convenience or of ease of calculation, or of simplicity in the argument by which the model was set up." Cf., also, *ibid.*, pp. 61–62: "We had then a sort of double theory—a mathematical theory of the idealized model and then a physical theory consisting of the statement that there was a correspondence between the idealized model and the actual physical system sufficiently close so that certain properties of the physical system were reproduced by the model. The point in making such an idealized physical model was that it had a mathematical theory simple enough to be handled. It presently appeared to reflection, however, that there was an unnecessary step here. . . . I think that the reason that this change of attitude was so long deferred was that it was not realized that there was an intermediate step—the idealized physical model was felt to be so much like the actual physical system, or at any rate the endeavor was to make it so much like the physical system, that the model was actually identified with the physical system." Cf., also, P. W. Bridgman, "Statistical Mechanics and the Second Law of Thermo-dynamics," *Reflections of a Physicist* (New York: Philosophical Library, 1950), pp. 154–55. For another account of the relation and the difference between material and formal models cf. A. Rosenblueth and N. Wiener, "The Role of Models in Science," *Philosophy of Science*, XII (1945), 317: "A material model is the representation of a complex system by a system which is assumed simpler and which is also assumed to have some properties similar to those selected for study in the original complex system. A formal model is a symbolic assertion in logical terms of an idealized relatively simple situation sharing the structural properties of the original factual system."

215. G. Tarde, *Social Laws: An Outline of Sociology*, trans. H. C. Warren with a Preface by J. M. Baldwin (New York: Macmillan, 1907), p. 61: "After these lengthy preliminaries, the time has come when it would be in place to set forth the general laws governing imitative repetition, which are

to sociology what the laws of habit and heredity are to biology, the laws of gravitation to astronomy, and the laws of vibration to physics. But I have fully treated this subject in one of my works, *The Laws of Imitation*, to which I may refer those who are interested in the subject. Nevertheless, I think it important to bring out here what I did not make sufficiently clear, namely, that in the last analysis all these laws flow from a higher principle—the tendency of an example, once started in a social group, to spread through it in geometrical progression, provided the group remains homogeneous." Cf., also, *Les Lois de l'imitation: Étude sociologique* (Paris: Alcan, 1895), p. 95: "Society is imitation, and imitation is a kind of somnambulism." Tarde gave theoretic statement to a principle that had often been stated in its practical implications. Frédéric Le Play, thus, having set forth the problems faced by France after the Revolution, recommends two means, suggested by the study of history, by which a people can save itself from complete decadence (*L'Organisation du travail* [Tours: Mame, 1870], chap. vi, par. 62, pp. 380–82): to imitate the best practices of foreigners and to return to those of its own practices in times of prosperity which remain in harmony with the necessities of the present times. "The imitation of models has been practised without intermission by all the peoples who have understood how to maintain themselves strong and prosperous. It constituted a principle of government for the Romans. It was in even more habitual usage among the Greeks; it was even taught by Socrates with a precision to which the moderns have been able to add nothing. Reform by imitation has likewise been applied to the government of France, under the ancient social regime, by the most perspicacious sovereigns. At the present time, finally, our governors are putting it to use, with feverish activity, to regain the advance which they had permitted rival peoples to take in all that relates to the manufacture of armaments of war." Wundt makes use of imitation to explain the origins of art and to trace its evolution from magical to memorial and finally to imitative art as these are differentiated by different uses of imitative devices (W. Wundt, *Elements of Folk Psychology: Outlines of Psychological History of the Development of Mankind*, trans. E. L. Schaub [London: Allen & Unwin, 1916], pp. 94–109 and 457–66). Eisler uses imitation to explain—with the aid of quotations from Schiller and Jefferson—the origins of lycanthropy (R. Eisler, *Man into Wolf: An Anthropological Interpretation of Sadism, Masochism, and Lycanthropy* [New York: Philosophical Library, 1952], pp. 33 and 110–11).

216. J. M. Baldwin, *Thought and Things: A Study of the Development and Meaning of Thought, or Genetic Logic* (London: Swan Sonnenschein, 1906), I, 87: "The very important fact of imitation, used by others as well as by

the present writer in connexion with the development of the consciousness of self in its social relations, again illustrates this fundamental motive in
the development of fancy objects. The child imitates the act of another, and
in so doing what before he had only observed, comes to feel how the other
feels. He thus learns to distinguish the arena of his direct feeling (the inner)
from the larger range of representative experience (the outer) from which
this feeling was and may still be absent. This is, I think, quite true; and it
is important as a step toward the rise of the 'subjective' as such, of which
we are to treat below." Cf., also, J. M. Baldwin, *Social and Ethical Interpretations in Mental Development: A Study in Social Psychology* (5th ed.;
New York: Macmillan, 1913), p. 114: "First, we may say that each of the
situations which arises from his effort to reproduce the copy *is an invention
of the child's*. It is so because he works it out; no one else in the world knows
it nor can reproduce it. He aims, it is true, not at doing something new;
he aims at the thing the copy sets for him to imitate. But what he does differs both from this and from anything he has ever done before." Cf., also,
the more recently elaborated theories of J. Piaget, *Play, Dreams and Imitation in Children*, trans. C. Gattegno and I. M. Hodgson (New York:
Norton, 1951), and N. E. Miller and J. Dollard, *Social Learning and Imitation*
(New Haven: Yale University Press, 1941).

217. Yrjö Hirn, *The Origins of Art: A Psychological and Sociological Inquiry* (London: Macmillan, 1900), pp. 74–76.

218. Bertrand Russell, *Our Knowledge of the External World as a Field for
Scientific Method in Philosophy* (Chicago: Open Court, 1915), pp. 58–59.

219. P. W. Bridgman, *The Nature of Physical Theory*, p. 117.

220. John Dewey, *Experience and Nature* (2d ed.; New York: Norton,
1929), pp. 357–68.

221. Jean-Paul Sartre, *L'Existentialisme est un humanisme* (Paris: Nagel,
1946), pp. 21–24.

222. W. J. Verdenius, *Mimesis: Plato's Doctrine of Artistic Imitation and
Its Meaning to Us* (Leiden: Brill, 1949), p. 36: "I have argued that Plato's
doctrine of artistic imitation is based on the conception of art as an interpretation of reality and that this principle is still a sound basis for our
theory of art. This is no new discovery, for the interpretative character of
art seems to become more and more recognized in different quarters."
Verdenius alleges the importance of his theory of imitation for the practice
as well as the criticism of art and quotes Proust's statement that only the
servant of the Muses who feels himself "not an inventor, but a translator"
will be a master.

223. Jean-Paul Sartre, *L'Imaginaire: Psychologie phénoménologique de
l'imagination* (Paris: Gallimard, 1940), pp. 239–42. Sartre uses the por-

trait of Charles VIII to illustrate the problem of what constitutes an "image" in much the same fashion as Duns Scotus uses the statue of Hercules. The distinctions that are brought out in the two analyses are similar, but Sartre uses them to distinguish kinds of things, Duns Scotus to distinguish kinds of knowledge. What happens, Sartre asks (*ibid*., pp. 232–33), when I grasp the portrait of Charles VIII *as* image of Charles VIII? "I immediately cease considering the picture as forming part of a real world. It is no longer possible for the object perceived *on* the picture to be susceptible of being altered by changes in the surrounding milieu. The picture itself, as a *real thing*, can be lighted up more or less, its colors can peel off, it can burn. This is because it possesses—for want of a 'being-in-the-world' which is limited to consciousness—a 'being-in-the-midst-of-the-world.' Its objective nature depends on reality grasped as a spatio-temporal whole. But if, on the contrary, I grasp Charles VIII as image on the picture, the object apprehended can no longer be subjected, for instance, to changes of lighting. It is not true that I can light up more or less the cheek of Charles VIII. . . . Likewise, if the picture burns, it is not Charles VIII as image which burns, but only the material object which serves as *analogon* for the manifestation of the imaged object." Duns Scotus differentiates the meanings of "image" according to what is perceived and what is known; cf. *Reportata Parisiensis*, Book II, Dist. 3, Quaest. 4, n. 2 [*Opera omnia*, XXII, 597]): "*Image* is used in two ways:—In one way as the *species* in the eye is called a *visible image*. In another way as the *image of Hercules*, and in this way the image leads to the knowledge of that of which it is an image, because it is known first, and it does not lead to the knowledge of something else unless it is first known as it is in the image. For *what is signified* is never known through a *sign*, unless the sign is known first as well as that it is the sign of such a thing." Cf., also, *Opus Oxoniense*, Book II, Dist. III, Quaest. 9, n. 324 (II, 313): "*Image* is employed in one way for a *likeness precisely imitating* or *representing*, because it does not represent because it is known, but precisely because it is the *reason of knowing*.—It is employed in another way for that which imitates something which is other than itself and which it represents *because it is known*. —In the first way the species white in the eye is an image; in the second way the statue of Hercules is an image of him."

224. M. Dufrenne, *Phénoménologie de l'expérience esthétique* (Paris: Presses Universitaires de France, 1953), I, 389.

225. Erich Auerbach, *Mimesis: Dargestellte Wirklechkeit in der abendländischen Literatur* (Bern: Francke, 1946).

226. Kenneth Burke, *A Grammar of Motives* (New York: Prentice-Hall, 1945), p. xv.

227. Francis Fergusson, *The Idea of a Theater: A Study of the Art of Drama in Changing Perspective* (Princeton: Princeton University Press, 1949), esp. pp. 25 ff., *"Oedipus:* The Imitation of an Action," and pp. 48 ff., "The Rational Imitation of Action: Principles of Racine's Dramaturgy." Fergusson distinguishes between the imitation of action and the rational imitation of action (*ibid.*, pp. 48–49): "In the chapter on Sophocles' *Oedipus,* we endeavored to find our way through the words, characters, and changing events of the play to the one action which Sophocles was imitating; and this action was seen as the clue to the coherence of the whole complex structure. It then appeared that one might think of the life, or hidden essence of the tragedy, as having been realized in the poet's successive acts of imitation: in plot, in character, in reasoned exposition and dialogue, and in choric odes. So Sophocles would have adumbrated the one essence, basing his art upon the primitive and subtle histrionic sensibility and the ceremonial make-believe of the Greek tragic theater. It is very clear that Racine and Corneille did not understand the art of drama as the imitation of action in just this way, though they thought their plays were tragedies in the Greek sense, and obeyed Aristotle's principles. . . . They did not make the distinction between action and deed, nor between the plot as the formal cause or 'soul' of tragedy and plot as a rationalized series of incidents, intended to satisfy the discursive reason. But the life of their drama *is* the rational mode of action. When Racine says of his Phèdre, 'Her crime is rather a punishment of the gods than a *movement of her will*,' he has his eye upon the action of that character, as I understand the word, though only action in the rational mode. They assumed this mode of action as self-evidently the one shape and substance of truly human life. They assumed that the audience assumed it; and so they took the art of drama to be, not that of imitating and celebrating action as a central mystery, in various modes and from various angles of vision, but rather that of demonstrating with the utmost clarity, economy, and harmony, an essence already given and accepted." Cf., also, F. Fergusson, *Dante's Drama of the Mind: A Modern Reading of the Purgatorio* (Princeton: Princeton University Press, 1953), p. 93: "On this notion Aristotle built up his theory of the arts as 'imitations' of action, in their various media, and in various ways— imitations, not of the literal surfaces of life, but of the underlying spirit. It is as imitations of the spirit's variegated life that the arts have meanings wider than that of literal fact; *general* significance akin to that of philosophic systems."

228. Kenneth Burke, "A 'Dramatistic' View of 'Imitation,'" *Accent*, XII (1952), 230. (Italics Burke's.)

229. André Dhôtel, "Rhétorique fabuleuse," *Cahiers du sud*, XXXVI

(1949), 8. This conception of imitation is, of course, restricted neither to the modern period nor to the Western world; Waley reports a like conception in a fifteenth-century Japanese treatise on the *nō* plays; cf. Arthur Waley, *The Nō Plays of Japan* (London: Allen & Unwin, 1921), p. 46: "Imitation (*Monomane*).—In imitation there should be a tinge of the 'unlike.' For if imitation be pressed too far it impinges on reality and ceases to give an impression of likeness. If one aims only at the beautiful, the 'flower' is sure to appear. For example, in acting the part of an old man, the master actor tries to reproduce in his dance only the refinement and venerability of an old man. If the actor is old himself, he need not think about reproducing an impression of age."

230. *The Idea of a Theater*, p. 230.
231. *Art as Experience*, p. 90.
232. *Reason in Art*, p. 146.
233. Cf. J.-P. Sartre, *L'Être et le néant* (Paris: Gallimard, 1943), p. 38: "The concrete is man in the world with that specific union of man to the world which Heidegger, for example, calls 'being-in-the-world.' To interrogate 'experience,' as does Kant, concerning the conditions of possibilities, or to effectuate a phenomenological reduction, as does Husserl, who would reduce the world to the state of a noëmatic correlative of the conscience, is to commence deliberately with the abstract. But one will no more succeed in restoring the concrete by the summation or organization of elements which one has abstracted from it than one can, in the system of Spinoza, attain substance by the infinite summation of its modes." Sartre had, in the preceding pages, argued that "modern thought" has made considerable progress in reducing the "existent" to the series of appearances which manifest it, thereby suppressing a number of dualisms that embarrassed philosophy. The critical examination of forms of thought and the phenomenological study of intentionalities result in like dualisms which preclude all possibility of attaining to, much less starting from, the existent and the concrete. The transformations of history that accompany this simplification of arguments are striking. Aristotle, Thomas Aquinas, and Descartes have taken their places among the precursors of existentialism for some of Sartre's opponents and disciples, and the history of philosophy must be written in terms of dualisms created and resolved. Cf., also, J. Łukasiewicz, *Aristotle's Syllogistic* (Oxford: Clarendon, 1951), p. 12, where commenting on quotations from Keynes and Copleston in which it is suggested that formal logic is so called because of its relations to the "forms of thought," Łukasiewicz remarks: "In both quotations I read the expression 'form of thought,' which I do not understand. Thought is a psychical phenomenon and psychical phenomena have no extension. What

is meant by the form of an object that has no extension? The expression 'form of thought' is inexact and it seems to me that this inexactitude arose from a wrong conception of logic. If you believe indeed that logic is the science of the laws of thought, you will be disposed to think that formal logic is an investigation of the forms of thought. It is not true, however, that logic is the science of the laws of thought." Aristotle's logic is formal, Łukasiewicz concludes, because it treats syllogisms as pure rules stated in letters, employing only variables and logical constants. Łukasiewicz is correct in observing that Aristotle's logic is not based on "laws of thought" (in either Aristotle's or Łukasiewicz's sense of "thought"), but he is mistaken in denying that it is based on what idealist logicians of the recent past meant by "laws of thought." Łukasiewicz apparently feels no incongruity in the argument he uses—the restriction of the meaning of "form" to "physical shape" when he must know that "form" has no such restricted meaning for Aristotle, and the simple reduction of any logic that is based on "forms of thought" to psychologism when a glance into a volume of idealistic logic would have been sufficient to suggest that, whatever its errors, it is neither "psychology" nor "mnemonics." The transformation of history which accompanies this simplification of arguments is striking. Aristotle's logic becomes "formal" and a step toward "formalistic" logic as conceived for the first time by the Stoics. Stoic logic had not been studied before nor had the aspects and portions of Aristotle's logic that prepared for it. Łukasiewicz then shows convincingly that Aristotle failed to live up to the formalist theses discovered in his work, but he does not consider the hypothesis, for which there is abundant evidence even in the citations he employs, that Aristotle sought the "formal" basis of logic neither in the forms of thought nor in the forms of discourse.

234. Wilhelm Dilthey, *Gesammelte Schriften* (Leipzig: Teubner, 1924), VI, 103.

235. *Ibid.*, pp. 112–13.

236. *Ibid.*, p. 115.

237. Cf. *Eislers Handwörterbuch der Philosophie*, ed. R. Müller-Freienfels (2d ed.; Berlin: Mittler, 1922), p. 417: "*Nachahmung* (μίμησις, *imitatio*) ist die *Nachbildung* von Objecten durch genaue Dartsellung derselben. . . ."

238. *Die Einbildungskraft des Dichters* (*Gesammelte Schriften*, Vol. VI), p. 135.

239. *Ibid.*, p. 138.

240. *Ibid.*, p. 186. Cf., also, "The Typical in Poetry," *ibid.*, pp. 185–88, and the treatment of the typical in the creations of imagination in "Poetic Imagination and Madness," *ibid.*, pp. 90–102.

241. *Beiträge zum Studium der Individualität* (*Gesammelte Schriften*, Vol. V), pp. 279–80.
242. *Ibid.*, p. 277.
243. *Gesammelte Schriften*, VI, 242.
244. Karl Groos, *Die Spiele der Menschen* (Jena: Fischer, 1899), p. 423: "Nun, die äussere Nachahmung ist, wie wir soeben gesehen haben, schon selbst zugleich ein inneres Nacherleben, und die äusseren Körperbewegungen haben einen Hauptzweck darin, eben dieses innere Nacherleben und diese Selbstversetzung zu ermöglichen."
245. *Gesammelte Schriften*, V, 308.
246. *Ibid.*, VI, 247.
247. Oversimple use of semantics and history has impoverished some of the recent discussions of imitation. In 1936 I published an essay on "Literary Criticism and the Concept of Imitation in Antiquity," in which I contrasted Aristotle's conception of imitation to four other ancient conceptions of imitation. After the publication of *Critics and Criticism: Ancient and Modern*, ed. R. S. Crane (Chicago: University of Chicago Press, 1952), in which the essay was reprinted, this statement of the Aristotelian conception of imitation was the subject of extended criticism by Professor Eliseo Vivas. The philosophic issues he raises are obscured by the semantic and historical arguments by which he states and supports them. When the three are separated, they illustrate strikingly the way in which a dubious philosophic argument may be supported by arbitrary semantics and dogmatic history.

(1) Professor Vivas' semantics reduces to the simple assertion that the Aristotelian conception of imitation, in my statement of it, obliterates the essential difference between mere copying and genuine creative activity. To make this point, he quotes bits from my statement in two essays in which he reiterates the charge. "According to a contemporary interpreter of Aristotle, Richard McKeon, artistic imitation is 'the presentation of an aspect of things in [a] matter other than its natural matter.' And this is possible because 'the form joined to matter in the physical world is the same form that is expressed in the matter of [the] art.' . . . But it [*sc.* contemporary aesthetics] argues that the Aristotelian account does not do justice to the creative process" ("Literature and Knowledge," *Sewanee Review*, LX [1952], 564). "The members of the Chicago school hold, with McKeon's version of Aristotle, 'that the artist separates some form from the matter with which it is joined in nature . . . and joins it anew to the matter of his art, the medium which he uses.' But thus stated this account is obviously not adequate, since it fails to consider what happens during the process of artistic creation and as a result it obliterates the essential differ-

ence between mere copying and genuine creative activity" ("The Neo-Aristotelians of Chicago," *ibid.*, LXI [1953], 142).

The most simple answer to the question whether, in fact, my account obliterates the distinction between "mere copying" and "genuine creative activity" is to restore the context of the three bits chosen by Professor Vivas from my statement: "Aristotle says relatively little concerning the process of imitation, and that little has been subject to great differences of interpretation; yet what he says of natural objects and their production and of artificial objects and their making affords sound basis for reconstruction of his theory of imitation. The natural object, composite of form and matter, acts according to the natural principle of its being; in imitation *the artist separates some form from the matter with which it is joined in nature—* not, however, the 'substantial' form, but some form perceptible by sensation—*and joins it anew to the matter of his art, the medium which he uses.* The action which he imitates may be 'natural' to the agent, but the artist must attempt to convey not that natural appropriatenesss and rightness, but rather a 'necessity or probability' suitably conveyed by the materials of his art. It is for this reason that 'a likely impossibility is always preferable to an unconvincing possibility.' The analysis might be illustrated from the various arts. The man who sits for his portrait assumes a posture which is determined by the laws of gravitation, by the anatomy of the human body, and by the peculiarities of his habits; the painter must justify the line he chooses not in terms of physics or anatomy, but in terms of the composition which appears in the colors and lines on his canvas. A man performs an action as a consequence of his character, his heritage, his fate, or his past actions; the poet represents that action as necessary in his medium, which is words, by developing the man's character, by expressing his thoughts and those of men about him, by narrating incidents. For Aristotle, consequently, imitation may be said to be, in the fine arts, *the presentation of an aspect of things in a matter other than its natural matter*, rendered inevitable by reasons other than its natural reasons; in the useful arts it is the realization of a function in another matter or under other circumstances than those which are natural. It is no contradiction, consequently, that the artist should imitate natural things, and that he should none the less imitate them 'either as they were or are, or as they are said or thought to be or to have been, or as they ought to be.' Art imitates nature; *the form joined to matter in the physical world is the same form that is expressed in the matter of* the art. Art does not abstract universal forms as science does, but imitates the forms of individual things. Yet, just as the form of man differs from man to man, so the actions of the historical Orestes differ from the actions presented as probable or necessary for Orestes in the plot of a play; and if

Orestes had no historical counterpart, the play would still, in this sense of imitation, be an imitation of the actions of men" (*Critics and Criticism*, p. 162).

The most obvious and persistently reiterated motif of this exposition of Aristotle's conception is the *difference* between the object of art and the object—natural, legendary, or ideal—which it imitates. If imitation were mere copying, the stress would be put on the *likeness* of the two and the fidelity of the artist to the object he imitates. Almost as great emphasis is put on the consequence that follows from this distinction, that the object of imitation need not be an object that existed prior to the work of art and independent of it: legendary, ideal, and even invented characters and actions may achieve probability and possibility better than actual historical occurrences. As Aristotle says (*Poetics* 9. 1451^{b}27–33): "It is clear from the above that the poet must be more the poet [i.e., the maker] of his myths or plots than of his verses, in as much as he is a poet by virtue of imitation, and it is actions that he imitates. And if he should happen to take a subject from actual history, he is none the less a poet for that, since some historical occurrences may very well be in the probable and possible order of things; and it is in that aspect of them that he is their poet." Only by adroit selection is Professor Vivas able to assemble phrases that seem to suggest that imitation emphasizes likeness to an antecedent object, that is, copying, rather than transformation of a matter represented, that is, ποίησις, or making. There are enough indications in the exposition to suggest a semantic problem to a reader who puzzled over why Aristotle chose to call this process "imitation," when he might have given greater emphasis to the difference between the actions of a man and the incidents of a plot by calling the same process by which the poet makes his play, with scarcely a change of phrase, "creation." Moreover, the essay in which the exposition occurs was written to assist such a reader to reconstruct the semantics of Aristotle's use of the term, for it is not simple and arbitrary but reflects the whole structure of his philosophy. Aristotle's conception of imitation was constructed in opposition to the Platonic doctrine (which was continued by later dialecticians, including the idealists and the Romantics of the nineteenth century) according to which two imitative processes are differentiated, one which copies or mirrors contingent, particular things, and another which embodies transcendent values and expresses inspiration, enthusiasm, madness, and genius. Aristotle rejected that distinction: his refutation of the doctrine of Ideas on which it depends entails a denial that there are any aesthetic values other than those which the poet encounters either in nature (in the things and men about him and in the powers and habits of his own and other minds) or in art (in the objects made by artists which imitate things and move men). The distinction between reproductive copying and poetic making can be made by examining the qualities that distinguish them in the objects made, but that distinction is rather less important than the double distinction, on the one hand, between history, which presents the thing that has been, and poetry, which presents a kind of thing that might be (*Poetics* 9. 1451ᵃ36–ᵇ33; cf. *ibid.* 23. 1459ᵃ17–30), and, on the other hand, between better and worse devices of poetic composition, in which some, but far from all, defects can be traced to too literal adherence to an existent model (*ibid.* 25. 1460ᵇ6—1461ᵃ9). These distinctions are distinctions found in works of art and in other objects. They do not require excursions into "the subjective capacities of man," which involve questions about artists and men, not about art. Aristotle does, of course, treat those questions in their proper place: the psychological powers involved in sensibility and in making in the *De anima*, art as an "intellectual virtue" in the *Nichomachean Ethics*, the influence of art as an educational and social instrumentality in the *Politics*.

The negative phase of Professor Vivas' semantics is supplemented by a positive phase. Having disposed of the "theory of imitation" because it obliterates the distinction between mere copying and creative activity, and having expounded his conception of artistic creation ("One thing we know about the artist, and that is that he has a passion for order, in response to which he shapes or informs experiential subject matter into a self-sufficient and relatively novel object"), he acknowledges that the processes of creation involve problems of discovery. At this point he restores the context which he had suppressed when he used phrases from my statement to show that imitation means copying and grants, with a disparaging aside concerning the art of learned exegesis, that the theory of imitation might have some relevance to what he is saying ("Literature and Knowledge," *op. cit.*, pp. 587–88). "But how shall we resolve the contradiction involved in the claim that the artist creates novel objects and that he *discovers* the hidden reality of our practical, commonsense world? The contradiction is only apparent, not real, since the two assertions were made from different points of view. From an external point of view, there is novelty in his product and spontaneity is involved in the process. From the standpoint of the artist, however, we grasp a different aspect of the creative process, since what the artist does is not to invent something new but to extricate out of the subject matter at hand its own proper structure or order. If this is what the theory of imitation intends—and there are some passages in the *Poetics* which, with the usual tucking and pulling that constitute the art of learned exegesis, could be used to justify this interpretation—it is a valid theory, and in this respect at least is not necessarily in conflict with expression theories that emphasize the novelty or uniqueness of the work of art. If this is true, McKeon's statement in the article referred to above is justified when he tells us that 'it is possible for the doctrine of imitation to persist in all essentials even when the term has disappeared.' What the artist does, as we have already seen, is to wrench from his subject matter something that is not fully realized in it, or that, life being the bungling thing it is, is realized in a different manner than it would be if it were designed to meet the demands of the aesthetic order exclusively. . . . But the structure is no more invented by him than it is by the physicist when the latter discovers the laws of the physical world and expresses them in the tools he has at hand. The writer *discovers* this structure, in the sense that the forms and the substance of his work are found by him in the data of experience which is the subject matter of his art." Unfortunately Professor Vivas misinterprets Aristotle as badly when he professes to agree with him as when he refutes him. For Aristotle, imitation does not mean copying existent things, nor does it mean discovering the structure of art objects in the data of experience. According to Aristotle, a dramatic poet *imitates* the actions of men, but he *makes* his plot or myth and, therefore, his poem. He represents nature or life or the actions of men, that is, he finds his subject matter in what he imitates; he makes a poem, that is, he arranges and presents that subject matter in a form which it did not and could not have apart from his work. Life (whether or not it be thought to be bungling) has a structure which determines possibilities, probabilities, and necessities; but, when the poet takes his material from life, he provides another structure for what happened and constructs probabilities and necessities by his art. This is why, in the beginning, the finest Greek tragedies, as Aristotle points out, were based on the histories of a few houses—the families of Alcmeon, Oedipus, Orestes, Meleager, Thyestes, Telephus, and a few others. The successive versions of the Orestes story did not discover or even approximate an identical structure, nor did they even repeat the same facts or emphasize the same forces or relations; they made the same lines of action plausible for different reasons and constructed different tragedies. Professor Vivas departs from the theory of Aristotle, not on the question of whether art is imitation or creation, but on the question of what art imitates. Professor Vivas reifies needlessly when he makes the "aesthetic order" something objective to be discovered by the artist in the data of experience, and he analogizes excessively when he supposes that the artist discovers it as the physicist discovers the laws of the physical world with the aid of scientific instruments. Aristotle could properly object to this theory of what the artist does on the grounds that it reduces imitation to mere copying of a pre-existent structure of reality.

(2) Professor Vivas supports his interpretation of what Aristotle means, not by semantic analysis of the text of Aristotle's statement or of mine, but by historical evidence. He alleges historical facts and uses historical arguments. He alleges as *historical facts* that it was "generally believed until about the end of the eighteenth century" that the function of literature was "to imitate something which exists prior to the act of imitation and independently of it" (*ibid.*, p. 563), that "contemporary aesthetics almost universally rejects or simply ignores the classical theory" (*ibid.*, pp. 563–64), that the "Chicago School of Criticism" defends "the theory of imitation" and that apart from the members of that school it has "very few open defenders" (*ibid.*, p. 565), that "the Chicago group has not given the consideration that they deserve to the arguments on which the theory of imitation has been jettisoned by modern aestheticians" ("The Neo-Aristotelians of Chicago," *op. cit.*, p. 143), but, on the other hand, that the theory of imitation cannot be "dismissed as easily as some aestheticians—Gotshalk, for instance—have done" (*ibid.*). These alleged facts are all false. The Aristotelian theory of imitation is not stated in simple formula: "the function of literature" is "to imitate something which exists prior to the act of imitation and independently of it"; there were many theories of imitation besides the Aristotelian, but even lumping them all together, they were not "believed" without question or interruption until the end of the eighteenth century and they were not "jettisoned" in nineteenth- or twentieth-century aesthetics; the "Chicago group" is far from being alone in "defending" the theory of imitation today, and they "defend" it only in the sense that they show that Aristotle's distinctions provide illuminating and subtle means of analyzing the aesthetic qualities of a poem and that their influence on poets and philosophers would be difficult to explain if they depended on a simple-minded confusion of artistic making with mere copying: they do not "defend" Aristotle's distinctions in the sense of holding that they are or ever have been the only means by which to state or consider the problems of literature.

Professor Vivas has derived his historical facts from Dilthey, and the *historical arguments* he uses depend on the authority of Dilthey. "As Dilthey pointed out in 1887, the principle of imitation became untenable when idealistic philosophy deepened the search into the subjective capacities of man and grasped their autonomous force. After Schlegel and Schelling it is no longer possible to defend an account of the creative act which tells us that the artist joins to the medium of his art the form he separates from nature" (*ibid.*, p. 142). But, although Professor Vivas cites the authority of Dilthey without repeating the argument on which Dilthey bases his conclusion, he does appeal to an argument which is similar in form. Throughout history, from the uses which the Greeks found for the term "imitation" to the discussion of imitation today, the problematic theory of imitation, according to which art imitates nature, has been opposed by the dialectical theory of imitation, according to which art approximates philosophy and imitates unchanging values. Professor Vivas' authorities employ such a dialectical theory. According to Dilthey, the theory that art imitates nature is untenable because art imitates types; according to Friedrich Schlegel, classic art is distinct from Romantic art, yet Romantic poetry is truly poetry only in so far as it shares in the principle of classic poetry and it is working toward a coming synthesis of poetry and science which will be the joint triumph of imagination and intelligence; according to Schelling, art and philosophy both represent Ideas, but art manifests the Infinite not through "prototypes" but through "reflected images." Professor Vivas also has a theory of the relation of literature to knowledge ("Literature and Knowledge," *op. cit.*, p. 590): "There is a kind of congruence, or pre-established harmony, between the work of literature and actual life. But it is not one in which literature imitates life. Rather the relation is, so to speak, 'normative,' in the sense that it tells us, not what actual life is like, but what it would be like if it had the wisdom or the good fortune to possess the economical interrelatedness that art possesses. What literature, therefore, gives us is a symbolic construct of what life ought to be like in order to answer the demands of aesthetic apprehension of it." Such a doctrine has an immense advantage when it is used to criticize other doctrines. It becomes a *historical argument* when it is applied to the work of earlier philosophers (even those who worked only a decade ago) to commend the element of truth contained in their statement while remarking the insufficiencies that make that statement untenable in the light of later data, more adequate theory, or the promise of what is to come from the use of another approach. Professor Vivas says, after quoting from Malraux, "This is true. But it is not the whole truth" (*ibid.*, p. 582). He can repeat the same judgment of any other philosopher: Aristotle's theory of imitation is untenable, but it might be interpreted to be valid; I. A. Richard's doctrine was justified when he formed it but is inadequate (*ibid.*, pp. 570–71); Bergson's theory has an "irrefragable content of truth," but we need not accept its "theoretical wrappings" (*ibid.*, p. 583); and the "Platonic myth of poetic inspiration" likewise has "a profound truth" (*ibid.*, p. 589).

(3) Professor Vivas' *philosophic argument* depends on this semantics and this history. Imitation means copying. Dilthey showed in 1887 that the principle of imitation was untenable. The argument runs somewhat as follows: since the concept of imitation is untenable because Dilthey said so

Notes to Page 213

(whether or not Dilthey's conception of the imitation of types is tenable), therefore anyone who uses the concept in the twentieth century, or for that matter before (however carefully he may differentiate imitation from photographic reproduction), necessarily obliterates the distinction between mere copying and artistic creation. Professor Vivas reinforces this argument by pointing out that I quote a hundred critics (in another essay in which "imitation" is treated only incidentally) but make no mention of Schlegel, Schelling, or Dilthey, and refer to only a few of the aestheticians "who in our day have followed on the tracks of the idealists" (ibid., pp. 142–43). He even acknowledges that this is argument by indirection and that his reasons are indicated rather than stated: "What I am saying is that there are good reasons why modern aestheticians were forced to abandon the Aristotelian theory of imitation, and that these reasons have not received the careful consideration that they deserve by the Chicago neo-Aristotelians" (ibid., p. 142). I shall not pause to consider facts alleged (although it is worth mentioning that Professor Vivas flatters me in calling me an Aristotelian—I hope that I have learned something from reading Aristotle's works, but Professor Vivas would find it difficult to trace the arguments or the conclusions of the two essays he criticizes back to Aristotle) or to examine the logical form or the rhetorical commonplaces of the argument (although Professor Vivas would do well to give some thought to both) or to puzzle over the device by which he hedges his conclusion by affirming its contrary (although the artist does not imitate nature, since that would be copying, he does reproduce a pattern which he discovers in nature and he wrenches something from nature that is not fully realized apart from art)—I shall concentrate on the difference between Professor Vivas' conclusion and the Aristotelian doctrine of imitation. Dilthey's formulation affords some help in finding an undistorted statement of this difference. The principle of imitation is an "objective" principle, that is, by its use art is examined in the context of natural objects and attention is focused on characteristics of art objects, which are not shared by natural objects and which are relevant to the understanding of art and the development of criticism. Professor Vivas says that no account of either the creative process or the created object which pushes to the background or ignores the all-important fact that the artist adds to what his senses give him can be acceptable. It would seem to follow that theories of aesthetics and criticism must be based on the "subjective" principle, that is, the work of art must be considered, not in relation to other objects which the artist and the audience experience, but only in relation to the creative act which, Professor Vivas adds, can be observed in some of its aspects but which has not yet been analyzed scientifically.

〚 284 〛

The theory is stated so vaguely that it would obviously be unfair to give it precise meanings or to try to follow its implications, but the arguments by which it is set up have interesting implications. Instead of using semantics to explore the different meanings that have been attached to an important term like "imitation," the meanings evolved in twenty-three hundred years of discussion are reduced to a single meaning that is so obviously inadequate that it is hard to imagine how the term could ever have been used in that sense (and one does not go to the texts in which it was used to find out whether it had that sense). The alternative to "imitation" (which means copying) is "creation" (which means adding), and we are asked to put our faith in inquiries that might be made into the creative processes of the artist without considering the hypothesis that what is added might also be discovered in the work in which it is added. Instead of using history to explore the changes in art and in theories of art, the insights achieved and the inadequacies discovered, history becomes a means of demonstrating that all theories (or more accurately the only preceding theory) were obviously wrong until a hundred and fifty years ago when the foundations of a preferred theory were laid. Professor Vivas' efforts to be historically up to date land him anachronistically in a form of Romantic theory that was beginning to lose force and attractiveness almost fifty years ago, and his attachment to that theory blinds him to everything that has happened in aesthetics and criticism during the past few decades that might break the unanimity of "contemporary aestheticians" as his history reconstructs them. Finally, instead of using philosophic arguments to state assumptions, analyze data, draw inferences, test hypotheses, and examine the rival claims of alternative theories, he uses semantic arguments to reduce alternatives to absurdity and historical arguments to show that they are untenable.

248. Henri Matisse, quoted by H. Read, *Art Now* (London: Faber & Faber, 1933), pp. 72–73.

Index of Persons

Abailard, Peter, 106
Achilles, 8, 33, 71, 266
Adams, Henry, 17
Addison, Joseph, 177–78
Aeschylus, 103
Agathon, 30, 32, 33, 34, 35, 45, 229
Ahab, Captain, 24
Alcestis, 33
Alcibiades, 32, 34, 35, 52, 229
Alcmaeon, 87, 238, 281
Alembert, Jean d', 181, 267, 268
Alexander of Aphrodisias, 64, 237
Alexander the Great, 97, 98, 172, 266
Alexander of Hales, 125, 244
Alfarabi, 264
Ambrose, St., 15
Amyclas, 240
Anaxagoras, 56, 63, 64, 73, 74, 97
Anaximenes, 64
Antigone, 8, 36
Apelles, 121
Aphrodite, 8, 36
Apollo, 36
Apollonius of Tyana, 146
Aquilius, 252
Aquinas, St. Thomas, 44, 106, 275
Archelaus, 33
Arete, 40
Aristophanes, 32, 34
Aristotle, 7, 9, 10, 18, 23, 25, 26, 28,
  39, 40, 43, 50, 54–88, 89, 97, 98,
  106, 108, 112–13, 114, 126, 139, 140,
  141, 159, 167, 175, 179, 194, 195, 196,
  201, 203, 209, 210, 226, 235, 237,
  238, 239, 240, 246, 251, 258, 264,
  265, 268, 274, 275, 276, 277, 279,
  280, 282, 284
Aristoxenus, 238
Asclepiades, 240
Aspasia, 97
Athenaeus of Naucratis, 31, 39, 40,
  229, 251
Athene, 147
Auerbach, E., 194, 273
Augustine, St., 6, 15, 17, 41, 42, 44, 83,

84, 103, 122–24, 125, 126, 143, 230,
  231, 242, 243, 244, 245, 246, 249
Autolycus, 39, 229
Avicenna, 264

Bacchus, 127
Bacon, Francis, 45, 127–28, 131, 140,
  206, 246
Bacon, Roger, 264
Baldwin, James M., 185, 270, 271, 272
Balzac, Honoré de, 24
Balzac, Sieur de, 247
Batteux, Abbé Charles, 180, 267
Baumgarten, A. G., 147–49, 151, 161–
  62, 252, 254, 258
Beatrice, 45
Bembo, Pietro, 233
Benivieni, Girolamo, 45
Berengar of Tours, 43, 44
Bergson, H., 71, 283
Boethius, 103, 143, 248, 249
Boileau, 132, 177, 201, 266
Bonaventura, St., 125, 244, 245, 246
Boswell, J., 46
Bottom, 104
Bréhier, E., 84
Bridgman, P. W., 188, 270, 272
Bruyne, Edgar de, 264
Buckle, Henry Thomas, 17
Bunyan, John, 25
Burke, Edmund, 178, 266
Burke, Kenneth, 194, 195, 273, 274
Burnet, John, 70, 235

Caesar, 172, 266
Callias, 32, 38, 39, 229
Callicles, 37, 57, 98
Callicrates, 97
Carlyle, Thomas, 18, 86
Carneades, 145
Carroll, Lewis, 71
Castelvetro, 176
Castiglione, Count Baldesar, 233–34
Castorp, Hans, 225
Cavalcanti, Guido, 232

Index

Index

Schopenhauer, A., 225
Scipio, 266
Seneca, 123, 137, 242
Settembrini, 224
Sextus Empiricus, 155, 240, 250
Shakespeare, W., 106, 202, 204
Sharp, Becky, 104
Shorey, Paul, 237
Simmias, 56
Simon Magus, 43
Simonides, 179
Simplicius, 237, 251
Smith, Adam, 181
Socrates, 8, 18, 23, 32, 33, 34, 35, 36,
    37, 38, 49, 51, 52, 56, 57, 59, 62,
    74, 77, 84, 96, 97, 102, 104, 111,
    121, 225, 236, 238
Solomon, 232
Solon, 68
Sophocles, 106, 274
Sophron, 224
Spence, Joseph, 180, 181
Spencer, Herbert, 185
Spengler, Oswald, 17, 83, 84
Speusippus, 40
Spinoza, 49, 71, 206
Stanley, Thomas, 232
Stewart, Dugald, 185
Sülzer, Johann, 256

Tamberlane, 24
Tannery, P., 70, 71
Tarde, G., 185, 200, 270, 271
Tasso, 176, 230
Tatianus, 252
Telephus, 281
Tennemann, W. G., 84
Tertullian, 41, 137
Thales, 62, 73
Theaetetus, 57
Themistocles, 97
Theognis, 133
Theophrastus, 145
Thespesion, 146

Thompson, Anstruther, 185
Thought (personified), 43
Thrasymachus, 57
Thucydides, 16, 19, 20, 66, 84, 90, 95,
    98, 238
Thyestes, 281
Timaeus, 56, 77
Timon, 240
Timotheus, 80
Tolstoi, Leo, 183
Toynbee, Arnold, 17, 84
Twining, Thomas, 181, 182, 268

Ueberweg, Friedrich, 18, 84

Varro, 39
Vega, Lope de, 202
Vergenius, W. J., 193, 272
Victor, C. Julius, 252
Virgil, 40, 106, 176, 209
Vischer, F. T., 185, 200
Vivas, E., 277–85
Voltaire, 103

Waley, A., 275
Webb, Daniel, 181
Weber, Max, 200
Werther, 172
Whitehead, A. N., 7
Wiener, N., 270
Wilhelm Meister, 172
Winckelmann, Johann, 181
Windelband, W., 84
Wundt, W., 271

Xenarchus, 224
Xenophanes, 103
Xenophon, 31, 32, 38, 40, 229

Young, Edward, 181

Zeller, E., 84
Zeno the Eleatic, 56, 70, 71, 237
Zeno the Stoic, 241
Zeus, 77, 123, 146, 147
Zoroaster, 69

Index of Subjects

Thought, Action, and Passion

Beauty—*Continued*
   art and, 119, 139, 144, 253,
257; experience and, 258, 261;
fancy and, 134; judgment and, 151,
259; order and, 117, 135; purpose
and, 254; sense of, 140, 250, 263;
vision of, 22
   hierarchies of, 34, 36, 135,
231–32, 144, 161, 225; kinds: artificial and natural, 119, 139, 144, 164,
252, 253; divine, 234, 244; ideal,
121–23, 126, 178, 233, 267; moral,
252; of order, 135; sensible, 135,
233, 249
Beckonings, 124
Being and becoming, 14, 72–74, 76,
83, 109, 111, 121, 123, 142, 198,
201, 219, 240
Beliefs, concepts, and doctrines as
particularizations of themes, 1–29
(11–13, 26–27), 108–9, 117–19,
140, 199–201, 206, 210–11, 214–21
Book, 121, 125, 128, 138, 171, 268

Catharsis, 215, 260
Causes, 19, 25, 73, 76–78, 90, 115,
122, 125, 133, 146, 150, 191, 198,
257, 266
Change, 1, 72–76, 226
Character of peoples, 68–69, 90–94,
236; *see also* Manners
Charity; *see* Love
Christian, 6, 8, 41–42, 107, 122–26, 231
Civilization; *see* Culture
Classes, 83, 91, 219, 220
Cognitive, 13, 16, 23, 102, 151, 153,
165, 169, 190, 193, 197
Commonplace, 13, 108, 116, 130, 140
Communication
   as a principle, 119–20, 156–57,
163, 186–87, 191, 197, 218; distinguished from expression, 14, 23,
166–67, 192–93, 216; problems of,
213–21; *see also* Expression; Imagination; Imitation
   community and, 100, 261; of
concepts, 153, 160; criticism and,
195; of emotions, 152, 163; love
and, 16; signs and, 168
Community, 1–5, 12, 16, 42, 100,
135, 163, 166, 169, 214, 260

Comparison, 129–30, 162, 178, 183
Composition, 109, 268, 278, 280
Concepts: beauty and, 152, 160, 254;
existence and, 190; intuition and,
164; representation and, 194;
types and, 204; *see also* Beliefs
Concupiscence; *see* Love
Consensus, 4–5, 10, 51, 131, 161, 192
Content: expression and, 131, 133,
183, 192, 193, 216; form and, 5,
116, 117, 192, 193, 216, 224–25
Copy: idea and, 109–11, 150–51,
162, 171, 182, 253; image and,
109–10, 122, 124; invention and,
272; *see also* Creation; Imitation
Creation
   as a principle, 119–20, 207,
212, 218; copy and, 146, 171, 194,
277–78, 279, 280, 284–85; expression, communication, and, 23,
192, 216; imagination and, 146,
157, 200; imitation and, 112, 123,
139, 180, 184, 255, 256, 257, 279,
281
   of art, 14, 143, 167, 189, 195,
203–4, 219, 227, 241–42; of self,
187, 189–90; of universe, 76, 124–
25, 138–39, 155, 159
   as making, 23, 215; as re-
arranging, 150; as representation,
194
Criterion: of action, 214; of art,
196–97; beauty, 152, 247; knowledge, 143–45, 147, 249–51; philosophy, 217, 225, 238; rhetoric,
161; taste, 254
Criticism: as a technique or art, 10,
25, 148, 150, 221, 254; theories of,
106–7, 108–9, 119, 132, 192–93,
200, 215, 217; fine arts, 155, 157,
173–82, 183–84, 197, 216, 217,
252, 272, 285; historical, 146, 184;
literary, 195, 201, 212; philological, 146, 184
Culture (or civilization): art, 193,
195; community, 11, 93, 163, 166,
185, 210, 213–15, 217, 219–20,
257; history of, 1–5, 74–79, 85–86;
philosophy and, 187, 189
Cycles, historical, 76–80, 96; *see also*
Ages

Index

Index

History
as a technique or art, 10–12, 14, 16–22, 23, 54–88, 173, 216–17; historical methods: causal or logistic, 17, 86–87; disciplinary or problematic, 18, 87, 175, 184, 212; epochal or dialectical, 17, 18, 82–83, 85–87, 183, 212; exemplary or operational, 17–18, 86–87, 187
action and, 90, 157, 265, 271; criticism and, 221; method and, 128; myth and, 5, 14, 226, 238; philosophy and, 54–88, 198, 204, 205, 207, 208–11, 275–76, 277, 282–83, 285; philosophy of, 17, 84–85; poetry and, 127, 179, 216, 279, 280; science and, 85, 87, 127; theory and, 1–6, 11, 14; theory of, 78–81
of art, 175, 220; of criticism, 175; Geistesgeschichte, 85, 200, 212; of literature, 146; of philosophy, 18–19, 54–85, 175, 217, 235–39, 275; of science, 175; of symposia, 46; of themes and doctrines, 8–10; semantics, historical, 206, 208, 210, 212
Holoscopic; see Methods
Human behavior, 2–4, 21, 130, 258; as a theme, 20

Ideal: action, idea, and, 1, 52–53, 89–91, 93; art and the, 154, 183, 265; beauty and, 121, 178; imitation and, 164, 175, 177, 186, 193, 256–57; material and, 113; real and, 147, 215, 259–60
Ideas
things, virtues, and, 25; as principles, 155, 164, 220, 233, 283
aesthetic, 153, 160; association of, 191, 197; comparison of, 178; emotions and, 258–60, 262, 269; eternal, 113, 117, 279; of fact, 204; history and, 1, 16–18, 54, 211; ideal and, 91, 256–57; imitation and, 180, 267; impression and, 150–51, 171, 182, 253; language and, 162, 258; simple, 142; sublimity and, 252; of value, 204; see also Concepts
Idol, 114, 127, 132, 162

Image
equality and, 126, 242–43; likeness and, 124–26, 242–43, 245; shadow and, 245; vestige and, 245
of expression (i.e., figure of speech or form of art), 158, 184, 265; of things (i.e., reflection, resemblance, or expression), 111, 121, 122, 124, 128, 130, 146, 155, 158, 176, 244–45, 249, 252, 273; of thought (i.e., sensible, imagined, or ideal), 114–15, 132, 134, 137, 155, 158, 170–71, 204, 233, 244–45, 247, 256
Augustine on, 123–24; Bonaventura, 125–26; Cicero, 121; Democritus, 114–15; Epicureans, 122; Plato, 111
Imagination
as a principle (distinguished from expression and imitation), 109, 119–21, 125, 146–47, 155–58, 173–74, 179–80, 182–83, 193, 200–203, 215–16; (distinguished from perception, emotion, and judgment), 143–55, 173–74, 184
different conceptions of: dialectical, 154–55, 158–59, 178–79; logistic, 149–50, 162–63, 170–71, 177–78; operational, 147–49, 161–62, 178; problematic, 150–53, 159–61, 166
kinds of, 145–55; as a faculty or criterion, 127, 132, 144–45, 253, 254–55; as an imprint or tablet, 136–37, 247, 249, 250; as a passion, 251; apprehensive, 144; creative, 146–47; rational, 146, 250
art and, 146–47, 155, 170; beauty and, 119, 125, 144–55; creation and, 119, 200, 212, 218, 244; fancy and, 111, 124, 134, 155, 170; imitation and, 196, 266; intelligence and, 283; logic and, 188; madness and, 276; poetry and, 127, 129–31; science and, 130, 141; sublimity and, 252; thought, feeling, and, 260, 261, 269; unity and, 195
different conceptions of, 145–55, 158; Academic, 145; Apol-

lonius of Tyana, 146–47; Bacon, F., 127; Baumgarten, 148–49; Bonaventura, 125; Coleridge, 155; Descartes, 129; Dewey, 261; Dilthey, 201–4; Epicureans, 144; Hobbes, 132; Hume, 150–51; Kant, 151–52; Longinus, 147, 251–52; Malebranche, 135–37; Russell, 188; Santayana, 170; Sartre, 193–94; Stoics, 144

Imitation

as a theme, 5–9, 10, **22–26, 102–221,** cf., 239–85; as a principle (distinguished from expression and imagination), 109, 119–21, 125, 146–47, 155–58, 173–74, 179–83, 184–85, 193, 200–206, 215–16; (distinguished according to object or nature imitated: [1] ideal or eternal model, [2] nature or action, [3] art, artist, or agent, [4] appearance, idea, or pleasure), 22–23, 26, 109, 112, 115–17, 123, 137–41, 173–74, 184–86; (and according to characteristics attributed to universe) : political—Roman, 120–22; religious—medieval, 122–26; scientific—seventeenth century, 126–37

different conceptions of: dialectical, 109–11, 137–39, 158–59, 164, 175–77, 184; logistic, 113–15, 140–41, 162–63, 171–73, 176, 184; operational, 111–12, 139–40, 161–62, 168–69, 175–77, 184; problematic, 112–13, 140–41, 159–61, 166–67, 175–76, 184

action and, 114, 123, 124, 126, 130, 133, 136, 176, 181, 195, 265–66, 278; art and, 22, 108–41, 159, 171–72, 180, 185, 195, 196, 215–16, 220, 262, 272, 277, 279, 283–84; beauty and, 109–14, 185, 275; creation and, 112, 120, 123, 139, 146, 180, 184, 255, 256, 257, 279, 281; imagination and, 196, 266; nature and, 112, 120, 123, 178; social and moral, 91, 93, 120, 135–36, 184–85, 256, 270–72; physical, 185, 188–89, 256, 269–70

Aristotle on, 112–13, 114; Augustine, 122–24, 243–44; Bacon,

F., 127–28; Baldwin, 271–72; Baumgarten, 149; Boileau, 266; Burke, E., 266–67; Cicero, 121–22, 241; Coleridge, 155, 255; Croce, 164, 259; Democritus, 113–15, 176; Descartes, 128–32; Dewey, 167, 261–62; Dilthey, 201–4; Dryden, 265; eighteenth century, 180–81; Eisler, 271; Hirn, 185; Hobbes, 132–35, 178; Hume, 150–51; Isocrates, 111–12, 114; Kames, 268; Kant, 152–53; Le Play, 271; Longinus, 147, 252; Machiavelli, 265–66; Malebranche, 135–36; Marcus Aurelius, 123; Plato, 109–11, 113; Plotinus, 123; Quatremère de Quincy, 256–57; Renaissance, 176; Rousseau, 267–68; Santayana, 171–72; Seneca, 123; Sophists, 111–12, 114; Tarde, 270–71; Twining, 269; Wundt, 271; Young, 268; recent analyses, 193–96, 272–75, 282

Impressions: as a theme, 124, 146, 186; actions as (i.e., imitation or empathy), 136–37, 185; ideas as (i.e., copy or image), 114, 150, 162, 171, 182, 253, 256; things as (i.e., stamp or passion), 127, 136–37, 145, 159, 164, 245, 249, 250, 259–60; see also Image; Vestige

Imprint, 124, 249

Inquiry into themes and techniques, 1–2, 11–12, 26–29, 56

Insight, 14–15, 57, 71, 82, 175, 214, 217, 223, 225, 226, 285

Inspiration, 14, 109, 114, 115, 117, 251, 260, 279, 283

Institutions, political and social, 31–33, 47, 76, 78–79, 90–94, 185, 186, 213

Instrument, 10, 12, 14, 22, 49, 188, 260

Interpretation, 16, 18, 25, 65, 75, 93, 125, 127, 201, 209–10, 272; kinds of, 45, 105–7, 141, 175; see also Hermeneutic

Intuition: as a theme, 14; discovery and, 129; expression and, 163–66, 193, 259; faculty of, 143; imagination and, 152–53, 178, 253, 255;

Index

intellectual, 154; mystical, 15; unity of, 195

Invention, 12, 94, 127, 128, 130, 131, 154, 161, 162, 182, 188, 189, 216, 221, 255, 256, 257, 272, 281

Irony, 154, 169, 223

Judgment: as a principle (distinguished from perception, imagination, emotion), 119, 145–46, 151–52; action and, 92–94, 96, 214, 220; aesthetic, 254, 263; art and, 176, 183, 254, 256, 266; faculty of, 151; memory and, 133, 137; moral, 162, 259

Knowledge
    action, art, and (or doing, making, and knowing), 1–5, 14–15, 19–21, 23, 25, 89–91, 102–4, 114–17, 125–26, 142–43, 156–57, 179, 182–86, 213–14, 223–24, 226–27, 262, 273; related dialectically: knowledge and wisdom, 14, 109–11, 154–55, 242; related logistically: knowledge and science, 113–14; distinguished operationally: knowledge and opinion, 111–12; distinguished problematically: knowledge, action, and art, 112–13, 151
    advancement of, 21, 52, 126–30, 192, 265; art and, 189; experience and, 134, 164, 259; history and, 199, 211, 217; imagination and, 253; play and, 171

Language
    action, art, and, 111–12, 156–57, 186, 214; as a principle (distinguished from action, experience, and operation), 162–63, 197–98; see also Communication; Expression
    different conceptions of: dialectical, 158–59; logistic, 162; operational, 161–62, 167–69, 262–63; problematic, 159–61
    artificial, 187; beauty and, 268; community and, 93; form and content of, 116–17, 130–31, 217, 221; imagination and, 136–37, 153; logical, rhetorical, poetic, 159;

ordinary, 131, 158; passion, sentiment, and, 145, 159, 162, 258; philosophy and, 159; poetry and, 173–74, 215, 225; propriety and, 131, 134, 161–62; reason and, 257; signs and, 159, 168

Law
    divine, 123; moral and political, 7, 9, 14, 91, 93, 110, 138, 186, 224, 268; natural and scientific, 130, 221, 238, 271, 281
    of art, 256; of association, 152, 159; of imitation, 185, 270; of thought, 276; of understanding, 151–52

Light, 125, 162, 231

Likeness: beauty and, 126; copy and, 113; equality and, 242–43; ideal and, 121; image and, 109, 111, 123, 124, 242–43, 245, 273; imagination and, 146; imitation and, 255; order and, 122; passions and, 159; shadows, vestiges, and, 125, 245; science and, 129–30

Literature, 177, 190, 192, 204, 251, 282, 283

Logic as a technique or art, 10, 11, 13, 130, 149, 159, 163, 187, 188, 190, 194, 249, 264, 276

Logistic as a technique or art, 10; see also Methods

Love
    as a theme, 5–6, 8, **13–16**, 19, 20, 22, **30–53**, 111, 225, 229–34; kinds of, 33–34, 37–38, 44, 135–36, 225–26: animal (bestial), 23, 233; charity, 6, 8, 41–44, 47, 48, 230; courtly, 8, 44; delectation, 44; desire, 8, 36–37, 49–50, 151, 156; divine (heavenly), 6, 33, 39, 41–42, 48, 231, 233; family, 37, 41; friendship, 8, 37, 41, 49–50, 234; human (earthly), 33, 36, 39, 41–42, 48, 231, 233; ideal, 13, 50; lust (concupiscence), 37–38, 42–44, 230; mystical, 15, 42, 44, 48; parental, 41; romantic (poetic), 8, 36–37, 41–43, 48–49, 102; scientific (cosmic), 33, 36, 41–42, 49–50; sexual, 8, 15, 33, 37, 39, 41, 44, 50; social (communal,

Index

natural genius and imitation, 148–49, 153

as a principle, 45, 250, 266; as bodies in motion, 113–14, 141, 264 action and, 170; creation and, 160; education and, 94; ideal and, 154, 267; ideas and, 269; imagination and, 247; interpretation of, 5, 127; laws of, 130, 221; love and, 135, 234

beauty as natural or artificial, 164, 252, 253; language as mirror of nature, 168–69, 263; language as natural or conventional, 158, 162

Necessity: as a theme, 25; as a principle, 76–77, 238; freedom and, 154–55; poetic, 24, 113, 139, 278, 281

Novelty (or new), 1–4, 94, 98, 134, 165, 168, 193, 199, 211, 226, 261, 272, 280, 281

Obscurity, 131, 137, 248
Operation, 10, 186, 187, 190, 191, 197
Operational; see Methods
Opinion, 14, 110, 111, 128, 142, 178, 249, 250, 251
Order, 37, 109, 112, 122, 133, 134, 135, 136, 149, 155, 161, 166, 204, 227, 238, 250, 256, 280, 281

Pain, 119, 149, 150, 151, 250, 266
Painting, 135, 160, 178, 179, 180, 181, 187, 193, 248, 255, 260, 267, 278
Paradox, 111, 169; Zeno's paradoxes, 70–72, 237, 267
Passion, 109, 144, 145, 156, 158, 159, 171, 178, 182, 183, 184, 186, 191, 197, 204, 218, 221, 250, 251, 258, 265, 266, 268, 269, 280
Pattern, 91, 124, 241, 284
Perception: as a principle (distinguished from imagination, emotion, judgment), 119, 143, 147–49; forms of, 147; of beauty, 151–52; creation and, 167; expression and, 166, 216, 260; figures and, 162; image and, 114; imagination and, 144, 155, 170; imitation and, 109,

186, 219; pleasures and, 159, 202; sensible, 121–23, 150, 171
Phantasm, 124, 132, 148, 149, 251
Philosophy
as a technique or art, 10–12, 13–19, 22–24, 30–53, 220, 229–34; history of, 18–19, 54–85, 175, 217; of history, 17, 54–56, 58; origins of, 68–70; principles of (see Expression; Imagination; Imitation); differences of (see Methods)
art and, 155, 176–77, 179, 183, 187, 189, 190, 214, 283; criticism and, 143, 144, 147, 154, 182; history and, 4, 128, 198–201, 205–7, 209–13; invention and, 127; language and, 159; poetry and, 24–25, 102–7, 114–15, 129–30, 132–34, 154, 158, 203, 223–25; politics and, 120–22; religion and, 120, 122–26; science and, 13, 109–10, 113, 120, 126–41
Play, 160, 171, 172, 173, 184, 191
Pleasure: as end of action and art, 22, 176; art and, 117, 119, 120, 140, 184, 193, 221, 254, 256, 265; beauty and, 110, 114, 144, 149, 151, 162, 169; good and, 151, 251; imagination and, 177–78, 266; imitation and, 109, 135, 141, 202, 241; love and, 38; poetry and, 174, 176; reality and, 191–92, 249, 250
Plot: action and, 105, 196, 215, 224, 279, 281; perfect, 89, 101; soul of tragedy, 117; unity of, 176
Poem, 24, 25, 138, 193, 195, 281
Poet, 129, 154, 158–59, 201, 203, 204, 208, 215, 224, 225, 227, 233, 242, 252, 260, 274, 279
Poetic as a technique or art, 10, 13, 107, 108, 130, 144, 148, 159, 175, 203
Poetry
as a technique or art, 12, 13–16, 22–26, 102–221; different conceptions of, 107, 173–76, 202; as creation, 203–4; emotive, 13; expression, 191; imitation, 109–10, 112–13, 132–33, 176, 196, 203, 256, 281; inspiration, 110, 114, 129; learning, 127, 145; making,

109–10, 112–13, 191; madness, 36, 110; noncognitive, 16, 102, 165, 169, 190; operation, 190–91; reality, 154; reproduction, 203–5, 265, 283; *see also* Production

kinds of, 127, 133; relation to other arts, 179–82; interpretation of, 45, 106–7, 145, 170, 175; art as, 34; language and, 131, 133–34, 158–59; philosophy and, 24–25, 102–7, 114–15, 129–30, 132–34, 154, 158, 183, 187, 192–93, 203, 212, 213–16, 223–25

Practical (or doing): relation to knowledge and production (i.e., knowing and making) (*see* Knowledge); fables and, 127; imitation and, 109–13, 123, 265, 271; reason and, 151, 182; theory and, 19–20, 148, 156, 182, 188, 189; *see also* Action

Precision, 11, 14, 57–58, 82, 188

Presentation, 144, 145, 170, 255, 278

Principles

philosophic, derived from nature of things, 109–24, 126–41, 179, 182, 191, 219, 266, 272, 278, 284; from the processes of thought, 119–20, 124–26, 141–55, 183–84, 256; from determinations of action, 119–20, 156–57, 162–71, 186–87, 191–92, 218, 271; from structure of language, 119–20, 156–57, 162–71, 177, 186–87, 191–92, 218; oppositions of, 139–43

of action, 7, 90–93, 99–100; aesthetic, 263; of art, 155, 160, 265, 272; creation as, 207; custom as, 269; dialectic and, 62–63; existence as, 190; historical, 4, 84–88; ideal beauty as, 267; imitation as, 171, 180–82, 274, 283; methods and, 197; philosophic, 75–76, 192, 198–99; physical, 128, 130; pleasure as, 172, 191; rational, 254; spirit as, 153; of taste, 150–52

Probability: aesthetic, 162; imagination and, 250; natural, 139, 279, 281; philosophic, 142, 145; poetic,

24, 113, 139, 278, 281; scientific, 13, 188

Problematic; *see* Methods

Problems

of themes and techniques, 1–4, 11, 14, 19, 22, 157, 173–75, 216–17, 219; of art and common values, 219–20; of art and emotions, 221; of art and social circumstances, 220; of artistic language and content, 220–21

aesthetic, 139–40, 144, 193, 197, 209, 212; dialectic and, 60–65; historical, 75–78, 208–10, 212; inquiry and, 187, 190; linguistic, 168; philosophic, 182, 188, 197, 198–200, 206–7; practical, 93, 96, 101; science and, 72–74, 120, 126–28, 156; semantic, 206–8, 212

Process, 4–5, 14–15, 76

Production (or making)

relation to knowledge and practical (i.e., knowing and doing) (*see* Knowledge); as a principle (distinguished from expression, communication, operation), 165, 173, 186, 190–91

appreciation and, 165, 189, 259, 261; art as, 112, 132–33, 173, 196, 203, 215, 219, 268, 279, 280; genius and, 153; imagination and, 152, 160; imitation and, 22, 109–13, 123, 149, 172; pleasure and pain, 250–51; self, 190

Proportion, 109, 119, 131, 136, 141, 218

Purpose, 13, 152, 208

Reality: as a theme, 18; appearance and, 111, 126, 140; dialectic and, 158, 164, 182, 183; fantasy and, 191; human, 190; imagination and, 146–47, 249; imitation and, 114, 257, 259, 272, 273, 275, 281; interpretation of, 5; knowledge and, 189; poetry and, 154; process and, 14; representation and, 194

Reason

as a criterion or principle of knowledge, 143, 147, 273; as a faculty of the mind, 127, 129–31, 151,

Index

160, 182, 197, 200, 231, 233, 255; as a principle of things, 76–77, 123, 126, 238, 257; as a statement or argument, 158
    analogical, 148, 162; art and, 175; beauty and, 149–50, 253; discursive, 274; history, semantics, and, 212; imagination and, 250; imitation and, 136; language and, 137; sense and, 147; will and, 225
Religion, 15, 47, 93, 219
Renaissance, 10, 45–46, 126, 138, 163, 175–77, 179, 187, 195, 208, 234
Representation: as a theme, 124, 216; as appearance or idea, 132; in art, 194, 244; of a class, 265; concept and, 151–52, 153, 160, 254; feeling and, 272; of ideas, 155; image and, 137, 245, 273; as imitation, 132–33, 166–67, 172, 215, 262, 279, 281; intuition and, 163–64; of life, 281; medium and, 196; of mind, 154
Reproduction: as a theme, 216; art and philosophy as, 205; of experience or type, 203–4; of ideal fact, 260; imagination and, 152; imitation and, 167, 171, 178, 215, 280; invention and, 272; mechanical, 164, 184, 284; representation and, 194; taste and, 259
Resemblance, 133, 178, 266
Revolution, 4–5, 143, 224
Rhetoric: as a technique or art, 10–16, **19–26, 89–101,** 108, 142, 187, 196, 239; action and, 140; aesthetics and, 148, 177; expression and, 130; imitation of art and artist in, 111–12, 115–16, 121, 122, 140, 147, 161, 175; interpretative, 175; obscurity and, 137; pragmatics and, 169; speech and, 159, 160; style and, 32–33, 149, 221; wisdom and, 156
Right: (opinion), 14, 110; (freedom), 21–22, 99–100
Roman, 107, 120–33, 135, 156, 163
Romantic, 49, 154, 183, 202, 203, 211, 285

Science: art and, 23, 76–80, 102–3, 124, 127, 129, 140–43, 156–57, 165, 179, 186, 189, 191, 197, 223, 225, 278; criticism and, 254; experience and, 197; experimental, 169; genius and, 160; history of, 6–9; imitation and, 185, 205; philosophy and, 13, 109–10, 113, 120, 126–41, 177, 214, 227; politics and, 138; practice and, 2–4, 23; principles, 198; progress of, 213, 253; relations of sciences, 11, 264; reproduction and, 203; of sensible cognition, 148, 254
Scientific; see Methods
Sculpture, 179, 181, 253, 267, 268
Seal, 124, 146, 249
Semantics, 167, 168, 198, 199, 206–8, 212, 213, 277, 279, 283, 285; historical, 175, 206, 207, 210, 212; philosophic, 207
Semiotic, 148, 156, 161, 168
Sense: aesthetic, 140; beauty and, 169, 263; communication and, 160; as criterion, 143, 249; expressiveness and, 166; as faculty, 151, 184; fantasy and, 191; image and, 114, 132, 162, 253; imagination and, 144–45, 147, 150, 170, 247, 250, 251; imitation and, 171, 178, 256–57; pleasure and, 254, 269; poetry and, 204; taste and, 152; thought and, 161
Sensible: beauty, 233, 268; cognition, 148; quality, 194, 240
Sentiment, 150, 162, 193, 218, 252, 253, 258, 260
Shadow, 124, 125, 134, 245
Sign, 114, 124, 142, 156, 159, 161, 162, 168, 169, 262, 273
Skill, 129, 139, 140, 152, 267
Society, 2–4, 7, 11, 120, 123, 132, 136, 178, 183, 184, 185, 197, 211, 213, 266, 271; as a theme, 20
Sophistic as a technique or art, 10, 74–75
Speech, 130, 160, 162, 176, 217, 252
Spirit: as a principle of the mind, 153, 160; beauty and, 135; dialectic of, 83, 113; freedom of, 91–101; gifts of, 129–31; imitation of, 274; intuition and, 163; matter and, 142,

Index

192, 193, 196, 203, 204, 208, 213, 214, 215, 217, 219, 220, 224, 238, 263, 279, 283

Vestige (footprint), 122, 124, 125, 137, 145, 146, 244, 245, 246

Virginity, 40–41, 43

Virtues: ideas, things, and, 25, 111, 116, 144; imitation and, 93, 109–10, 112–13, 156, 159, 242, 265; language and, 258; licentiousness and, 37; pleasure and, 251; teaching of, 36–37, 99, 132–33

Way, 125, 261

Whole, 13, 116, 166, 167, 245, 246, 257, 261, 273

Will, 127, 143, 155, 156, 184, 186, 200, 225, 244, 274

Wisdom, 121, 125, 129, 146, 156, 214, 217, 226, 227, 233, 234, 237, 251, 265

Word, 2, 111–12, 114–15, 116, 121, 137, 142, 156–58, 161, 162, 164, 170, 176, 180, 183, 192, 196, 250, 252, 263, 268–69, 278